CANADA

MINNESOTA

Red River of the North

Lake Superior

Bismarck

Duluth

Northern Pacific

Railroad

Fort Rice

DAKOTA TERRITORY

Cheyenne River Agency

St. Paul

Mississippi River

Fort Sully

ort ierre

ver

Missouri River

Yankton

Sioux C

NEBRASKA

Oregon Trail River

Co. Bluffs

Platte

MISSOURI

KANSAS

THIEVES' ROAD

THIEVES' ROAD

The Black Hills Betrayal and Custer's Path to Little Bighorn

TERRY MORT

Prometheus Books

59 John Glenn Drive
Amherst, New York 14228

Published 2015 by Prometheus Books

Upper cover images from the Denver Public Library,
Western History Collection, B-696 and B-115

Lower cover image from the Library of Congress,
John C. H. Grabill, LC-DIG-ppmsc-02503

Jacket design by Grace M. Conti-Zilsberger

Maps by Rick Britton

Inquiries should be addressed to
Prometheus Books
59 John Glenn Drive
Amherst, New York 14228
VOICE: 716–691–0133
FAX: 716–691–0137
WWW.PROMETHEUSBOOKS.COM

19 18 17 16 15   5 4 3 2 1

Library of Congress Cataloging-in-Publication Data Pending

ISBN 978-1-61614-960-4 (cloth)
ISBN 978-1-61614-961-1 (ebook)

Printed in the United States of America

CONTENTS

❧

6 CONTENTS

INTRODUCTION

Only connect.

— E. M. Forster, *Howards End*, 1910

[He] trusted God was love indeed
And love Creation's final law
Tho' Nature, red in tooth and claw
With ravine, shriek'd against his creed

— Alfred, Lord Tennyson,
In Memoriam A.H.H., 1849

I n the summer of 1874, Brevet Major General George Armstrong Custer led some one thousand men—cavalry, infantry, civilian teamsters, and scientists—on an exploration of the Black Hills of South Dakota.[1] The expedition consisted of ten companies of cavalry, two companies of infantry, an artillery detachment to service three Gatling guns and a three-inch-caliber rifled artillery piece. Officers included Custer's brother Tom, as well as a number of others whose names would appear on the "killed in action" list two years later at the Little Bighorn. Youngest brother, Boston, went as a civilian guide even though he knew nothing of the country and spent most of his time wandering away and getting lost. He, too, would be killed at the Little Bighorn. Brevet Lieutenant Colonel Fred Grant, son of the president, went as an "acting aide" to Custer and an observer for General Philip Sheridan. He had apparently inherited his father's taste for alcohol, if not his ability as a soldier. But he was a good companion, and Custer liked him. Custer also surely understood that a solid relationship with Fred made very good political sense. It wouldn't help Custer in his subsequent entanglements and disputes with the president, but he was not to know that in 1874. The regiment would be divided into two battalions.

Major George Forsyth would command one battalion; he was on loan from General Sheridan's staff. Known as "Sandy," Forsyth was no stranger to combat with Indians; he and fifty or so frontiersmen had held off many times their number at the Battle of Beecher's Island, six years before. (It was not much of a battle in terms of casualties, but it was a long siege of nine days; several intrepid messengers rode for help. The arrival of the celebrated Buffalo Soldiers lifted the siege. Had they not, Forsyth, who was badly wounded, and the others could not have survived.)

Custer liked Forsyth and made a point of requesting that he be made available for this assignment. Major Joseph Tilford commanded the other battalion. He was not a Custer favorite, and in fact the two disliked each other. There was rarely any middle ground between affection and the reverse in Custer's relationships with other officers. Tilford was not particularly enthusiastic about the assignment. He was stationed at Fort Rice in command of the Seventh Cavalry's several companies there and would just as soon have stayed in garrison enjoying whatever comforts that post might offer. But there was no alternative to Tilford just then, and so Custer ordered him to go. Major Marcus Reno, who would go on to controversy and notoriety at the Little Bighorn, was on detached service doing surveying work along the Canadian border.

The regimental band went along, as did a collection of seventy-five or so Arikara and Santee scouts, including Custer's favorite, Bloody Knife. Also along as a guide was "Lonesome" Charley Reynolds, so called because of his natural diffidence—or his atypical behavior in a line of work usually featuring colorful characters full of tall tales and braggadocio. But Reynolds did not lack courage, and he would have an important role in the expedition and an equally important influence on the events that followed. He, too, would die at the Little Bighorn, along with Bloody Knife.

Custer also invited five newspapermen. The General was keenly aware of the value of publicity, and these journalists would play an important role by obliging him. One of the reporters, Samuel Barrows, wrote for the *New York Tribune*. Barrows had been along on Custer's 1873 Yellowstone River expedition that surveyed the valley for the Northern Pacific Railroad. Barrows had dispatched colorful and laudatory accounts of Custer's battles with the Sioux along the Yellowstone. Another reporter, William Curtis, worked for the *Chicago Inter Ocean* and the *New York World*. Curtis had not known Custer before this time, but he soon fell under the sway of the general's personality—Custer could be charming when it suited him. And Curtis's reports would significantly influence subsequent events. A third journalist, William Knappen, worked for the *Bismarck Tribune*. His attitudes toward the expedition and the Indian situation accurately reflected majority western opinion that was impatient or, more accurately, furious with the handling of Indians in general and the Black Hills in particular. The other two reporters were from St. Paul papers. St. Paul was vitally interested in the Seventh Cavalry, since the commanding officer of the regiment was stationed there, as was the commander of the Dakota Department, General Alfred Terry. Civilian scientists also were part of the expedition. Their assignment was to assess the geology and flora and fauna. A photographer was there to record events. The chief engineer, Brevet Lt. Colonel William Ludlow, and his assistants would map the region. Civilians managed the supply train that consisted of one hundred and ten wagons. And there were two civilian "practical miners"—so named by the newspapers and rosters to distinguish them from the scientific corps.

The expedition left from Fort Abraham Lincoln near Bismarck, a rough-hewn town on the upper Missouri River, and the western terminus of the Northern Pacific Railroad. They would be gone two months: July and August. The troops and their civilians would travel some three hundred miles southwest across the Plains and Badlands before reaching the Black Hills, which by the time they arrived seemed like an oasis, as indeed they were, of a kind. Given the size of Custer's force (larger even than the one he took to the Little Bighorn), he felt he could handle anything that came along. But he knew he was going into potentially hostile territory. (In a letter to Terry he said: "I am confident the Indians do not intend to strew flowers on our pathway.")[2] And he knew he might very well be outnumbered if it came to a fight. Trying to understand the odds before he left, Custer communicated with a regional Indian agent who told him the best estimate of Sioux and Northern Cheyenne in the different agencies of the North Platte and Missouri was more than three thousand warriors, most of whom were armed with "one or more pistols, exclusive of other arms. All have bows and arrows. About one-half of the warriors remaining at the agencies have repeating rifles, all others breechloaders. I have known Indians at the White River Agency to have as many as 3000 rounds of ammunition for a single gun . . . fully three fourths of all enumerated are hostile."[3]

Apparently, Custer might need all the men he had and, perhaps, then some.

The stated objective of the expedition was to explore the area and find a location for a permanent military installation—a fort. The proposed fort was a response to Sioux and Cheyenne attacks on the settlements to the south—settlements below the boundary of the Sioux reservation (essentially the southern border of South Dakota). The army needed a post near the Nebraska border to interdict, or discourage, warriors heading from the reservations to the southern settlements and travel routes. As General Sheridan put it: "by holding an interior point in the heart of the Indian country we could threaten the villages and stock of the Indians, if they made raids on our settlements."[4]

Custer had another objective, however, one that was unstated (and even officially disavowed) by the army but well understood by the civilians (and troops)—both those on the expedition and those watching and cheering the effort. That was to determine whether there was gold in the Black Hills. For decades there had been rumors and stories about potentially rich gold deposits in the Hills, but no one knew whether those stories were true—or, more accurately, whether there was enough gold to justify the risks of looking for it. The remoteness and inaccessibility of the Hills coupled with Sioux enmity had been historical barriers to thorough investigation. But Custer's expedition was probably strong enough to deal with any war parties, and his practical miners were there to determine whether the rumors of gold had some basis in fact.

Though this objective was kept sub rosa, there is no doubt that Custer was intent on making the discovery, if there was anything to discover. As Lieutenant James Calhoun, Custer's adjutant and brother-in-law wrote: "The Commanding Officer of the Expedition has expressed a desire on many occasions to explore the Black Hills, believing that it would open a rich vein of wealth calculated to increase the commercial prosperity of this country. Having this object in view, he made known his impressions through the recognized military channels—which were favorably received."[5] The "which" in this case of course refers to Custer's recommendations, not those of the military channels. So it's fair to wonder whether the idea for the expedition originated with Custer or Sheridan. Given their close personal relationship it's likely that they were of the same mind about the expedition's goals, stated and otherwise. Two birds with one stone.

There was some difficulty about the whole project, though—the Black Hills were part of the Sioux reservation, granted by the 1868 Treaty of Fort Laramie. Under the treaty, no whites other than "officers, agents and employees of the government"[6] assigned to, or servicing, various agencies were permitted to enter the reservation. In fact, the army was responsible for intercepting or evicting any civilian individuals or outfits that entered the Hills or any part of the reservation. And in the period after the 1868 treaty until Custer's expedition (and even afterward), the army did just that. As General Terry warned in a letter to the *Sioux City Times*, any enterprise heading for the Black Hills would be illegal and "the consummation of which it will be my duty, under the law, and my instructions to prevent by the use, if necessary, of the troops at my disposal."[7] The very idea that US troops would use force to prevent US citizens from exploring useful land, given away to hostile Indians, raised more than a few hackles among western politicians and editorialists—to say nothing of regular citizens. Nor did the army have much sympathy for this assignment. But they did it. Note that the army prevented white settlers from going into the Black Hills even before the treaty. In 1867 General William T. Sherman wrote to Terry: "I agree with you perfectly that we are not in a position to permit an invasion of that region, for no sooner would a settlement be inaugurated than an appeal would come for protection. . . . You may therefore forbid all white people going there at present and warn all who go in spite of your prohibition, that the United States will not protect them now, or until public notice is given that the Indian title is extinguished."[8] Sherman was simultaneously worried that the "invasion" would stir up the Sioux and that his limited resources would be stretched by a called-for additional post. Note, too, that Sherman refers to the Indians' "title" to the land,[9] and this was before the treaty legalized that title.

Custer also took a hand in the business when a group of fifty civilians from Bismarck organized to explore the Black Hills for gold. Their leader, said Custer, was "the keeper of a disreputable house opposite this post." Custer went on to say: "From the irresponsible character of the leader, and many men who are likely to form the party, no good results are to be expected from this projection. While great harm and embarrassment to our relations with the Indians is almost sure to follow."[10] Custer had a notice posted in the *Bismarck Tribune* warning the locals that he would use troops to prevent the expedition. The citizens of Bismarck were a rough crowd, mostly. As Custer's wife, Elizabeth (Libbie), said: "[They were men] whose lawless life as gamblers and murderers had so outraged the sentiments of the few law-abiding residents that they had forced them to depart."[11] No doubt Custer knew that not only would that expedition violate the treaty, but that these kinds of men were more than likely to make trouble with the Sioux.

On the other hand, the same treaty restrictions did not apparently apply to the army's ability to penetrate the Hills. The army determined that, as representatives or employees of the federal government, they were authorized to go where civilians were excluded—under the somewhat ambiguous terms of the 1868 treaty. As temporary employees of the army, the civilian members of the expedition were also legal, although the usual distinction between the letter of the law and the spirit certainly applied to these civilians, to say nothing of the reporters who were certainly not federal employees. There were perhaps enough fig leaves to cover this expedition, but only just.

National and international economics and politics were some of the driving forces behind Custer's expedition—to the extent that looking for gold was an unspoken objective. The United States and most of Europe were in the grips of a terrible economic depression. The economies of these countries had recently become intertwined through a combination of trade and international finance. (Odd as it may seem, it is possible to trace the connections between the 1873 collapse of the Russian wheat market and Custer's mission—as will be described later.) If Custer could find gold in the Black Hills, there would be a significant and positive ripple effect throughout the sagging US economy. But as importantly, the US Treasury was still trying to dig out from under the mountain of debt incurred during the Civil War—debt that was denominated in gold and would therefore have to be repaid in gold. In short, gold mattered to more than just the rough-and-ready prospectors who found it. They would sell it, one way or another, through the banking system, and the gold would be bought by the Treasury, monetized, and then used to pay federal debts. The availability—and possibility—of gold therefore affected national political and economic decisions. Consequently, the Black Hills Expedition was more important than just a reconnaissance in force, and there was more to be looked for than just a site for a fort. There were also reports that the Hills contained other valuable resources, beyond the gold. The land was said to be ideal for agriculture, ranching, and timbering. It was well watered and wooded, with broad meadows for grazing or farming. Game animals were plentiful. As a result of these circulating stories, the Hills were a source of continuing and violent frustration among white westerners, who were enduring the difficulties of the depression, like their cousins in the east. Plains farmers whose crops were devastated by hordes of grasshoppers thought longingly of the reported fertility of the Hills. Town builders on the treeless Plains thought with equal longing of the vast timber resources. That such a magnificent combination of natural resources should lie undeveloped and unused, except by the occasional Sioux hunting party, outraged the western settlers. As the *Yankton Press & Dakotaian* editorialized:

> This abominable compact [the 1868 Fort Laramie Treaty] with the marauding bands that regularly make war on the whites in the summer and live on government bounty all winter, is now pleaded as a barrier to the improvement and development of one of the richest and most fertile sections in America. What shall be done with these Indian dogs in a manger? They will not dig the gold or let others do it. . . . They are too lazy and too much like mere animals to cultivate the fertile soil, mine the coal, develop the salt mines, bore the petroleum wells, or wash the gold. Having all these things in their hands, they prefer to live as paupers, thieves and beggars; fighting, torturing, hunting, gorging, yelling and dancing all night to the beating of old tin kettles.[12]

The "old tin kettles" reference is a nice bit of condescension. But you could hardly find a more succinct expression of western attitudes toward the Indians in general and the 1868 Treaty of Fort Laramie in particular. Besides, not all the hostile bands had signed the treaty. Sitting Bull and his followers had ignored it and had stuck to their traditional way of life, which meant hunting, wandering, and occasionally raiding. Other bands agreed and settled on reservations, but that did not stop raiding. For many warriors the reservation was a convenient sanctuary and, in times of need, a source of rations. The treaty was a weir, not a dam, in the river of violence; it caused a slight pause, but there was more to come downstream.

Since so few westerners had actually seen the Black Hills or their reputed riches, the stories told by a few mountain men who had been there gathered mythic status over the years. The Hills were a jewel in an Ethiope's ear, and the problem was how to disengage the ear from the Ethiope. Or, to change the metaphor, westerners felt themselves to be collectively a current-day Tantalus, but a Tantalus who was being punished not by the gods but by detested eastern bureaucrats—and self-appointed humanitarians and parsons—policy makers who understood neither economics nor the difficulties and dangers endured by the western settlers. Let those eastern Pecksniffs spend a night on the Plains, where there was no help for miles and the darkness went on forever, and let them listen to the howls of wolves and wonder whether the wolves walked on four legs or two. Let them understand the terror of the night and afterward view the hideous mutilation of Indian victims—and then let them come and deliver their sermons and wave their treaties. Philanthropy had a way of evaporating the closer one came to the tribes—although, in fairness, a handful of dedicated missionaries lived among the tribes and tried to spread their message of peace. But for most pioneer settlers, the West was red in tooth and claw. That was the truth of it, as far as they experienced it. And in the years immediately after the Civil War, they were not far wrong. In exchange for enduring those dangers, the settlers wanted opportunity. That's why they had come to this remote and dangerous place. And the Black Hills were the most glittering of opportunities, so they believed. There hung the fruit, all the more tantalizing for being viewed through the prism of imagination and rumor. But standing in the way were ignorant or asinine eastern preachers and politicians—and a treaty that was nothing more than a piece of paper signed by bureaucrats and agreed to by illiterates who had little, if any, intention of abiding by the terms. So said the westerners, if not unanimously, then close to it.

In short, the western press and population hated the treaty and warmly endorsed Custer's expedition. They saw it for what it was—the thin edge of the wedge.

To say that looking for gold (and other resources) was an unpublicized objective is not to suggest that the stated military objective was a fiction to cover a gold-hunting expedition. On the contrary, the military and economic objectives were, in this case, perfectly congruent. That congruency was typical of this period in which the federal government and private enterprise cooperated closely on a number of projects deemed to be in the national interest. If people managed to get rich in the process, so much the better. Further, the army's role in settling the west went well beyond battles with native tribes. It involved mapping and collecting scientific information about the largely unknown territories. Officers who had been trained at West Point—especially those who did well academically—were primarily engineers, surveyors, and scientists, since that was the primary focus of the Academy's curriculum. The best performers were well prepared for scientific and topographical missions. Militarily, the story was slightly different. Officers were trained in the traditional Napoleonic tactics: artillery preparation followed by a massed bayonet charge with cavalry waiting to exploit defensive gaps or lapses, or to block enemy maneuvers. The carnage of the Civil War was to a very real extent the result of the Academy's tactical curriculum, which was hardly different from those of the European academies. The Academy prepared the professionals for war between nation-states, and although the tactics were wasteful and suicidal, the officers at least could tell themselves they were following the rules. Unfortunately, the Academy graduates were totally unprepared for the task of finding and fighting Indians. That subject was considered a waste of time at the Point. As a result, there were no rules to follow.

But the key point is that Custer's expedition was by no means unique or unusual in combining military and scientific/geographic objectives. The army did not see them as separate missions. If you were going to fight over a ground, you needed to know what it looked like. And if your country had acquired vast new territory—even if it was uninhabited and uncontested—

it was your job to map it and discover any indications of natural resources. As an example, the five initial surveys of potential transcontinental roads (initially stagecoach and ultimately railroad) were conducted before the Civil War by junior officers of the army. And well conducted, too. Finally, most of the West was federal territory. Who but the army was available to survey and evaluate it?

Until Custer's expedition, the Black Hills were mostly terra incognita, as far as white settlers and the army were concerned. The Hills are a mysterious island rising from the Plains. They appear from the Plains to be a citadel with no access points. And it is a mighty citadel, at that; they cover more than forty-five hundred square miles and sit along the border between southeastern South Dakota and Wyoming.

The very inaccessibility of the Black Hills raises questions about whether the interior of the Hills would be a good location for a fort. Supplies would be a problem; there were no navigable rivers close by. The Hills were cut by deep ravines and rivers and streams and were guarded by escarpment, so that although the environment would be healthful by comparison to forts on the Plains or along rivers, the fort would be a difficult place from which to observe and maneuver. A fort there might be nothing more than an island in an island. The difficulty of finding access into the Hills had been one of the barriers to exploration, especially to white civilians and soldiers who depended on wagon trains for supplies. Further, a fort in the Hills exposed the troops to increased risk of attack. As Lt. Calhoun said during the march to the Hills: "The prevailing impression is that the Indians will not attack us until we get into the interior of the Black Hills, when they will have a decided advantage over us. Bushwhacking with unseen enemies is a game of warfare not to be desired."[13] Bushwhacking with unseen enemies was not a subject taught at West Point, nor was it the kind of thing the army was good at.

In fact, the army never did build a fort in the Hills proper. It wouldn't be until 1878 when Fort Meade was built next to Bear Butte on the northeastern edge of the Hills. That was in response to cries for protection from the mining towns that had sprung up after Custer's expedition. So it's fair to wonder which expedition objective really had the highest priority. On the other hand, Custer's thorough scout through the interior of the Hills may have convinced him that the Hills, beautiful as they were, were not a good site for a fort and led ultimately to the Bear Butte location.

Over the previous decades some intrepid explorers and prospectors had penetrated the Hills, but they had been driven out or killed by the Sioux, who had earlier driven the Kiowa, Cheyenne, and Crow tribes from this territory. But in the days before the Sioux were feeling overwhelmed by white civilization, they were not so unfriendly. Indeed, in 1846 the youthful historian Francis Parkman joined a band of Oglala Sioux on a brief expedition into the Black Hills to cut lodge poles. He describes the inaccessible nature of the Hills: "[No] white man with us had ever seen the difficult and obscure defiles though which the Indians intended to make their way. I passed them afterwards and had much ado to force my distressed horse along the narrow ravines and through chasms where daylight could scarcely penetrate."[14] One of Parkman's companions, a "vagrant Indian trader" named Reynal, spoke of the gold in the Hills: "Many a time when I have been with the Indians, I have been hunting for gold all through the Black Hills. There's plenty of it here; you may be certain about that." But Reynal went on to say, "It won't do for a white man to be rummaging too much about these mountains. . . . I believe myself that it's no good luck to be hunting about here after gold."[15] Reynal was typical of the type of men who spread stories about gold; he no doubt hoped that being married to an Oglala woman offered him some protection. Parkman's book, *The Oregon Trail*, was published in 1849—a year that was significant in the story of gold. In the 1850s there were two army expeditions, but both of these merely skirted the outer edges of the Hills, and one, led by Lt. Gouverneur Warren, was turned away by the Sioux. (Warren went on to become one of the heroes at Gettysburg, the man who recognized that Little Round Top was undefended and moved troops there just in time.)

Another source of stories about gold was the peripatetic Jesuit missionary, Father Pierre-Jean De Smet. He was generally respected, and his accounts could hardly be dismissed, although General Sheridan described him as spreading "dreamy stories."[16] Still, De Smet was no garrulous mountain man whose stories might be discounted as the usual tall tales. More than one westerner said to himself that there must be something to it.

The Sioux had a particular regard for the Hills as a hunting ground and, for some, as a sacred place. Indeed, Francis Parkman called the Hills "a hunter's paradise." When the buffalo in their mysterious ways made themselves scarce, the Sioux could retire to the Black Hills where elk, deer, and antelope were plentiful. Indeed, the Sioux called the Hills their "meat pack." (In fact, the Sioux preferred deer to buffalo for flavor and for the softness of its skin, but of course the buffalo herds were vast and provided almost everything the Sioux required—food, clothing, utensils, lodge coverings, sinews for rope, even glue.)

As far as the Sioux were concerned, the Black Hills belonged to them, originally—and most legitimately to the Sioux—by right of conquest, and more recently under the 1868 Treaty of Fort Laramie, in which the whites granted to the Sioux something, in their eyes, they already owned. If the white man wanted to put something on a sheet of paper, well, that was no substitute for grim and obvious reality, for the unwritten laws of war. But if the treaty meant a cessation in the troubles, then fair enough. And if it could keep greedy miners and frontiersmen out of the Hills, so much the better. Like other native tribes anywhere, the Sioux dreaded the discovery of precious metals in their territory. They knew a gold strike would release a torrent of white miners. And what had been a pristine wilderness, rich in game animals, would be degraded by miners grubbing around in the placers and sluice boxes and returning at night to wretched muddy mining camps offering gambling, whiskey, and loose women. To the Sioux this would be a tragedy of multiple dimensions—economic, aesthetic, environmental, and spiritual. It was unthinkable. Black Moon, a Hunkpapa Sioux, reportedly said that any Indian who showed the gold fields to white men should die.

But the rumors would not die. Lt. Calhoun wrote: "I have read in a newspaper of an Indian squaw going into one of our forts some years ago (I believe it was Fort Laramie) and offering to barter or sell a lump of gold about the size of an egg, which she said was obtained from the Black Hills."[17]

Without the help of any Sioux informers, however, Custer's expedition did find gold. There were no egg-sized nuggets, and it was not a bonanza. But it was enough. It was the news the westerners wanted to hear. It was the political and economic leverage they needed. And from the moment of Custer's first reports of the discovery, Sioux ownership of the Black Hills was doomed, just as they feared it would be—but not before a fight, for

Custer's expedition was also a significant cause of stirring up, or reigniting, the hostilities of all the Sioux tribes, hostility that resulted in the battle at the Little Bighorn two years later. It was said that George Custer dug his grave—and, as importantly, the graves of 262 men—when he led an expedition into the Black Hills of South Dakota in the summer of 1874.[18]

Is that true? And if so, how did it all come about?

CHAPTER ONE

WAR, TAXES, DEBT, AND THE RESULTANT LURE OF GOLD

> *War reflects culture. Weaponry, tactics, notions of discipline, command, logistics—all such elements of battle arise not just from constraints of terrain, climate and geography, but also from the nature of a society's economy, politics and sociology.*
> —Victor Davis Hanson,
> *The Father of Us All*, 2011

E very war the United States had fought in its young history had resulted in some form of debt, but the policy of the government had always been to retire that debt as soon as possible. The very idea of a national debt was abhorrent to the political heirs of Thomas Jefferson and Andrew Jackson, all of whom worried that borrowing from capitalists would give a handful of wealthy bankers an undue influence over the government—to the detriment of the rest of the population. But the Civil War made many politicians, and ordinary citizens alike, reassess their attitudes about debt. In truth, there was no alternative. The Civil War was unlike previous American wars, not only in the scope of death and devastation but also in the unprecedented size of the financial obligations left in its wake. In 1860 the national debt was $60 million. By war's end it was $2.6 billion (30 percent of the gross domestic product [GDP]). And by the time of Custer's expedition into the Black Hills, nine years later, the debt had only been reduced to just over $2. 25 billion—roughly 24 percent of the GDP.[1]

And to the general public the national debt was not some vague abstraction; it was on people's minds.

When Custer reported the possibility of gold, the *Yankton Press &*
Dakotaian trumpeted: "Struck it at last! Rich mines of gold and silver
reported found by Custer. Prepare for lively times! Gold expected to fall
by ten percent. Spades and picks rising! The national debt to be paid when
Custer returns."[2]

There in a single headline is the synthesis of a number of key themes
surrounding Custer's expedition—the euphoria of unsubstantiated and
inflated claims. Picks and shovels were all that would be required, because
the gold was in placers, so that any amateur with a strong back could
hope to get rich (no mining expertise or capital equipment required). The
"strike" was so potentially rich that the price of gold would drop (price
being subject, of course, to supply and demand). Even the national debt
would be retired through the ripple effect of economic boom times and
the increase in taxes to the Treasury. Further, there would be an increase
in the nation's supply of gold that would ultimately find its way into the
federal Treasury and be used to retire US Treasury bonds—bonds that
were denominated in gold, meaning that the interest and principle must be
paid in gold specie, not paper currency. And if the price of gold dropped,
the Treasury could acquire gold at reduced prices and thereby reduce the
debt that much faster.

Small wonder that people were excited by the news from the Black
Hills. That the issue of national debt made headlines in a western paper
dedicated to promoting the benefits of western expansion underscores the
political importance of the debt. It also reflects the fact that a new gold
strike was important to more than just a few thousand professional and
amateur prospectors. It was national business. True, the gold was on Sioux
land, guaranteed by solemn treaty, but that legal difficulty would prove to
be a flimsy barrier against the momentum of larger national concerns. In
a matter of a couple of years, the Sioux title to the Black Hills would be
extinguished. And during that time, Custer and 262 of his troopers would
be killed at the Little Bighorn. Did they die for gold and for the national
debt? That's probably an overstatement. But had there been no national
debt, would the government and the army have turned their backs on their
treaty obligations? That's a different question.

THE NATIONAL DEBT

The Civil War cost more than early war hawks, or anyone, for that matter, could possibly have imagined. At the start, almost everyone thought it would be a short war and, therefore, relatively inexpensive by any measurement. (The first call-up of Union volunteers asked for only three-month enlistments.) That sort of optimism is a common preamble to war—and, in fact, quite often contributes to the decision to commence hostilities. Usually, it is a miscalculation. The "butcher's bill" for the Civil War has traditionally been placed at 620,000 lives from combat and disease, although recent studies suggest the number was closer to 750,000.[3]

Beyond the dead were uncounted maimed and scarred, physically and psychologically. And these were just the military casualties and do not include the desolated families of the killed and wounded. There is no way to assess the damage suffered by civilians who lost their livelihoods or lost the fathers, husbands, and brothers who provided for them. Thankfully, there were relatively few civilian casualties from combat, despite massive property losses. The Battle of Gettysburg, for example, was fought for three days within and on the near outskirts of that tiny village, but there was only one civilian killed (twenty-year-old Jennie Wade, making bread in her kitchen, was hit by a stray bullet), while on the nearby battlefields there were fifty thousand casualties, all told. Unlike the wars of the twentieth century, civilians were not considered legitimate targets, except by rogue guerrilla bands or marauding renegade troops. There was some local score settling, which is a feature of most, if not all, civil wars. On the other hand, historian James MacPherson estimates that there were at least fifty thousand civilian deaths—not from combat, mostly, but rather from crime, disease, and starvation—cooperating evils of war, but not war itself.[4] The 620,000 (or more) dead and hundreds of thousands of wounded wore uniforms. Perhaps there is a certain nobility in that, especially in contrast to the indiscriminate savagery of most wars, ancient and modern.

The war also cost nine billion dollars in property losses—cities and towns destroyed, farms and plantations devastated, factories and railroads ruined. That is nine billion 1865 dollars—roughly 128.6 billion in today's inflated money.[5] And it would be a virtually impossible task to calculate the "opportunity costs"—the losses of productivity while the men were away from their farms and workshops and during the period between destruction and reconstruction of the Southern economy. Of course, there was a war dividend for the Union manufacturers and suppliers of military equipment, food, and livestock. The meat-packing industries in Chicago, for example, enjoyed an explosion of business as the Union army was introduced to the dubious pleasures of processed rations.

The day-to-day financial cost of conducting the war very nearly brought the federal government to its knees and ultimately ruined the Confederacy, which suffered most of the losses to property and productivity—to say nothing of a catastrophic 9,000 percent inflation rate on its paper currency and the attendant impoverishment of its citizenry. When the war was finally over, much of the South lay in ruins, and the North had a national debt of staggering proportions—a debt that, as mentioned, had to be paid off in gold. And ahead lay the financial, social, and political complexities that would come under the rubric "Reconstruction," a Gordian knot that politicians would have to untangle without Lincoln's unique moral and political leadership. And it would not go smoothly.

At the beginning of the war it quickly became apparent—and appalling—to Lincoln and his Secretary of the Treasury, Salmon Chase, that the existing system of federal taxation could not support the cost of equipping, feeding, training, and maintaining the massive armies that the war suddenly required. Before the war the US regular army mustered approximately sixteen thousand officers and men, but when the first Union call for volunteers summoned seventy-five thousand men, existing logistics systems were overwhelmed. Soon after, there were further calls-ups and ultimately the draft, so that by war's end more than two million men had been or currently were under Union arms. The corresponding number of Confederates was nine hundred thousand.[6]

Prior to the war, the primary methods of federal taxation were tariffs and, occasionally, excise taxes. Tariffs were external taxes on imported goods. Tariffs were therefore favored by the manufacturing states, primarily of the northeast, because they protected local industries against otherwise cheaper foreign imports produced by underpaid European labor. Politicians who supported the concept of tariffs said that such taxes also protected American workers, not just the manufacturers. This sort of argument may have had some merit, but it was as much a political as an economic argument, because it was designed to prove to labor that their political representatives were looking out for their interests as well as for the interests of the wealthy owners. Tariffs protected jobs, and the politicians who instituted them to raise necessary government revenues said they deserved the political support of workers and owners alike. What's more, tariffs were indirect taxes and comparatively palatable, because the average person did not have to reach into his pocket to pay the tax. And although that same average voter paid the tax in the form of higher prices for imported goods, that sort of indirect tax was less noticeable. Not coincidentally, tariffs also allowed domestic producers to increase their prices and profit margins—a further tax on the average consumer.

The agrarian interests and regions, especially the South, disliked tariffs. Tariffs made necessary imports (or their domestic equivalents) more expensive. Further, those regions had little if any manufacturing that needed protection. Nor did southern planters worry overmuch about discontent among their labor force. Plantation slaves obviously could not go on strike, nor could they vote. Additionally, the southern cotton growers worried that high tariffs would bring retaliation against them by their European (largely British) customers.

If there had to be taxes of any sort, opponents of tariffs preferred excise taxes. These were internal charges on goods and services and could be selectively applied. Luxury goods that were the province of the wealthy might be taxed (carriages, jewelry, etc.), while various necessities such as tobacco and flour could be exempted. The list of items that could be taxed shifted according to need and political expediency. Excise taxes, therefore, had the potential to be somewhat progressive, depending on which goods were taxed and which were exempt. That appealed to Americans, who were touchy about the differences between the wealthy and everyone else. Class envy and regional economics therefore had a bearing on the political debates about how best to raise money to operate the federal government.

Not at all surprisingly, the issue of tariffs versus excise taxes broke down along party lines, with the Northern Republicans supporting tariffs and the Southern Democrats opposing them.

When secessionist Democrats left Congress, the debate over excises versus tariffs became academic. The Republicans were in control, facing the thorny question of how best to finance a war that no one but a handful of firebrands and fanatics really wanted. The sightseers who accompanied the Union troops to Bull Run expecting to see something like a military parade accompanied by an exciting whiff of gun smoke and a few saber charges were no more shocked than the Union politicians who realized what lay before them. It quickly became clear that revenues from existing tariffs would not be nearly enough to support the hemorrhaging of cash that accompanied the sudden and appalling hemorrhaging of blood. True, tariffs could be raised—and they were (tariffs rose from 20 percent in 1860 to 47 percent by 1864). And although revenues from tariffs amounted to more than $300 million during the war,[7] they still fell well short of requirements. Other sources had to be found—and quickly. Like most of those in government and in civilian life, Secretary Chase no doubt assumed that a year or so would be enough to see a military conclusion to the rebellion. Even so, his estimates of the first year's operations were woefully off the mark. In fact, the first year of the war cost the Union $532 million—well beyond Chase's estimate of $318 million. Federal tariffs and other taxes that year brought in only $55 million.[8] Bank loans made up the difference, but the bankers soon began to get nervous; early Union defeats did not help matters.

Although the Republicans controlled Congress, that did not mean clear sailing for the administration's policies. Secretary Chase proposed a tax on property, but here again regional differences caused resistance. Representatives from western farm states howled in protest, because the property tax would fall heavily on their constituents while exempting those (primarily easterners) whose wealth consisted mostly of stocks and bonds, not farmland. It was an early version of the Main Street versus Wall Street divide that had been, and obviously still is, an evergreen staple of American culture.

News of the fighting damaged alternative fund-raising efforts. As financier and economist Robert D. Hormats writes: "With steady news of the Union's defeats in 1861, public confidence fell sharply. Uncertain over the outcome of the war, nervous investors withdrew large amounts of gold from Northern banks to the point that in December most of them suspended specie payments and stopped purchasing government bonds. . . . Lincoln despaired that 'Chase has no money and tells me he can raise no more.'"[9] (As mentioned, federal government bonds were denominated in gold, and the primary buyers of these bonds were banks. But when the banks' depositors began withdrawing gold, the banks were less able either to honor their paper banknotes with gold specie or to invest in government bonds.)

In response, Congress agreed to impose a tax on wealth and income. To avoid alienating the mass of people Lincoln needed to support his war policies, a 3 percent tax was levied only on incomes of more than $600 a year—a level that seems ridiculously low by today's standards. But in 1861 fewer than 3 percent of the population "qualified."[10] Further, in the final agreement between the House and Senate, incomes over $10,000 were taxed at 5 percent. Over the course of the war that percentage would rise to 5 percent on incomes between $600 and $5,000, 7.5 percent on incomes between $5,000 and $10,000, and 10 percent above $10,000. Moreover, Congress devised an estate tax. Rates ran from .75 percent to 5 percent based on the size of the estate.

But even the income and estate taxes were not enough: "And for the first time since the War of 1812, Congress imposed excise taxes, assessing them on a wide range of items, including liquor, tobacco, commodities, jewelry, playing cards, telegrams, leather, licenses and other legal documents. It also levied taxes on utilities, banks, insurance companies, railroads and ferry boats."[11]

Politics affected the form and volume of taxes. Congress and the administration had to raise funds by any reasonable means, of course, but they wanted the majority of voters, the lower- and middle-income people, to believe that the taxes were fairly imposed, that the wealthy were paying their share. There would soon be a widespread feeling in some quarters in the North that it was "a rich man's war and a poor man's fight," that the wealthy were profiting from the surge in manufacturing and finance, while the poor men, volunteers or draftees, were suffering on the battlefield. The combination of across-the-board new taxes plus early and catastrophic battlefield defeats created a toxic political brew that Lincoln and his administration had to manage with all possible deftness. Accordingly, all these new taxes contained loopholes and deductions designed to appease certain constituencies and to avoid imposing hardships on those least able to pay. Farm produce and raw materials for manufacturing were exempt from excises, for example. State and local taxes were deductible from federal income taxes, as were some excise taxes. To appease homeowners, mortgage interest was also deductible. And for all practical purposes, Congress removed the detested property tax by suspending it and then not reinstituting it when the two-year suspension expired.

It was one thing to impose new taxes; it was something else to collect them. In the past federal taxes were collected by the states and passed on to the federal Treasury. The opportunities for inefficiency in this system and the experience of past wars, such as 1812, in which states' collection of taxes was a hit-or-miss proposition, motivated the administration to propose a new government agency—the Bureau of Internal Revenue. Initial reaction was predictable: "One of the most obnoxious . . . of all its features is that which creates an army of officials whose business it is to collect this tax." So said Rep. Roscoe Conkling of New York.[12] But by 1862, when it became apparent that the war would neither be short nor financially manageable under the current tax-collection methods, Congress recognized the need for a more efficient collection and approved the new bureau. Robert D. Hormats observes: "War, and in this case war to maintain the very unity of the nation, meant Congress was willing to greatly strengthen the federal government's financial powers, which would have been highly unlikely in more tranquil times."[13] The new bureau, by the way, offered politicians new opportunities for patronage. They could give supporters new government positions in return for their support, both political and financial. So the new Bureau of Internal Revenue was not a universally detested incubus.

The debate over the form and level of taxation reflected the two major and abiding divisions in American political philosophy. The Jeffersonians viewed America as a land of independent yeoman farmers and artisans who did not need or want a strong central government. In their view, the smaller the central government, the lower the need for taxation and the lower the probability that the monied interests could gain undue influence over the government. On the other side was the Hamiltonian idea of a strong central government supported by a centralized financial system. The debate over taxation was therefore one aspect of that larger philosophical argument that the Civil War, ultimately, would settle. War swept aside the Jeffersonian arguments against expanded federal powers; through the new Bureau of Internal Revenue Washington was expropriating a former prerogative of the states.

Lincoln signed the sweeping new tax legislation on July 1, 1862.

BIRTH OF THE GREENBACK

The same centralizing dynamic was occurring with the money supply and the banking system. Before the Civil War the only federally produced money was in coins—gold, silver, and copper. And since these precious metals were scarce, there was a limited supply of minted coins. There was no US central bank to issue federal currency. The charters of the First Bank of the United States and the Second Bank of the United States had both been allowed to expire (in 1811 and 1836, respectively) by Jeffersonian and Jacksonian objections to the very idea of centralized, in other words, national banking. Here again was the fear that financiers who ran the banks and who raised money for the government, through their own investments and through their depositors and customers, would exercise too great an influence on government. The interests of the "monied classes" would take precedent over the interests of small-town and rural America. The First and Second Banks of the United States operated through a number of branches in key commercial cities. They had a wide depositor base and could issue banknotes that were acceptable throughout the country, unlike the notes of state-chartered regional banks whose notes were generally acceptable only within the state or region. When the First and Second Banks of the United States were scuttled, nationally accepted banknotes disappeared.

As a result, when the Civil War broke out, the money supply, aside from the federally minted coins, consisted of a bewildering array of banknotes issued by state banks: "In the years immediately before the Civil War, roughly sixteen hundred state-chartered banks dotted the American landscape, each issuing its own notes. Roughly seven thousand varieties of banknotes were in circulation. Some were issued by legitimately state-chartered banks, but many were of dubious quality or simply counterfeit."[14]

As mentioned, these banknotes circulated locally or, at best, region-ally. When taxpayers used them to pay their federal taxes, the Treasury could only use them to purchase war supplies within that region or state. As a result, the varying reliability and convertibility of thousands of different state banknotes greatly complicated the problem of procuring military supplies from the private sector. Manufacturers in other states would not accept out-of-state banknotes as payment for war supplies. That was understandable. After all, a banknote was nothing more than a promise to pay the holder the face value of the note in specie (i.e., gold or silver coin). But manufacturers or farmers in other regions had no way to verify whether that promise was any better than the paper it was written on, or whether the bank was still in business, or even whether it had been simply the product of a counterfeiter's imagination. Then, too, there was the very real possibility that the bank had suspended specie payments because of a lack of gold.

It soon became clear to the administration and Congress that a national currency was desperately needed—a currency issued by the federal government that would be legal tender throughout the country. In principal, a paper currency works well only as long as it is convertible into specie. In that way the paper currency, which obviously has no intrinsic value, is nothing more or less than a reliable receipt for gold or silver—a twenty-dollar paper receipt for one twenty-dollar gold coin. But the federal Treasury needed more money than it had gold to back it, and so after much political wrangling the Treasury issued paper "greenbacks," so called because of the color of the ink on the reverse side of the note. The money was not convertible into gold or anything else, for that matter. Its value rested solely on a *legal requirement* that it be accepted for all transactions, private and public—except for payment on government bonds (which were denominated in gold and were to be respected as such in order to protect the principal value and the viability of future borrowings) and customs duties—an important source of gold to the Treasury. The greenback was legal tender for all other transactions. It had value because Congress said it had value.

There was a great deal of wrangling over the constitutionality of this measure, but in the end constitutional questions gave way to military necessity. Even Salmon Chase, who first abhorred the idea of an unsupported paper currency, told Congress in February 1862: "Immediate action is of great importance. The Treasury is nearly empty."[15] Despite the institutional memory of the disastrous inflation of the Continental paper currency during the Revolution, Congress bowed to necessity. The Legal Tender Act of February 1862 authorized an issue of $150 million greenbacks. Ultimately that figure would rise to $450 million. Not surprisingly the greenback did not hold its face value. During the course of the war it bottomed out at roughly thirty cents on the dollar. As Congressman George Pendleton, an Ohio Democrat, said: "The wit of man has never discovered a means by which paper currency can be kept at par value except by its speedy, cheap certain convertibility into gold or silver."[16] The government may say it's worth a dollar, but if the local merchant wants three greenback dollars for a silver dollar's worth of flour, it doesn't matter what the government says. The law may require the merchant to accept the greenback, but the law could not make him accept it at face value or prevent him from adjusting his prices, which amounts to the same thing. What's more, the infusion of so much money into the northern economies combined with scarcities because of military requirements fueled the classic formula for inflation—too much money chasing too few goods. So the combination of doubts about a paper currency backed by nothing and the rapid increase in the supply of those dollars along with the explosion of government purchases in the private market all contributed to inflation and the depreciation of the greenback. It's a wonder things weren't worse than they were. As it was, annual inflation in the North ran to 25 percent.[17]

Still, the greenback fared far better than its Confederate counterpart, the "blueback." As mentioned, by war's end it would take nine thousand bluebacks to buy a silver dollar's worth of plug tobacco. With few other sources of funds, because of poor credit, blockaded imports and exports, and a small manufacturing base, the South resorted to printing money. The result was predictably disastrous. But from their point of view, they had no alternative, except surrender.

Then in a move that would warm the hearts of most Hamiltonians,

Congress passed the National Bank Act of 1863. The act was designed to create a national banking system, but without the contentious presence of a central bank. The act allowed state banks to qualify for a national charter by requiring them to buy Treasury bonds that amounted to one-third of the bank's capital. The bank was then authorized to issue banknotes in the amount of 90 percent of the total value of its holdings in Treasury bonds. These banknotes carried the name of the bank, but they looked like greenbacks and were acceptable nationwide; in effect they became a second national currency. To some they may have appeared even safer than the greenbacks, because they were at least backed by the banks' holdings in Treasury bonds, which, in turn, were denominated in gold. The Treasury motivated banks to convert to a national charter by levying a 10 percent tax on the banknotes of state banks, so the banks got in line. By the end of the war there were sixteen hundred nationally chartered banks in the states of the Union.[18]

But even with new and accelerated taxes and nationwide currencies, it was clear that the Union could not run the war on a cash basis. In other words, revenues from taxes alone—regardless of their form—could not provide enough money to support day-to-day military operations. Like a home builder whose construction costs exceed his income by a wide margin, the federal Treasury (and its Confederate counterpart) had to borrow. In fact, the new taxes were designed not only to raise cash for day-to-day operations but also to bolster the federal government's creditworthiness by demonstrating to potential lenders that there would be a predictable and reliable stream of future revenues that could pay off the debt over the term of a loan. Federal officials intended to borrow long term to fund the short-term military operations. Even if the war stretched out several years, as it obviously did, that would be relatively short compared to the twenty-year (redeemable in five years) and sometimes forty-year (redeemable in ten years) loans the government sought. These long-term loans were structured as Treasury bonds, in other words, securities, which meant they could be sold (and resold) to other institutions or to the public, unlike traditional bank loans. An investor paid for the bonds in gold specie and expected to receive his interest and, eventually, the principle, also in gold. The longest-term bonds paid 6 percent interest (for a brief period the

Treasury allowed investors to pay for the bonds with greenbacks, but they discontinued this practice in 1863).

An army may march on its stomach, as Napoleon said, but it stays in the field, supplies itself, and fights on credit.

THE BUSINESS OF CREDIT

> *Beautiful credit! The foundation of a modern society. Who*
> *shall say that this is not the golden age of mutual trust?*
> —Mark Twain and Charles Dudley Warner,
> *The Gilded Age*, 1873

Credit. In the simplest commercial transaction, a seller provides a product to a buyer, who, in turn, promises to pay for the product within a certain time period, say, thirty days. The seller is therefore a lender, a creditor, whether he thinks of himself that way or not. If the competitive conditions allow, the seller may build an interest rate into his price to pay for the cost of having to borrow from his bank to cover the thirty-day period while he is out of pocket.

The glue that holds these credit transactions together is trust and its close cousin, confidence. The seller trusts the buyer to pay him in thirty days; the bank trusts the seller to repay his short-term loan regardless of whether the seller's customer pays on time or at all. Meanwhile, the bank's depositors trust that the bank will have the depositors' money on hand when they call for it, whether the bank's borrower pays on time or not.

Banks are intermediaries. They borrow from one source, for example, investors, such as depositors, and lend to another, for example, businesses and individual borrowers. Aside from their capital, they do not *have* money—they *raise* it from one source and invest it in another, hoping to make a profit on the difference between the two transactions. Under normal and simplified circumstances, there is a positive spread between the interest rate they pay to depositors and the rate they charge to borrowers. As with any kind of credit, both transactions are based on promises. The bank promises to return the depositors' cash upon demand, and the borrower promises to pay back the money according to the established terms of the loan. These terms are spelled out in legal documents, which, in theory, strengthen the promise, or at least spell out remedies, if the promise is broken. A fundamental function of the bank is to evaluate the strength and validity of the borrower's promise—to evaluate his credit quality. The rate the bank charges the borrower is, in part, a function of the borrower's creditworthiness. The stronger the borrower, the less he pays in interest, at least in theory. The depositor, likewise, should evaluate the quality of the bank's promise to have sufficient funds available to meet its obligations to the depositor. The bank operates on the assumption (statistically established) that not all the depositors will want their money at the same time, so that the bank can lend out more than it retains in cash reserves. Further, the bank can supplement depositors' "investments" by selling bonds and equity to boost its capital and by borrowing from other financial institutions.

This system of promises, otherwise known as credit, is the foundation of commerce. In the simplest of examples, a wheat farmer can borrow from his bank in order to have sufficient cash to plant and harvest his crop. If the farmer's credit is a little shaky, the bank may require collateral, such as the title to the farmer's land. In some cases, the farmer may pledge the actual wheat. The farmer then plants his crop, harvests and sells it, repays the loan with the proceeds and keeps whatever is left. If there is any left. If the market for wheat changes, that is, if the price of wheat on the open (and increasingly international) markets plunges, the farmer will not be able to cover his loan, and he may therefore lose his collateral—his farm. And if that happens during a period of economic downturn, the bank may not be able to sell the farm (or sell it for the value of the loan) and so may find itself short of cash when the time comes to repay its depositors and other lenders and investors.

While confidence and trust may seem like different words for the same thing, in fact they are slightly different. A lender may have confidence that a borrower is able to repay a loan, but he may not trust the borrower to do so. And the reverse is true. A lender may trust the sincerity of a potential borrower but lack confidence that the borrower will be able to repay over the life of the loan. The longer the term of the loan, the greater the risk and therefore the lower the confidence. This sort of judgment is especially true in large international loans to sovereign governments. Governments may change radically, through war, revolution, or civil war, and the new government may disavow the loans, even though they have the where-withal to pay.[19] At the risk of stating the obvious, trust and confidence have an emotional component. Facts, such as careful financial analysis, can influence trust and confidence, but so can rumors and herd instincts. Bubbles occur when confidence and trust are too high, panics arise when they are shattered for some reason that is often unrelated—or is an overre-action—to objective realities. When markets are poised on a knife edge, a single report from a respected source can tip the scale one way or the other. (Custer himself wrote two such reports. The first in 1873 went a long way toward panicking the financial markets. The other, the following year, had a more positive effect. More on this later.)

As mentioned, banks borrow from each other, and there is an ever-shifting interbank rate, both domestically and internationally. During the post–Civil War period, the Bank of England was the chief source of international lending and therefore set the interbank rate for its customers among the financial institutions. And so a second fundamental function of a bank is to structure its loans so that they are compatible with the terms arranged with the bank's lenders. For example, a bank may lend at a long-term fixed rate (as in a mortgage) and yet borrow on a short-term floating rate and may, therefore, run into difficulties when short-term rates rise above the long-term interest the bank is receiving. Further difficul-ties arise if the bank has lent out money and does not maintain sufficient cash reserves, and a panic (caused by any number of extraneous causes—war, political upheavals, etc.) causes depositors to demand their cash all at the same time. That generally results in the bank's closing its doors, leaving the depositors and lenders holding an empty bag. (In the nineteenth century there was no Federal Deposit Insurance Corporation [FDIC] and no Federal Reserve, so US investors in bank deposits needed to pay careful attention to the creditworthiness of their bank. Many, however, did not.) Some of those other lenders were banks, so that when one bank defaulted on a loan, the lending bank lost the money, and, if that lending bank had also borrowed from a third bank, the domino effect came into action and a nationwide crash occurred.

What's more, the domino effect always spreads to other sectors of the economy, because when banks fail (or, fearing the future, raise interest rates and thereby curtail lending) businesses that rely on credit to keep operating also suffer and eventually either cut back on production or go out of business altogether. Employees lose their jobs, and the economy goes into free fall.

A complicated bond financing employs the same basic cast of characters—borrower, lender, and intermediaries—usually in multiples. A bond is nothing more than a loan structured as a tradable security and backed by a future stream of revenue. Investors (lenders) advance money to a borrower (a corporation or sovereign government) and in return accept the borrower's bond, which is the borrower's promise to pay a specified (usually fixed) rate of interest during the term of the bond and to repay the principal amount when the bond matures. The fixed rate of interest is called the coupon. In the nineteenth century the lenders in these transactions were in most cases banks, and these banks were generally also intermediaries, that is, they borrowed from other banks and from their depositors to fund their own investments. As mentioned, bank lenders made money on the difference between the interest they earned on their loans, including bonds, and the interest they paid to their lenders, for example, their depositors, other banks, or buyers of the bank's bonds. They also made money by reselling the bonds on the open market (trading/speculating) or by acting as an agent for the borrower and selling bonds to their list of individual clients, for which they received a commission from the borrower. Usually, in large transactions in which governments were the borrowers, there were many banks involved in the transaction, operating in both capacities—lenders and intermediaries. Bonds were more liquid investments than traditional loans, because they could be sold on the open market. But they could also lose principal value if, for some reason, the borrower came under a financial cloud, or if the interest rates had risen at the time the bond holder wanted to sell. Higher interest rates mean lower bond values, as a general rule.[20]

Doubts about the creditworthiness of the borrower also affected the price of a bond on the open market—to say nothing of its salability. The key ingredients in bond financing as in any form of credit were trust and confidence in the promises of a borrower. Bond investors naturally wanted to know how the borrower intended to pay the interest and repay the principle. Where was the money coming from, not only short term, but in the future, for the life of the bond? Was that revenue stream secure? What outside events might damage the borrower's creditworthiness? Using bonds to finance a war was especially tricky, because events on the battlefield affected investor confidence. And those events—victories and defeats—had an unsettling unpredictability about them and affected an investor's assessment of the risk of lending. (Bond issues and bond sales would continue throughout the Civil War; they were not a one-time event. A one-time bond issue would have been less exposed to sudden battlefield shocks, known as "event risk." Continuing bond issues, however, were to some extent hostages of Fortune.) And the higher the risk, the greater the return the investor demanded, in other words, higher interest, which meant that more money would be needed for debt service on the bonds. This demand for higher interest could be reflected in a lower market price for fixed rate bonds, which would mean less money from the sale of the bonds. (If no one offered to buy the bond at par, the ultimate selling price, and therefore revenue, would obviously be lower.) In either case, there would be less money for military operations. And if the risks appeared too great, investors declined altogether, and financing dried up. What's more, nervous holders of shaky bonds would find few takers on the open market—or they would have to accept deep and ruinous discounts.

Grand strategy also affected investor confidence. Consider the Confederate position: the federal naval blockade virtually shut down southern cotton exports, with the result that planters could not export their product, and importers had virtually nothing coming into port, nothing on which to levy tariffs. Despite the fact that there were few major naval battles (*Monitor* and *Merrimack*, *Kearsarge* versus *Alabama* aside), Union sea power decisively reduced the Confederate tax base, which in turn reduced its ability to convince bond investors that there was—and would continue to be—a sufficient revenue stream to support Confederate bonds. What's more, even creatively structured bonds, such as those backed by future cotton revenues, were unappealing to foreign investors for the same reasons—future revenue streams were not reliable. If the cotton could not be exported, the revenue to pay principle and interest on the bond was an illusion. The blockade strategy therefore not only starved the Confederates' imports and exports but also destroyed investor confidence in the long-term viability of Confederate bonds, even as the Union's creative adjustments to its taxation, money, and banking strengthened investors' confidence in the federal government's creditworthiness. Battlefield success also helped significantly. The Federals' close-run victory at Antietam not only gave Lincoln the political leverage he needed to issue the Emancipation Proclamation; it also no doubt soothed the nerves of more than a few investors in Union Treasury bonds. Had that been another Union debacle, interest rates would likely have risen as investors demanded more return for the increased risk.

Those who did invest in Confederate bonds were in many cases Southern individuals who were motivated by patriotism, and as with most investments that are driven by emotion rather than rigorous credit analysis, the investors suffered. (Emblematic of that is the scene in *Gone with the Wind*, in which Scarlett O'Hara's unbalanced father shows her a box full of worthless Confederate bonds, believing them to be valuable. Like many true believers in The Cause, he invested with his heart and lost his fortune—and his mind. And although the dashing Rhett Butler made a lot of money evading the Union Navy, there weren't nearly enough blockade runners to offset Union sea power.) Southern banks that bought Confederate bonds in exchange for gold soon began to run short of specie. That, in turn, damaged the confidence of foreign and domestic investors who quite naturally demanded their interest and principle in gold.[21] (Given the fact that the Confederacy was gradually starving for credit and therefore for the means to continue fighting, it seems all that much more tragic that so many lives were lost in bloody stalemates, like the Battle of Petersburg, toward the end of the war. A containment strategy while the Confederacy financially bled to death would have saved countless lives on both sides. After all, lack of supplies greatly contributed to General Robert E. Lee's surrender. On the other hand, that is probably an oversimplification. Most likely the war-weary North would not have had the patience for such a strategy. Nor was General Ulysses S. Grant a patient commander. And Lincoln had long since grown tired of commanders like George B. McClellan, who was patient to a fault.)

JAY COOKE & COMPANY—SALESMEN

> *The whole country is opening up, all we want is capital to develop it. Slap down the rails and bring the land into market. The richest land on God Almighty's footstool is lying right out there.*
> *If I had my capital free, I could plant it for millions.*
> —Mark Twain, and Charles Dudley Warner,
> *The Gilded Age*, 1873

Not surprisingly, during the Civil War foreign investors had small appetite for US Treasury bonds—especially in the early stages of the war. They wondered whether the United States would prevail and whether the Confederacy would survive. And since the Treasuries of both governments were running short of gold, foreign investors, who had been aggressive buyers of bank and railroad stocks and bonds before the war, turned their backs for the most part on government bonds. That meant the treasuries of both combatants would have to look primarily to domestic sources for bond investors. Ordinarily that would mean selling bonds to the banks—a strategy that both treasuries certainly did employ. But the Civil War introduced a new category of bond investors—Middle America.

Lincoln, of course, came from a rural area and might have been expected to share the Jeffersonian aversion toward national debt, but the cost of the war gave him no choice. He had to borrow from any available source. That included the public. In fact, Lincoln was able to see a virtue in necessity, because he understood that if average Americans invested in Union bonds, they would have an additional stake in the war and in the policies designed to fight and win the war. Far from being a contentious issue, the national debt would thereby become a unifying force. As Lincoln said: "Men readily perceive that they cannot be much oppressed by a debt they owe to themselves."[22]

Enter Jay Cooke, Philadelphia banker. Cooke had already made a fortune in banking as a partner in his brother-in-law's firm. He had invested wisely in transportation companies—canals and railroads. In January of 1861 he opened his own bank—Jay Cooke & Company. The firm was essentially an investment bank; it funded itself with loans from other banks and investors and invested in the stocks and bonds of companies and acted as a sales agent for securities, especially federal Treasury bonds.

The scion of an abolitionist family, Cooke's greatest attribute was salesmanship, along with a messianic sense of mission and an elastic conscience. He fully supported the Union cause, was well placed in political circles, and soon became the primary sales outlet for government bonds. And his greatest contribution to the war effort was his quickly established network of salespeople. Twenty-five hundred agents around the country sold Treasury bonds in denominations as small as fifty dollars to individuals who had never invested in any kind of security before. Cooke took great care to advertise the bonds and explain how they worked. He touted their complete safety as an investment. He took out these ads not only in established newspapers but also in foreign-language papers whose readers were recent immigrants. He appealed to the public's patriotism, their belief in the cause, and their natural desire to make a little money, too. He kept in touch with his agents (who were not his employees but rather a collection of insurance salesmen, real estate agents, and local bankers) through the nationwide telegraph service.

Cooke's campaigns were extremely successful, and by the end of the war 5 percent of Northern families owned Union war bonds. Cooke had sold $1.6 billion worth of bonds, which was 25 percent of the total federal bond sales (and bond sales accounted for 60 percent of the Union's war costs).[23] Cooke and his partners and agents were paid commissions for the sale. By war's end his personal net worth was in the neighborhood of $10 million. He was the nation's preeminent banker, with a reputation for reliability and effectiveness, although there were naturally grumblings about some of his practices. This was to be expected in the competitive world of high finance. As historian M. John Lubetkin wrote: "Cooke bought members of Congress, bribed two vice presidents, built churches, gave vacations to penniless ministers, and combined qualities of money getting, corruption, farsightedness and piety in such successful proportion that he was venerated by the public, feared by politicians, and considered by all the country's leading banker."[24]

In just a few years Jay Cooke and George Custer would be joined in a common project—a project that would contribute significantly to the Panic of 1873.

The obscene costs of the war and the bonds issued by the federal government to cover the financial costs led to a large national debt that was still hanging over the economy during Grant's administration—and during Custer's 1874 Black Hills Expedition. And since that debt (US government bonds) was denominated in gold, any potential gold strike was, as mentioned, something that commanded political as well as commercial attention. Grant, the newly elected president, had been approached with the idea of repaying the government bonds in greenbacks instead of gold. But he rejected the idea. He believed in the gold standard and, what's more, believed in honoring the federal government's promises to its bond holders. Ultimately, he wanted to return the dollar to the gold standard— something that would not happen during his terms as president. (In 1879 the Treasury was required to buy back greenbacks at par, i.e., one greenback dollar for one gold dollar. The object was to retire the paper money from circulation. This is considered a de facto return to the gold standard.) But in his first inaugural address in 1869, Grant said that "to protect the national honor every dollar of government indebtedness should be paid in gold, unless otherwise stipulated in contract." Doing so would "go far to strengthen a credit which ought to be the best in the world."[25] Grant's position was not only honorable but consistent with the recently passed Fourteenth Amendment, as stated in Section Four: "The validity of the public debt of the United States, authorized by law, including debts incurred for payment of pensions and bounties for services in suppressing insurrection or rebellion, shall not be questioned. But neither the United States nor any State shall assume or pay any debt or obligation incurred in aid of insurrection or rebellion against the United States, or any claim for the loss or emancipation of any slave; but all such debts, obligations and claims shall be held illegal and void."

Union bonds would be honored; Confederate bonds would not. Investors who trusted and had confidence in the Confederacy had to swallow a very bitter pill. But Union investors would receive their interest and principal in gold specie.

CHAPTER TWO

GOLD IN MONTANA, DISASTER IN WYOMING

Satisfactory treaty concluded with the Sioux and Cheyennes.
Most cordial feeling prevails.
> —Indian Superintendent E. B. Taylor,
> Fort Laramie, summer 1866[1]

There is a treaty being made at Laramie with the Sioux that are
in the country where you are going. The fighting men in that
country have not come to Laramie, and you will have to fight
them. They will not give you the road unless you whip them.
> —Standing Elk of the Brulé Sioux to
> Colonel Henry B. Carrington, summer 1866[2]

Much of the settlement of the west started with the discovery of gold. It wasn't the sodbusters and cowboys who started the westward movement. They generally came afterward. There were some exceptions, as in Oregon and Texas, but more often than not, settlement followed the miners. When gold was discovered, first a trickle, then a flood of prospectors took a road, or sometimes blazed a trail, to the diggings. It was a geometric progression of hopefuls. It happened in much the same way each time during the nineteenth century—California, Colorado, Montana, Idaho, Nevada, Arizona, and New Mexico.

The gold and silver fields were always inconveniently remote, separated from centers of civilization by vast empty spaces inhabited by fierce and not so fierce tribes of Indians. The roads to the diggings were long and always dangerous, not just because of Indian hostility but also because of the inherent hazards of nineteenth-century frontier travel—oxen-drawn wagons traveling at a pedestrian pace, bad water along the route, inadequate food, sudden storms. Accidents and bad luck were as much a problem as native hostility. A ruptured appendix? A glancing cut from a ricocheting ax blade? A snakebite? A sudden lurch of a wagon and a foot run over? The kick of a mule? Cholera along the river? The trails west were literally scattered with skeletons and graves covered with rocks in a vain attempt to keep the wolves away from the bodies, young or old. Heading west to the mines of Nevada, young Mark Twain wrote that they traveled "always through splendid scenery but occasionally through long ranks of white skeletons of mules and oxen . . . and here and there were upended boards or small piles of stones which the [stagecoach] driver said marked the resting place of more precious remains. It was the loneliest land for a grave."[3] Those who dug the shallow grave knew very well they would never return to put flowers upon it.

And obviously it was not just the men who took to the trails. The women who made the journey, especially in childbearing years, were equally and, even more than equally, at risk. Most were there because of their husbands—with a few entrepreneurial exceptions—and because they also wanted to better their lives. They believed the dreams of gold, if not quite so fervently. Even so, imagine the terror of a teenaged wife, pregnant and forced to give birth along the trails, hundreds of miles from any help other than rough teamsters, a bewildered young husband, or, if lucky, a midwife with only the dimmest understanding of hygiene. Mostly the dreams that drove the emigrants west were the dreams of men; the women had their dreams, too, no doubt. They were probably a little different, but the women went, anyway. Brave souls.

The dangers were real, but they didn't daunt the Argonauts. Most of the would-be miners probably didn't understand or consider the risks very carefully. They bought Colt Navy revolvers and some ammunition and signed on to a wagon train heading for prosperity. And when they got there, they staked a claim and started digging. Reality would set in soon enough. But hopefulness would abide until it became impossible.

And around the mines it wouldn't take long for the rest of white civilization to sprout and grow—saloons, hardware stores, newspapers, farms, ranches, schools, railroads. Sometimes there was even talk of building a church. What came, in fact, were all the blessings and curses of the white society that would inevitably overwhelm the natives. Some prospectors would strike it rich; most would not. Some who struck it would hold on to their wealth; others would lose it and, with a shrug, go back to the diggings for more. But the shopkeepers and drummers and newspaper reporters and lawyers and doctors and parsons peddling everything from patent medicine to shovels to whiskey to eternal salvation could make a decent living without ever lifting a tool. Nor would prosperity elude the professional gamblers or the "soiled doves" who gave the miners a moment or two of pleasure in a tent city and, later, more elegantly, in a false-front saloon. (Mark Twain is a good stand-in for most of the young optimists who headed for the mines. Ignorant of anything having to do with actual mining, he failed quickly and comprehensively but found his way in the newspaper business in one of the boomtowns that inevitably grew up near the diggings.)

Watching this process unfold, the native tribes sooner or later understood that their way of life was being overwhelmed. Whether they could stop the process was a question they could not answer, but many were determined to try. It was the road through their hunting grounds that worried them most, for the road degraded the grazing and chased away the herds of game animals. Whatever the emigrants did when they got to the gold fields was less of a problem, although still real. But initially the Plains tribes were worried about the roads *through* their country. At first it was the wagon roads; soon after it would be the railroads.

Trying to protect the westward-bound rough-and-ready emigrants from the infuriated Indians was the army's job. Sometimes that meant aggressive campaigns against hostile tribesmen; sometimes it meant issuing orders to attack a village whenever they found one; sometimes it meant futile campaigns that wore out men and horses but discovered no Indians; sometimes it meant having great peace conferences and negotiating treaties with the tribes while delivering gifts of supplies and promises of more to come. There never was a consensus on how best to deal with these troublesome people, although most army officers and in fact nearly all of white society understood that the nomadic Indians' way of life was on the verge of extinction and that their only choice was to adopt white civilization's ways of doing things. That was an inevitable outcome, but to most white westerners, it was damnably slow in arriving. The only disagreement was about the means, not the end. Consequently, official policy lurched back and forth between confrontation and negotiation. Partly, the ambivalence stemmed from politics, mixed with genuine and fundamental disagreements about how best to deal with the tribes. Eastern philanthropists preached peace, without apparently understanding that it took all parties to want peace before peace treaties meant anything. Partly, it was economics—war was expensive; annuities and treaties were much cheaper, and promises cheapest of all, and the various corrupt post traders and Indian agents who profited from the system had their own agendas to protect. Partly it was ignorance and bewilderment about the Indian society and culture. A devout Quaker in Philadelphia—a sincere advocate for the Indians—could not really believe in a Sioux warrior who defined himself and his amour propre by the number of scalps he had taken and who would stand over his victim screaming in triumph before carving him into offal. Partly, it was the bureaucratic mindset of some negotiators who defined success as getting a few Indians to agree to a treaty, when in fact those who did agree did not speak for anyone other than their immediate circle and most likely did not understand all the elements of the treaty or even care about them. The decentralized and individualistic society of the Plains Indians did not lend itself easily to high-level diplomatic negotiations. But a bureaucrat who went back east with a signed treaty felt he had done his job and was happy to accept the scanty laurels of diplomatic success, perhaps knowing, or perhaps not wanting to acknowledge, that it was all a fraud—just one more in a Gilded Age that featured kaleidoscopic fraud.

The Bozeman Trail was a major element in this historical process. It was traced out in 1864 and substantially shortened the route between the east and the newly discovered gold fields of western Montana. Roughly five hundred miles long, the trail diverged from the Oregon Trail north of Fort Laramie in Wyoming and went northwest to Virginia City, Montana. Prior to opening the Bozeman Trail, emigrants and prospectors had to take steamboats up the Missouri and then trek across Montana to the western diggings. Or maybe they took a steamship around the Horn and came to Montana from the west. Or up through Utah from Salt Lake City (the trail was essentially the hypotenuse of the triangle, with Salt Lake being at the right angle). Regardless of how they came, it was a long way, and the Bozeman Trail shortened the journey.

John Bozeman and his partner discovered the trail and guided the first prospectors and their families from Fort Laramie northwest along the eastern edge of the Bighorn Mountains and into what was known as the Powder River country and from there west along the Yellowstone River. Well watered and awesomely beautiful, once into the Bighorns, the country was the favorite hunting grounds of the Sioux, Cheyenne, and Arapahoe—three tribes that were loosely aligned when they were not quarreling—three tribes that understood what was happening before their eyes. Their hunting grounds were shrinking, and now there was a detested white man's road running through the heart of them.

The Bozeman Trail was therefore a microcosm of western development. Its short history is directly linked to the story of Custer's 1874 Black Hills Expedition, because the Bozeman Trail led to the Red Cloud War, which, in turn, led to the 1868 Treaty of Fort Laramie that gave the Black Hills to the Sioux. The Red Cloud War was fought over a road. Or maybe the road was a symbol and a harbinger, not only to the whites but also to the Indians, revealing that the clash between the tribes and the encroaching whites was really a conflict of different ideas and attitudes, optimism on the one hand, desperation on the other—one way of life in the process of overwhelming another.

Colonel Henry B. Carrington's Civil War experience consisted of recruiting duty in Ohio and administering POW camps in Indiana. By all accounts he did a good job. But he had spent the war behind a desk and had not experienced the exhilaration, as Winston Churchill put it, of having been shot at and missed.[4] He was not a graduate of West Point, and without the benefit of combat experience, his military skills were limited, at best. Nor did he have a forceful personality or strong leadership abilities. Physically, he was unimposing. He was a political appointee who decided to stay in the army after the war. In short, he was hardly the man to choose to take on a dangerous assignment in a hostile region. But somehow he was given just such a job.

He was to command the Second Battalion of the 18th Ohio Infantry. His assignment was to build and garrison two forts along the Bozeman Trail. In addition to building the forts, Carrington was to protect the travelers along the trail—emigrants and gold seekers. As he understood it, his role was essentially defensive. And as happened so often in the settlement of the west, the army was assigned the job at least in part because the gold finds were important not just to the hardy pioneers who looked for it. It was national business. Hence, the army.

The battalion Carrington was given by no means resembled the unit that had fought successfully in Georgia with General Sherman, while Carrington was in Ohio. Two-thirds of the men were raw recruits brought in to replace the veterans who were mustered out. Many of the veteran officers remained, however. Moreover, the majority of men were armed with Civil War muzzle-loading rifles. They fired a .58 caliber Minié ball and had a range of up to one thousand yards. A well-trained soldier could fire perhaps three rounds a minute.[5] But Carrington's troops were not well trained, and worse, they were chronically short of ammunition, which made effective training that much more difficult. The army was in the process of phasing out the muzzle loaders in favor of a breech-loading rifle that fired metallic cartridges—a huge advance over the separate powder and bullet charges on the Civil War. But Carrington's command would not get replacement weapons until well after the disasters awaiting him and his men. The regimental band, however, carried seven-shot Spencer carbines, a weapon with less range and hitting power but greater rate of fire. The bandsmen could fight as well as play. Taking a band along might have seemed frivolous, but if there was one thing officers and men agreed upon, it was that a regimental band was important for morale. This was especially true for units that were going into the heart of the frontier to establish a presence in a country far from any aspect of civilization.[6]

Also part of the expedition were several officers' wives, including Margaret Carrington, and a few children. The total force numbered seven hundred men, and although they were infantrymen they also acquired two hundred horses from discharged volunteer troops. It was not unusual in the frontier army to use horses and even mules to provide transportation for infantry. Armed with long-barreled muzzle loaders, the troops could hardly fight as cavalry, but they could do scout duties and ride quickly to the scene of action at which point they would have to dismount and fight on foot (it would take an exceptional trooper to reload a muzzle loader on horseback). Infantry per se were better suited for garrison or defensive roles such as guarding slow-moving wagon trains. They were also the primary means of attacking fixed positions or lines of enemies, as they did in the Civil War. Unfortunately for the army, Indians did not believe in fixed positions. Obviously, the infantry could not compete offensively against well-mounted tribesmen, as common sense should have suggested and subsequent events would demonstrate conclusively. But an infantryman was much less expensive to maintain, roughly half the cost of a cavalry trooper, whose expenses included his horse. Congress was forever trying to cut costs, especially in light of the national debt left from the Civil War. So the frontier army, undersized to begin with, was chronically short of cavalry.

Carrington was apparently not too concerned about taking his "walk a heaps" (as the Indians called infantry) into the Powder River country. His job, as he saw it, was to build two forts and escort settlers' wagon trains when necessary. Infantry could handle those duties (most frontier forts were built by the troops, rather than civilian contractors). As for the Indians, Carrington was prepared to confront them with "patience, forbearance, and common sense."[7] If the Sioux and their allies had shared these sentiments, Carrington's plan might have had a chance of working, but patience and forbearance were not on the Sioux or Cheyenne agenda, and they had a different and perhaps more realistic notion of common sense.

Supporting the Carrington expedition were some two hundred wagons driven by civilian contractors. The army had experimented with using troops to drive supply wagons during the Mexican War, but the experiment was not a success, and from then on the army usually hired civilian teamsters, who, after all, were specialists and knew their business. (The owners of transportation companies, moreover, tended to be well connected politically.) Along for the trip was a herd of seven hundred beef cattle. The beef herds, the horses and mules of the teamsters, and the two hundred army horses were enough to degrade the grazing along the trail; it was one of many things that infuriated the Sioux. Their game animals were almost exclusively grazers, and their pony herds existed entirely on grass, unlike the army's horses that needed substantial amounts of grain to supplement their grazing. Further, the army was not the only force using the trail. The white settlers and their long trains of wagons, encouraged by the army's presence, were flooding up to the gold fields. (As an example of the impact on the environment, the ruts made by the wagons on the Bozeman Trail are still visible in some spots, today.) On the other hand, the cattle herd, horses, and mules were very tempting objects for raids. By stealing the livestock the Indians achieved a number of objects at once—they got the animals off the trail, converted them into food or additional mounts, and they reduced the army's capability and food supplies. There seems to be no doubt that the Sioux and their allies were sincere in wanting to close the Bozeman Trail, but while they were at it, they were happy enough to gather plunder and a few scalps. And the younger warriors could count coup and so give themselves great deeds to talk about around the campfires later.

The venerable frontiersman Jim Bridger was Carrington's guide. Bridger was into his sixties by this time, but he was still up to the job. He had been trapping and trading through the Rockies for four decades, and his knowledge of the tribes and his advice to Carrington were invaluable. For Carrington, any reasonable advice was welcome. It's hard to imagine a less well-prepared officer for this assignment. Or, more accurately, Carrington was well enough prepared for the assignment of building two forts, but that was not the most difficult task he would face. It would soon be his turn to experience the exhilaration Churchill referred to: being shot at by tribesmen who did not share Carrington's patience and forbearance. (Carrington would later suffer a gunshot wound to his leg, but this would happen after he had been relieved of command, and it would not come in combat but rather from an accidental discharge of his own pistol.)

When Carrington's force arrived in Fort Laramie in the summer of 1866, there was a great gathering of tribesmen, summoned there by agents of the Indian Bureau for yet another peace conference. Influential war leaders such as Red Cloud and Young Man Afraid of His Horses were there. These two

had been involved in fighting the previous year and were only mildly interested in what the white peace commissioners had to say. When they saw
Carrington's troops arrive and learned of their destination, Red Cloud and
his followers stormed out of the meeting, saying: "The Great Father sends
us presents and wants us to sell him the road, but White Chief [Carrington]
goes with soldiers to steal the road before Indian says yes or no."[8] Red Cloud
and his band headed north, intending to close the Bozeman Trail permanently. Meanwhile, Indian Superintendent E. B. Taylor managed to make a
treaty with those Sioux and Cheyenne who remained, probably because they
came from territories that were not threatened by the Bozeman Trail. And
no doubt some were sly or cynical enough to agree to the treaty, accept the
"presents," and then go off and forget about the deal. In any event, Taylor
felt justified in reporting that "cordial feelings prevailed." That report
encouraged emigrants and reinforced their natural ignorance of the dangers
that lay along the trail. A few months later Taylor was fired by his boss,
the Secretary of the Interior, Orville Brown, who said that Taylor was in
league with "rogues . . . robbing the Indians."[9] No doubt there was truth to
the charge, since the Indian Bureau was rotten with corruption, but that was
not Taylor's only sin; his knowingly false and optimistic report doomed
more than a few emigrants to violent death along the Bozeman. They came
carelessly and in small groups, too small for adequate deterrence or defense,
because they assumed the local Indians would only show themselves when
they came to beg for coffee or sugar. Easy pickings—for the Sioux.[10]

Carrington's first destination was Fort Reno, 169 miles northwest of
Fort Laramie. The fort was manned by two companies of "galvanized
Yankees," Confederate POWs who had signed on for frontier duty as a
better alternative to prison camp. Reno was a dilapidated disgrace of a
fort, and Carrington had originally intended to gather up any useful items
and supplies and then destroy the place. But he decided quite rightly that
emigrant trains would welcome any way station, however crude. So he
detached one company of troops to garrison the place and relieve the galvanized Yankees, who were in poor physical condition and in no mood to
continue their service, now that the Civil War was over.

The next leg of the expedition was a sixty-seven-mile march to the
forks of Piney Creek, a beautiful location on the east side of the Bighorn

Mountains. Here Carrington decided to build his first fort, to be named Fort Phil Kearny. There was ample timber close by, and Carrington immediately began the task of cutting and sawing materials for his fort. (He had brought along a steam-powered sawmill.) Unlike most western forts, Carrington's outpost would be surrounded by a log stockade with blockhouses on the corners to allow troops to cover the entire exterior walls. (Most frontier "forts" were nothing more than buildings grouped around a parade ground with no exterior walls—more like villages than citadels.) Work progressed quickly, and on August 3 Carrington felt comfortable enough to detach two more companies to head north and establish Fort C. F. Smith along the banks of the Bighorn River in Montana, ninety-one miles away. That left Carrington with five companies.

From the moment the troops arrived, Red Cloud and his allies wasted no time attacking the workers, stealing the stock as well as harassing the civilian wagon trains on the trail. Red Cloud appears to have been the presiding genius behind the Sioux and Cheyenne strategies, although it's always difficult to apply white notions of generalship and politics to the more independently minded tribesmen. But somehow he and the other major chieftains aggregated anywhere from fifteen hundred to two thousand Sioux, Cheyenne, and Arapahoe warriors, who constantly harassed the fort and the workers, as well as the trains along the trail. It was not difficult for Red Cloud and the other leaders to motivate the tribesmen; they all could see what was happening, and they all were interested in plunder and martial glory. They had both defensive and offensive reasons to attack the fort and the travelers on the trail. As things worsened and attacks accelerated, Carrington repeatedly sent messengers to Fort Laramie asking for reinforcements, for he felt he was more or less under siege. His attitude and tactical concept disgusted his officers, who advocated more offensive action against the hostiles. Carrington felt his duty was to build a fort—which he had done. But in so doing he had built walls that kept not only the Indians out but also virtually kept his command inside. The Sioux and Cheyenne, meanwhile, roamed at will beyond the gates.

Finally in November Carrington received forty-five new infantrymen and sixty cavalry—all of whom were new recruits and dubious horsemen. They, too, were armed mostly with muzzle loaders, so it hardly mattered whether they were expert riders or not, since they would have to fight on foot. Also arriving was Captain William J. Fetterman, an aggressive officer with the kind of Civil War combat experience that Carrington so sorely lacked—and so consciously regretted. In the slang of the Civil War troops, Fetterman had seen the elephant, and more than once. Soon after he arrived, Fetterman, who boasted that he could march through the entire Sioux nation with eighty troops, began to lobby for more aggressive action against the Indians. Other officers agreed. They got their chance a few weeks later. He and they would see an elephant of a different color.

The Sioux warriors' favorite tactic was the decoy. A small group of riders would attack some unit of the army and attract the attention of the fort. They would then withdraw and lead the troops into an ambush. They had tried it earlier in December, with some success, although the officer in charge in that attack did not follow aggressively and so escaped annihilation. But the Indians saw indications that the tactic could work against Carrington's troops. All that it required was a slightly more aggressive officer or a more persuasive decoy. All told, the Indian forces numbered something like two thousand warriors—more than enough to wipe out Fort Kearny, if the soldiers could be enticed to leave their walls. The warriors concealed themselves in the ravines on both sides of the Bozeman Trail that ran up to and over the Lodge Trail Ridge. The ambush was set about three miles from the fort, on the far side of Lodge Trail Ridge.

On December 21 a small number of warriors led by Crazy Horse attacked the wagon train bringing timber from the logging camp. It was the decoy. Carrington sent a relief force under Captain Fetterman, who, because of seniority, demanded that he be given command of the troops. He had, all told, two officers, seventy-six enlisted men and two volunteer civilians. It was a mixture of cavalry and infantry that marched to the rescue of the wood wagon train. In a grim sort of irony, Fetterman led eighty men, and he would get the chance to make good on his boast and march through a great portion of the Sioux nation. Carrington gave Fetterman strict orders not to chase the Sioux beyond the Lodge Trail Ridge, but the decoy was too tempting for the exasperated and turbulent Fetterman, and he passed over the ridge and out of sight. The Indians sprang the trap, killed every man, and stripped and mutilated the bodies.

The fight lasted less than an hour. Not able to see what was happening but sensing difficulty, Carrington sent a relief force, but they were too late. All that was left of Fetterman's troops were ghastly remnants.[11] Fortunately for the relief force, the Indians had left, or those troops would have been overwhelmed, too.

The scene at the battlefield would have revolted the most hardened soldier. Colonel Carrington's official report detailed the mutilations:

> Eyes torn out and laid on rocks; noses cut off; ears cut off; chins hewn off; teeth chopped out; joints of fingers, brains taken out and placed on rocks with other members of the body; entrails taken out and exposed; hands cut off; feet cut off; arms taken out from sockets; private parts severed and indecently placed on the person [usually shoved into the victim's mouth]; eyes, ears, mouth and arms penetrated with spearheads, sticks and arrows; ribs slashed to separation with knives; skulls severed in every form, from chin to crown, muscles of calves, thighs, stomach, breast, back, arms, and cheek taken out. Punctures upon every sensitive part of the body, even to the soles of the feet and palms of the hand.[12]

Collecting the bodies was like collecting cordwood. In the arctic conditions the bodies froze quickly, but even so the smell of blood or the sight of the carnage spooked the mules pulling the wagons. A civilian teamster and volunteer wrote: "When the first wagon had been half loaded, the mules began to lurch and kick, until they succeeded in throwing the men aside. Turning the wagon around they overturned it in their frenzy, and the bodies were dumped out before the animals could be recaptured and subdued. It was a terrible sight and a horrible job."[13]

It's not hard to imagine the reaction of the new recruits, or even the veterans of the Civil War. Not long ago many of them were starving as tenants, little more than serfs, on an Irish or German estate. They had come to the United States for opportunity. Now they were collecting the body parts of men they had known. What sort of place had they come to? What kind of people did this sort of thing? If this butchery was intended to frighten the soldiers, it worked. How could it not? The literate among them might begin to question James Fenimore Cooper's "noble savage." There was nothing noble about this battle. What sort of human would do this to another, dead adversary? And, worse, what if the victims were still alive as it happened? What then? Clearly, it was a new world these troops had come to. The mountains and the trail north were beautiful, but the underlying reality was something like a painting by Hieronymus Bosch. It was Hell.

Civilian frontiersman John "Portugee" Phillips volunteered to ride south for help. It took him four days to reach Fort Laramie. It was a ride of two hundred and thirty-six miles, all in a blinding snowstorm and grotesque cold. Phillips suffered for weeks thereafter from severe frostbite; his horse collapsed and died just after he reached Laramie. (He was not the only one who volunteered to go. Carrington wisely understood that sending multiple messengers was something of an insurance policy. But Phillips arrived first and so gets the lion's share of historical credit.) A relief force was organized and arrived at the beleaguered fort on January sixteenth, after being delayed by blizzard conditions.

Of course, there was an inquiry. The army didn't like disasters, so someone's head had to roll. Carrington was relieved of command. He and his wife and a small escort left Fort Phil Kearny in a hideous snowstorm, and it was along the way that he shot himself, accidently, in the leg. He was reassigned but left the army three years later, still under a cloud.

One inquiry (conducted not by the army but by the Interior Department) was able to catalog the results of the Indian attacks all along the trail. Their findings go some way toward exonerating Carrington by demonstrating that he was simply undermanned. The inquiry found that "between July 26 and December 21 the Sioux on the Bozeman Trail and in the vicinity of Fort Phil Kearny killed 5 officers and 91 enlisted men, killed 58 civilians and wounded 20, and stole 306 oxen and cows, 304 mules, and 161 horses. They made 51 hostile demonstrations against Fort Phil Kearny."[14] It went on to say that "the difficulty in a nutshell was that the commanding officer of the district was furnished no more troops or supplies for this state of war than had been provided and furnished him for a state of profound peace."[15] That was part of the problem, surely, but leadership and experience with Indian fighting were also sorely lacking, not only with Carrington but with the other officers of the battalion. As Jim Bridger had said to Carrington: "Your boys who fought down south are crazy. They don't know anything about fighting Indians."[16] (Lakota holy man, Black Elk, concurred. He said, "The cavalry of the Wasichus [whites] did not know how to fight. They kept together and when they came on you could hardly miss them."[17]) Fetterman certainly fit that bill. He had too much confidence in his own mettle and that of his troops, too little understanding of Indian warfare, too little respect for the Indian's martial spirit and skills, and too much contempt for Carrington to pay attention to explicit orders. As for Carrington, it's true that he ordered Fetterman not to follow beyond the Lodge Trail Ridge, but when issuing a direct order, a commander who has the respect of his subordinates is able to put the fear of God into them. It's easy to imagine Sherman's or Sheridan's style in issuing similar orders (Sheridan was known to be an artist with profanity). If either of them had said, "Don't go past the Lodge Trail Ridge," no junior officer would have gone a step beyond. But Carrington did not have that natural authority, and Fetterman feared neither Carrington nor the Indians, and so had no compunction about disobeying.

Fetterman's contemptuous relationship with his commanding officer and his impetuous aggressiveness are a lowercase version of future events involving George Custer and two separate commanding officers, neither of whom Custer thought much of. But until Custer repeated some of Fetterman's mistakes at the Little Bighorn, Fetterman's defeat was the worst in the history of the army's battles against the Indians.

The Indians did not rest on their laurels. They resumed harassing the forts as soon the weather began to moderate. The following summer saw two sharp fights, one at Phil Kearny, the other at Fort C. F. Smith. There was a difference this time, however, for the troops had recently been supplied with breech-loading Springfield rifles that fired a metallic cartridge. Although still a single-shot weapon, the new rifles could be reloaded in a fraction of the time it took to load the older rifles. When the Indians staged a frontal attack against a wood-cutting party, they were shocked by the volume of fire they received from troops hidden behind a corral made of wagon boxes—hence the "Wagon Box Fight." After taking more casualties than they could tolerate, the Indians retreated. So, too, at Fort C. F. Smith they attacked a collection of civilian and army hay cutters, but these men had also built barricades and had the advantage of repeating rifles. In both fights the Indians were driven off with severe casualties. In fact, Red Cloud later said he "lost the flower of his fighting warriors in the Wagon Box Fight."[18]

Subsequently there were discussions about peace, but Red Cloud refused to negotiate until his conditions were met—abandonment of the forts, including Fort Reno, and closure of the Bozeman Trail. Finally in November of 1868 Red Cloud arrived at Fort Laramie and agreed to the treaty, for the United States had accepted his demands. The army had abandoned the forts, and as the soldiers marched away they perhaps saw the smoke rising from the fires started by the Indians. In return, Red Cloud and the others agreed to live on a reservation that consisted of the current state of South Dakota west of the Missouri, including the Black Hills. The reservation lands totaled thirty-one million acres. The Sioux would also have the right to hunt in their normal territories outside the reservation, which included the Powder River country. Consisting of an additional nineteen million acres, this land was called, according to the 1868 Treaty, "unceded Indian territory," and was identified as "the country north of the North Platt River and east of the summits of the Big Horn Mountains." This land was adjacent to, but not part of, the reservation and so remained in a kind of legal limbo, although the treaty said that no white man could enter this area without Sioux consent (Article XVI).[19] They did not specify, however, the northern border of this territory. This was, of course, the favorite hunting grounds of the Red Cloud and Spotted Tail bands but also the preferred country of the non-treaty Sioux under Sitting Bull and Crazy Horse. The Sioux also agreed that they would cease hostilities and stop attacking white travelers or railroad construction crews and that "they will never capture or carry off from the settlements white women and children and that they will never kill or scalp white men or attempt to do them harm" (Article XI).[20] Red Cloud was acknowledged to be the most powerful of the Indian leaders, but even he could never enforce those restrictions on his younger warriors. He certainly knew that very well, but he signed anyway.

The Red Cloud War can be seen as a victory of sorts for the Sioux. Certainly the Sioux considered it a victory and viewed the treaty only as a sign that they were willing to live in peace. They did not care much for, or really understand, the fine print of the treaty. As far as they were concerned, the detested forts were gone, and life would go on pretty much as it always had. Red Cloud could take some satisfaction in having won his war. The army could also tell itself that the forts had become irrelevant since, after the Fetterman Battle, few if any emigrants wanted to use the Bozeman Trail. The intrepid Nelson Story, who in 1866 had defied Carrington's orders and driven one thousand head of Texas longhorns up the trail, had returned in 1867 with another herd and twelve wagons loaded with produce for the mining districts.[21] But he was the rarest of rare breeds and was most likely the last civilian to use the road. The hopeful and eager amateurs from the east and the hardy prospectors from everywhere finally knew better than to risk the Bozeman Trail. What's more, the Union Pacific Railroad was growing steadily west, so that emigrants would soon be able to take the train all the way to Salt Lake City and then head north to the mines from there. So from the army's point of view, there really was no reason to maintain the forts, now. Of course, that was largely a rationalization, but it was one the generals who negotiated the treaty, including General Alfred Terry, could live with, in exchange for peace, however fragile. (They would regret the loss of these forts during the campaigns of 1876, however.)

Red Cloud and Spotted Tail led their bands to the reservation. Other Sioux leaders, such as Sitting Bull, wanted nothing to do with the treaty, nor did they care anything about peace with the whites. They remained hostile roamers living their traditional life in their traditional hunting grounds. Between these two factions were hundreds of young warriors who were ambivalent about the peace. They spent winters on the reservation living off the government annuities, but when the spring came many gravitated to Sitting Bull and the old way of life—hunting where they liked and fighting their enemies—other tribes, like the Crow and Arikara, and the white settlers, miners, and travelers. This shifting constituency was a constant source of trouble and confusion to the army, which had the nearly impossible task of separating the hostile from the peaceful individuals—

impossible because the same individual was often both, depending on the season and the mood. Before the Red Cloud War it could be assumed that all the Sioux were hostile. But now that some had agreed to peace and agreed to live on a reservation, the picture became much more complicated. At first General Sherman felt some optimism about the arrangement, since the army could accept that any Sioux on the reservation were peacefully inclined and any off the reservation were hostiles. But he soon understood that the problem of the "summer rovers" made the army's task more, not less, difficult. It was the same problem encountered by invading armies in any guerilla war throughout history—partisan fighters protected by their countrymen and living among them were difficult to identify, much less encounter and defeat. And when the young warriors were roaming in the summer in the vast country of the Dakota and Montana territories, they were simply hard to find.

Red Cloud and his colleague Spotted Tail made a trip to the east in 1870. It was an eye-opening visit for both, and if the object was to overawe the two chieftains with the size and might of the US government and indeed the white civilization, it apparently worked. Or as one still militant Lakota warrior put it, "Red Cloud saw too much."[22] Both chiefs returned to their respective agencies and made no more war on the whites. The warriors who lived around Red Cloud and Spotted Tail were, however, another story. So, too, Sitting Bull.

And so, as of November of 1868, the Black Hills legally belonged to the Sioux. A piece of paper said so.

CHAPTER THREE

THE ADVERSARIES

THE SIOUX

> *The ideal male role was adjusted to risk, violence and self-assertion. To court danger and tempt death to an extent almost beyond reason, were prerogatives of success. To boast and brag of one's daring and one's achievements were the accepted rewards for the successful.*
>
> —Royal Hassrick[1]

> *The morning star symbolizes wisdom; intrinsic to that wisdom is the understanding that the life forms of the entire universe comprise a system of relationships with humans. Thus kinship is the central trope of the Lakota world.*
>
> —Raymond J. DeMallie[2]

T o Custer, the Sioux, and in fact all the Plains tribes, were profoundly different, although anthropologist Royal Hassrick's quote above could also easily describe Custer's own modus operandi. There were perhaps more similarities between the two warrior cultures than few whites could perceive or admit. But for most if not all of white culture, the Indians were savages. Even those who romanticized them and admired them from afar, like James Fenimore Cooper, put them in the category of "noble savages."

The word "savage" had several different meanings. In the nineteenth century it was commonly believed that cultures went through well-defined evolutionary phases. There were different terms for these phases depending on the particular anthropological theory, but basically the three major phases were Primitive, Savage, and Civilized. So the word "savages" in that context simply meant that the Indians were a step behind in their cultural development. With a little help from well-meaning missionaries, philanthropists, and an enlightened government, they could be guided to the next level. They could become civilized. While hardly complimentary, the term "savage" was descriptive of a state of evolution and was therefore not especially derogatory, except for the implicit cultural condescension. Another use of the term, perhaps related to the first, was simply as an alternative to "Indian"—a synonym in the sense that the French equivalent, *sauvage*, was used generically. (It should be noted that the French in North America generally had good relations with the natives they encountered— far better than their Anglo-American competitors—and were significantly less guilty of ethnocentrism. The first white men the Indians encountered were more often than not the *coureurs du bois*, the French-Canadian frontiersmen, trappers, and traders, men who often married Indian women and adopted many of the Indian ways.)

A third use of the word "savage" was the adjective that sprang to mind whenever a white person viewed the mutilated corpse of a settler or soldier. Or read about it. In this case, the word was used with venom and bitterness. Army Captain John Cremony described one particular Apache he knew as a "savage savage," illustrating the fact that the word was both an adjective and a noun.[3]

Despite the multiple meanings of the word, the common denominator was the widespread white belief that the Indians had no social structure, no sense of their history, no religion beyond superstitious offerings to inanimate objects or animal spirits, no arts, no science, and that culturally they were little better than wolves, who also traveled in packs and cooperated among themselves for the hunt. Indians in fact were worse than wolves, because they also gloried in war and in killing and mutilating their enemies.

The whites thought in terms of a strictly linear and inevitable cultural development—primitive to savage to civilized. Some cultures were slow in arriving, to be sure. But the process was inevitable. The European/ American understanding of history allowed no other interpretation and did not admit to, or even conceive of, the possibility of a parallel and distinct evolution of a culture that was a response to different environmental conditions and one that satisfied its members to the point that they sought no further evolution, desired no change. This is not to suggest that the culture of the Plains Indians was the equal to what we think of as Western civilization. It was certainly true that they had no developed literature (or literacy), science, architecture, or medicine. But it is to say that the Sioux response to their history and geography satisfied themselves and that they were content to have things stay exactly as they were. Their cosmology made sense to them, and it was far from unsophisticated, likewise their social structures and religion. Their only temptation in their contacts with the white men was technology—firearms, most notably. And, unhappily for many, alcohol. And it was this contact and gradual dependence upon it that partly contributed to unwelcome changes. But the Sioux did not look upon the whole of white culture with envious eyes or a sense of inferiority; quite the contrary.

But the Indian savagery, in all its definitions, was evidence of something otherworldly to the whites. Like all of his troops, Colonel Henry Carrington had been appalled by the mutilations at the Fetterman Battle, and the subject troubled him. Years later he talked with one of Red Cloud's fighters and questioned him:

> The key to the mutilations were [*sic*] startling and impressive. Their idea of the spirit land is that it is a physical paradise; but we enter upon its mysteries just as in the condition we hold when we die. In the Indian paradise every physical taste or longing is promptly met. If he wants food, it is at hand; water springs up for ready use; ponies and game abound; blossoms, leaves and fruits never fail; all is perennial and perpetual. But what is the Indian hell? It is the same place and profusion of mercies, but the bad cannot partake . . . with the muscles of the arms cut out, the victim could not pull a bowstring or trigger, with all other muscles gone, he could not put a foot in a stirrup or stoop to drink; so that while every sense was in agony for relief from hunger or thirst, there could be no relief at all.[4]

This may have been plausible as an explanation of the mutilation, but the theological gloss was not at all persuasive to the white civilization, even if they knew about it, which is highly unlikely. To them it was barbaric butchery, plain and simple. Viewed from the Sioux perspective, it's especially interesting that they were such aggressive warriors, since they knew if they were killed in battle, their enemies would mutilate them in exactly the same fashion, and paradise would turn into hell. (And, when their enemies were other tribes or barbarians like Colonel John Chivington and his men, they were not wrong. Chivington commanded a group of Colorado volunteers at the massacre of a Cheyenne village at Sand Creek.) It may also explain why the Sioux were so zealous in recovering the bodies of their slain comrades; it was always difficult to estimate their casualties, because there were rarely any bodies left on the battlefield. (On the other hand, Hassrick quoted the testimony of a warrior who said of a slain comrade that "it was good to be left in enemy territory."[5] So the subject is, as with most things about the Sioux, complicated.)

Regardless of the white prejudices and fears, the fact is the Sioux had a highly evolved culture, one that was perfectly adapted to their surroundings. Custer only glimpsed this culture, and not being conversant with their difficult language, he was at the usual disadvantage of one adversary trying to understand another alien culture and people. But he was right in understanding that the Sioux were very, very different.

Historian Francis Parkman traveled with a band of Oglala for several weeks in 1846 and echoed Custer's assessment:

> For the most part, a civilized white man can discover but very few points of sympathy between his own nature and that of an Indian. With every disposition to do justice to their good qualities, he must be conscious that an impassable gulf lies between him and his red brethren of the prairie [irony, noted]. Nay, so alien to himself do they appear, that having breathed for a few months or a few weeks the air of this region, he begins to look upon them as a troublesome species of wild beast, and, if expedient, he could shoot them with as little compunction as they would experience after performing the same office upon him.[6]

Of course, Parkman was generalizing about all the western Indians, but it's fair to say that if all Plains Indians were different from white men, the Sioux and their close allies were the most different of all.

The cosmology represented a system of great complexity and logical integration. The rank and order of the universal forces was a carefully conceived organization which explained not only how the world operated but mankind's role in relation to it.
—Royal Hassrick, *The Sioux,* 1988[7]

Who were these people, and where did they come from?

They had not always lived on the Plains, not always hunted the buffalo, and were not always the world's finest light cavalry. They used to hunt on foot. In the past it was the woodland creatures that they hunted—deer, elk, and anything else that came their way. They were stalkers of game and so were the opposite of their popular image. They had lived in the forests of Minnesota and were threatened by the Cree and Ojibwa, who had closer contact with French traders and who had consequently acquired firearms. The word "Sioux" is derived from an Ojibwa word *Nadowessioux,* which means "little snake," in other words, "enemy."[8] Pressured by their enemies, the Sioux began migrating west and into the buffalo-rich Plains. They had to fight tribes like the Omaha, Iowa, and Arikara for this territory, and by the middle of the eighteenth century they had consolidated their position. No one knows precisely when they acquired the horse, but most likely it was early in the eighteenth century. Their nomadic hunting culture then underwent a dramatic change. Suddenly their range could be extended and the buffalo more easily tracked and killed. The horse transformed their society, and in a matter of only a century the Sioux had changed from woodland stalkers of game to accomplished hunters on horseback and fearsome cavalry during time of war.

And just at the turn of the nineteenth century the Sioux attacked and evicted the Cheyenne, the Kiowa, and the Crow from the Black Hills. The Cheyenne would later ally themselves with their powerful neighbors, but the Crow, never. Interestingly, the Crow language falls under the broad family of languages known as Siouan, while the Cheyenne spoke an Algonquin language. As historian Alvin Josephy writes: "Among Indians there is little relationship among language groups and culture. Many contrasting ways of life, as well as sharply different cultural levels existed among people who spoke the same or related tongues. The rich, powerful Aztec of Mexico and the poor, timorous Gosiute of the Utah-Nevada desert were members of the same language family. At the same time, peoples like the Flatheads and Nez Perce, who spoke entirely different languages, could band together and lead the same type of life."⁹ The same could be said for the Sioux and Cheyenne as well as the Arapaho (also Algonquin)—the three tribes that annihilated Fetterman and his men.

There were three major divisions of the Sioux nation—the Teton Sioux or Lakota, the Santee Dakota, and the Yanktonai Nakota. These latter two divisions tended to stay to the east of the Lakota—most commonly identified as the "Sioux," the mighty warriors of the Plains.

There were seven major groupings of the Teton or Lakota tribe: Brulé, Sans Arc, Miniconjou, Hunkpapa, Blackfeet, Oglala, and Two Kettles. The largest and most famous were the Oglala, the Brulé, the Miniconjou, and the Hunkpapa. Each of these tribes had some agreed-upon territorial definition, but no hard and fast boundaries, and during the Red Cloud War, for example, warriors from the subtribes came together in common cause. The Oglala's territory was the westernmost and encompassed the northeastern corner of Wyoming and the western edge of South Dakota, including the Black Hills. The Brulé were to the southeast, the Miniconjou north of the Brulé, and the Hunkpapa, Sans Arc, and Blackfeet farthest north on both sides of the border between Montana and North Dakota. The smaller Two Kettles were wedged between the Brulé and the Miniconjou.

The total population of all seven Teton Sioux tribes was, not surprisingly, difficult to determine. Even when the tribes were on the reservation, the problem persisted, since corrupt Indian agents inflated their numbers in order to increase the annuities, which could then be co-opted by the agents and sold for personal profit. And, except in winter, warriors were constantly coming and going, sometimes to hunt, sometimes to raid. But a reasonable estimate of the Sioux population in 1850 was fifteen thousand.¹⁰ That number had probably increased gradually by 1874, when Custer went into the Black Hills. But regardless of the precise number, the Sioux were the largest and most powerful of the Plains tribes, and they knew it.

The whites who advocated peace with the Sioux were destined to be

disappointed, as long as the Lakota remained culturally intact and unde-
feated on the battlefield. True, Red Cloud (an Oglala) and Spotted Tail (a
Brulé) agreed to a reservation, but the only element that was even remotely
of interest to them, and slightly compatible with the Sioux way of life, was
the promise of regular rations. Like all hunter/gatherer peoples, the Sioux
endured famine now and then, when the buffalo unaccountably disappeared
according to the mysterious vagaries of their migrations. Winters could be
especially hard on the Indians. The treaty annuities, such as they were,
were a fallback position. So, too, were the Black Hills, where the hunters
could expect to find deer, elk, and antelope in any season. Moreover, the
Sioux who signed the 1868 treaty apparently did not object to living on the
reservation, since that country was more or less where they lived traditionally and, more to the point, because most of them did not understand the
limits that were placed on them under the treaty. To Red Cloud, Spotted
Tail, and their followers, the treaty simply meant they would refrain from
attacking the railroad, stage lines, and emigrant trains. In exchange, they
would be free from attack, and they would receive regular annuities. They
could also hunt in their usual hunting grounds, so in most ways, life would
go on pretty much as it always had. And, of course, the young men would
do as they always had done—wander, hunt, and raid their enemies—and
there was nothing anyone could (or wanted to) do about that. The other
provisions of the treaty, to the extent the Sioux understood them, could
easily be evaded or ignored. On the other hand, Sitting Bull, a Hunkpapa,
found nothing in the treaty that appealed to him, and he and his people
remained off the reservation and did not ask for or agree to peace. Their
territory was also farther north, so they were farthest removed from the
settlements, the central emigrant trails, and the ever-westward-moving
Union Pacific Railroad. But Sitting Bull and his Hunkpapa would soon
take the lead in attacking the Northern Pacific Railroad, when it began to
be built through the Yellowstone Valley to connect Duluth, Minnesota, to
the Puget Sound. Then it was their territory that was being threatened by a
road, and in this case, an iron road.

Now that many of the Sioux like Red Cloud and Spotted Tail were
more or less stationary on the reservation, many philanthropists and missionaries thought they would have a better chance to introduce Christi-

anity. Conversion to Christianity was regarded as a major step in moving the Indians from savagery to civilization. But most of the Sioux had little or no interest in the notion. They had their own well-developed and highly sophisticated cosmology and attendant theology. Their religious beliefs perfectly explained the world order as they experienced it, and they saw little in Christian doctrine that offered any value or even much in the way of spiritual complexity. As Hassrick writes: "The Sioux were a systematic people. They were organizers and classifiers. As the universe was intricately patterned into hierarchies and divisions, so was the nation."[11] Ironically, they would have been more at home with medieval scholastics and their elaborate hierarchies and systems than they were with the comparatively simple ideas of the Protestants. Of course, this is a generalization. Some formerly warlike Sioux (though not many) embraced the Christian doctrine. None other than Spotted Tail's beloved daughter converted, and her conviction heavily influenced his determination to accept and endure peace with the whites. But most Sioux ignored the missionaries' blandishments. They had a different understanding about how they and the rest of the world operated and had come into being. Nor could they respect these strange white shamans who preached peace. As difficult as it was for the honest, well-meaning missionaries to believe, most Sioux did not want peace, and especially not with their traditional and inveterate enemies like the Arikara and Crow.

The culture hero who appeared to the Sioux to teach them the proper way of life was called White Buffalo Calf Maiden. She delivered the sacred pipe and taught the Sioux seven key ceremonies that would protect them and allow them to flourish. When she finished she turned into a white buffalo and vanished. The identification of the avatar with the buffalo illustrates the way the Sioux integrated the natural and the supernatural. It's also significant that the culture hero was a female, for the buffalo cow was far more valuable than the bull. Her hide was thinner and more pliable and therefore more easily worked into the pieces that composed the tepee and clothing. Her flesh was also more palatable. White hunters routinely singled the cows for the same reason, so that the buffalo herds eventually dwindled to groups of bulls that were regarded as useless by most whites for anything other than target practice. It's impossible to believe, however, that during periods of scarcity and famine, that the toughest old bull would not have been used by the Plains tribes. It was eastern sportsmen, like Francis Parkman, who shot the bulls and took only their tails as trophies. (As estimable as Parkman's later work might be, his descriptions of buffalo hunting in *The Oregon Trail* makes for difficult reading.) It will come as no surprise that the Sioux did not hunt their game animals for sport. It was serious business to be accompanied by solemn ceremonies and rites of propitiation. The animals allowed some of their numbers to be taken to support the Sioux, but in return they expected respect and awareness of their sacred qualities.[12]

The identification of the culture hero and the buffalo underscores the outrage and disaster the buffalo hunters visited upon the Sioux. The destruction of the herds was more than an economic catastrophe to them; it was a philosophical and religious tragedy. Those army officers, like Sherman, who understood the economic impact of the destruction of the buffalo, probably had no inkling of the religious and cultural damage the buffalo hunters caused. Had they known, it's fair to wonder whether they would have cared. After all, they had been raised in a very hard school of war and were not especially interested in the poetic constructions of their own culture, much less those of an alien culture.

To the Sioux, the buffalo as well as the rest of natural life were elements of an overarching cosmic system, the head of which was *Wakan Tanka*: the Life Giver or the Great Mystery, under whom there were separate divisions of supernaturals, each of whom was able and willing to communicate with the human who followed appropriate rituals and ways of life. These subordinate gods were also part of the Life Giver. Collectively called the Controllers, there were sixteen of them arranged in a hierarchy: "Taken together these four major groupings [of four each]—the Superior Gods, the Associates, the Subordinate or Gods-Kindred and the Gods-like were the benevolent aspects of the Great Mystery—sixteen in one, yet only one."[13] These various gods had differing responsibilities in the universe. The Superior gods, for example, were embodied in the sun, the earth, the sky, and the rock. The sun god, Wi, was the chief among the Superior gods and was protector of the four cardinal virtues of the Sioux—bravery, fortitude, generosity, and wisdom. Hence the celebrated sun dance was a ceremony that linked the warrior to the four most important virtues in the Sioux culture.

Thus everything in the Sioux environment—animals and inanimate natural objects and even weather—had an element of the supernatural. And the sixteen Controllers were actually one—a concept of multiplicity that does not differ all that much from the Christian idea of the Trinity. But when well-meaning (mostly Protestant) missionaries came to the tribes with their Christian stories, the Sioux could be excused for thinking that these new explanations and ideas were a trifle thin and a little simplistic. Further, to the Sioux, Christianity completely overlooked the supernatural element in all forms of Nature. The Christian divinity, Protestant or Catholic, existed somewhere apart, invisible, whereas the Sioux recognized divinity in every element of the environment. What's more, the Sioux were also troubled by evil gods, so their theology had an element reminiscent of Gnosticism. The evil ones were organized in hierarchies, too, and the chief of them all was called Iya and was embodied in the cyclone.[14] Christians had expunged the Gnostic heresies and had come to deny the equality of good and evil and the battle between them. The Sioux thought otherwise. And, finally, a Sioux culture that revered conquest, rewarded raiding and warfare and glorified the warrior would find a religion personified by the Prince of Peace laughably alien and absurd.

The Sioux theology was, in concept, not all that different from other polytheistic religions in which the gods interact with humans and manifest themselves in differing natural phenomena and animals. That is not surprising. A preliterate culture without other forms of entertainment and communication had time to watch and listen to the "music of the spheres." Over time they would develop myths and legends that explained how it all worked. Moreover, the Sioux survived by understanding the ways of nature, the patterns of the weather, the migrations of the buffalo, the growth of the spring grass, the rain that nourished the grass, so it was natural that they endowed these elements with divinity and sought to propitiate them and encourage them to continue to provide health and survival for the people. They were dependent upon the good graces of the Controllers.

The Sioux believed the universe made sense. They believed they were at the center of it, that they were the chosen people. The nineteenth-century white civilization is routinely and quite fairly described as ethnocentric. But the Sioux were no different; they believed themselves superior to all other peoples.[15] Indeed, one of their creation myths said that the Sioux were the direct descendants of the First Man, who was guided from the underground by a wolf and who entered the world from a cave. Some versions place this cave in the Black Hills.[16] That may be in part an explanation for the name the Teton Sioux called themselves: Lakota—The Men. On the other hand, their environment was so harsh at times and their grasp on life so tenuous that they had no illusions that humans were in any way *the* significant element of the universe. They were a small part of the system and would have had no patience with the Renaissance (and Catholic) concept of the "Great Chain of Being," in which humanity stood just a step below the angels and above all other forms of life. Compared to most elements of Nature, the Sioux saw that humankind was pretty puny. But compared to the rest of humankind, the Sioux thought themselves superior. (This is yet another illustration of the gulf of misunderstanding between the Sioux and the whites, who, as mentioned, considered them backward and inferior savages, while the Sioux regarded the white men, and most other tribes, with lofty contempt.)

It was the office of the older men and women as well as the shamans to convey their cultural, religious, and tribal history. They were responsible for maintaining tribal identity. Winter time was best for stories, because they believed themselves safe from attack, and their ponies were unfit and useless for raiding because of lack of forage. Further, the Plains winter weather was so dreadful that there was very little else to do but work on crafts and tell the tribe's history and myths.

There were many stories to tell, a lot having to do with the interaction between the supernatural and the human and the animal worlds. The story of the Deer Woman is particularly revealing. She was the most beautiful woman in the world and routinely appeared to solitary hunters, enticing them into her lodge where she made love to them and then disappeared, taking with her the man's spirit and leaving him forever longing to find her again. The similarities of this story to John Keats's *La Belle Dame Sans Merci* and to William Butler Yeats's *The Song of Wandering Aengus* at the very least suggest some fundamental human commonality, something that psychologist Carl Jung might have described as operating from the "collective unconscious." (While this reference to Jung may seem a bit of a stretch, Jung did know of and appreciate *Black Elk Speaks*.) There is also a sinister aspect to the magical and sexually alluring woman (something psychologists like to ponder). In the case of the Deer Woman, she transforms herself into a deer and threatens to charge when the solitary hunter declines her invitation. In that case the hunter's only recourse is to raise his bow and offer to shoot, at which point the Deer Woman turns and disappears. It was often the role of a boy's grandmother to tell him about the Deer Woman and warn him not to succumb.[17]

Despite their different languages the Sioux and the Cheyenne share some remarkably similar stories. Like many Western tribes, they tell stories of the Trickster, who is variously a simple-minded butt of jokes or a malevolent force for evil, or something in between, and he is often "personified" by the coyote. In one story Coyote sees a flock of ducks and begins to dance on the shore to attract them. Being ducks, they are curious and swim over, whereupon Coyote invites them to dance while he sings, but he tells them they must keep their eyes closed, and if they open them their eyes will turn red. Of course, Coyote starts killing them, because, as usual, he is hungry, but one duck opens his eyes and warns the others. And that, according to legend, is why the freshwater grebe has red eyes. The stories in both the Sioux and Cheyenne languages are remarkably similar, including the business about the red eyes.[18]

Many stories were simple tales designed to entertain, for the Sioux, among themselves, had a keen sense of humor, generally. Other stories were more serious and were used to make an important social or moral point. There were stories of their heroes, which promoted the warrior ethic and motivated young men to emulation. There were stories of the interaction between animals and humans, all of which illustrated the interconnectedness of all forms of life. Most of the stories were used to illustrate how and how not to behave. The story of the Deer Woman is obviously a warning against a variety of temptations a young man can encounter and how to act when he is confronted. Phrased in metaphor and imagery, the stories affected the listeners more profoundly than any straightforward lecture on morality. And metaphor and imagery were perfectly adapted devices for a culture that was steeped in a kind of mysticism in which the natural and the supernatural are conjoined in most, if not all, experience. These things cannot be explained, or understood, or even approached by reason alone. This is yet another illustration of the vast differences between the Lakota (as well as other Plains tribes) and the white civilization that was gradually encroaching upon them. To the Lakota there was scarcely a difference between the dream and reality; in fact, truth and understanding often visited them in dreams. In that sense they retained a childlike (not childish) integration of imagination and perception of the irrational and rational, of the sacred and the secular. The white man obviously had no patience for this kind of dreamy mysticism; his only concession to the supernatural was his Christianity, which, in the majority of cases, was expressed in the stark images and strictures of Protestantism, a faith that celebrated work and achievement and rewarded those who could co-opt the natural resources and turn them into wealth—wealth to be accumulated for its own sake and as a symbol of the Protestant ethic and virtue. (Of course this is a generalization, and there were plenty of Catholics who were wandering in the west looking for profit through trapping and trading, but it is fair to say that the French Catholic frontiersmen and the missionaries—Jesuit and otherwise—displayed somewhat greater sensitivity and respect for the Indian cultures they encountered. No doubt this was to some extent a matter of self-interest and self-preservation. In the early periods of North American colonization, the French tried to recruit the tribes for wars against the British and American colonists. Later, they were often the first to arrive on the Plains to open trading relationships. Fort Laramie started life as a French trading post, as did a number of forts and cities on the frontier. On the other hand, Laramie, the fort and the nearby river, were named for Jacques La Ramie, a French trapper who disappeared and was assumed to have been killed by the Arapaho. So not all Frenchmen enjoyed cordial relations with the tribes.)

None of this is meant to suggest that the Sioux and their allies were mostly just wandering poets and philosophers. The richness of their mythology and theology should not obscure the fact that they were fierce and generally brutal tribes, enemies not only of the white interlopers but of neighboring and equally brutal tribes from whom they stole horses, ter-

ritory, and sometimes even corn, squash, and other crops of the more sedentary tribes, like the Arikara. These raids were an important element in
their economy and the social system, for raiding enemies and stealing their
horses were the primary ways for a warrior to distinguish himself and so
rise in the ranks. (It's no wonder that Custer admired them, in his way,
for the Sioux warrior and Custer defined success in remarkably similar
ways—the acclaim of the multitude after success on the battlefield.) The
Sioux lived by hunting, by raiding, and by gathering—fruits, berries, and
vegetables—this latter job generally, though not always, assigned to the
women. The men did not "work" in the sense that the white civilization
understood the term. Nor did they want to.

The Sioux were the strongest of the Plains tribes, and they actively
sought to extend their territory and hunting grounds. They were firmly
invested in the notion of the right of conquest, and they were fiercely
protective of their territory, as they defined it. In 1873 a large village of
Pawnee came to the North Platte River to hunt buffalo, and upward of a
thousand Sioux attacked them and killed two hundred. They did not spare
women or children.[19] In fact, none of the Plains tribes took prisoners very
often. Now and then they might kidnap a small child to raise as one of
their own, and occasionally they would capture a woman who would then
become more or less a wretched slave. But generally speaking, a village
that was attacked by an enemy war party could expect annihilation.[20]

According to the clearly defined value system of the Sioux, the chief
virtues of the warrior were, as mentioned, bravery, fortitude, generosity,
and wisdom. *Wisdom* was the hardest to attain and was usually a gift of
age, though one not given to everyone. But the ones who displayed wisdom
joined the council of elders that acted as the band's advisors on all important matters.

Generosity meant that the successful man should share with the less
fortunate. The Sioux admired individuals who were rich in material things,
but only if that same person gave away his possessions. In so doing he
would gain the praise of the people; in other words, charity was anything
but selfless. It was a means to social and political acclaim (perhaps this was
not unique to the Sioux). It was also a way of maintaining a modus vivendi
in a nomadic camp. People could not simply be left to starve if they were

too old or too inept to hunt. There was also a practical reason for generosity—a nomadic tribe could not be burdened by too many possessions,
since moving them would at some point become impractical.[21]

The Sioux had a keen sense of property value—mostly in the form of
crafts and, more importantly, horses. Horses were the primary medium of
exchange and were acquired through raiding, rather than breeding. The
wealthy warrior who gave away his horses, therefore, needed only to make
another raid on his enemies to get replacements—something he would do
anyway, since that was the warrior's vocation—and great joy.

Fortitude meant stoicism in the face of danger and pain, and *bravery*
of course meant fearless action in combat. Here again both of these latter
virtues were means of gaining acclaim—something the Sioux warrior
valued beyond all else.

There were many apparent paradoxes among the Sioux. In one sense
they were highly individualistic and recognized no final authority but their
own judgment. And yet they lived communally and had well-established
rules of conduct that could lead to banishment for offenders against the
order. They also had a well-defined class system. A man from a "good
family" had a much better chance to rise to political and military influence than someone from a poor, or less respected, family. The criteria for
the "good family" were well understood. First, of course, the members
must be successful hunters and warriors, men who had acquired and
continued to acquire wealth (but not accumulate or hoard it). They also
needed to be members of one of the warrior societies, which acted as tribal
policemen, especially during the communal buffalo hunts. These societies
were selective and were the fraternities of the younger men. Further, they
should have strong supernatural power that they obtained in their dreams
and vision quests. A young man undertook a vision quest by going off by
himself, fasting for several days, and awaiting the appearance of a supernatural, usually in the form of an animal, who then became a guardian
spirit. Visions could also come in dreams. As Black Elk said of his cousin,
"Crazy Horse dreamed and went into the world where there is nothing but
the spirits of all things. That is the real world that is behind this one, and
everything we see here is something like a shadow from that world."[22] And
finally they should in all their activities exhibit the four principal virtues.

A man whose family had distinguished itself in these ways had a much better chance to achieve his own distinction. For all his military success, Red Cloud was never revered the way other leaders were, because he came from an undistinguished family.[23] (His reputation also suffered because the non-treaty Sioux regarded him as one of the "hangs around the fort people." So, too, Spotted Tail.) But there was some upward mobility. As one warrior said, "There are places for each man. As you go along in life, you can work your way up. Some men get to the top, others never seem to make it. The old men who have been leaders see in the good young men the future leaders and help them raise themselves."[24] The "top" in this case was wealth (denominated mostly in horses); political influence; and the affection, respect, and acclaim of the tribe. Talent might be recognized and rewarded, but it could also be obscured by humble antecedents. The Sioux hierarchies were both social and political, although political leaders exercised only moral and rhetorical power. They could not expect to issue orders and have them always obeyed. But a leader's influence was affected by his reputation; the greater the respect, the more likely his advice would be heeded. As Lakota historian Joseph Marshall III writes: "If a man was capable of acting bravely in the midst of the most violent, chaotic and frightening of circumstances, [combat] he was capable of bravery and honor in the time of peace. The benefit to the people was twofold. Their fighting men were totally committed to the defense of families, home, and homeland, and the lessons of courage and honor learned under the most difficult of circumstances would serve to benefit all of the people in any circumstance."[25] There's an element of non sequitur here, since a warrior who is successful in battle need not necessarily have good peacetime judgment or intelligence. But the Sioux apparently thought otherwise.

The Sioux method of waging war involved pitiless treatment of the enemy: torture and ritual scalping and mutilation of the dead. Hassrick explains: "Taking a scalp was closely associated with the retaliatory aspect of warfare [that is, avenging a slain comrade], but scalping implied a much more involved concept than simple eye-for-eye desire for vengeance. For the scalp was a badge of honor, a sign of victory and a symbol of life itself all in one. Scalping was no mere bloodthirsty act of the savage mind but a ritualistic necessity for men who believed that the human spirit was somehow in and of human hair."[26] The scalp might then be turned over to a relative of a slain warrior who then believed that the spirit of the lost one had been retrieved and returned. Or it could be given to the women who would then perform a ritual victory dance while displaying the scalp (or other body parts) on a stick.[27]

War was an opportunity for the warrior to display his prowess and to gain fame—a curious but pervasive motive among a people with an almost dual personality that valued cooperative, communal living and at the same time individual accomplishment and self-aggrandizement. Counting coup was the zenith of achievement in combat. This meant touching an enemy (alive or dead) before comrades could do it. It was self-proclamation. Eagle feathers were the reward for coups (and significantly, the Black Hills were a favorite place to hunt eagles).

This desire for the acclaim of the tribe affected the Sioux fighting tactics. To display almost fanatical courage in battle led warriors to fight as individuals, and many planned ambushes could be ruined by the eagerness of a single warrior to dash ahead of his comrades. This makes the Fetterman ambush all the more remarkable, for it seems that Red Cloud and the other headmen were able to impose discipline. On the other hand, no soldier survived, and it's possible that some warriors did jump the gun, but only after Captain William Fetterman and his men were far enough into the trap. As Black Elk said: "The cavalry of the Wasichus [whites] did not know how to fight. They kept together and when they came on, you could hardly miss them."[28]

Esteemed ethnologist (and Black Hills Expedition member) George Bird Grinnell wrote:

Much has been written about the great chiefs, Sitting Bull, Red Cloud, Spotted Tail, Crazy Horse and American Horse of the Sioux and Tall Bull, Dull Knife and Roman Nose of the Cheyenne. They have been described as great leaders and in a fashion this is true. Besides being themselves brave, these men were orators, able to stir the emotions and were looked up to with much respect. Some of them were great warriors, but in battle not one of them could have given an order that would have been obeyed, for among the Indians there was no such thing as discipline. If some great warrior wished to charge the enemy, he would say "Now I am going," and if a group of young men felt disposed to do so they would follow him. But if Red Cloud or Sitting Bull had picked out two or three hundred men and ordered them to charge the enemy in a body no attention would have been paid to the order. The individual Indian fought just in his own way and took orders from no one. . . .[29]

The Sioux tendency to fight as individuals led many in the army to believe that the army's firepower and discipline could offset the warriors' better horsemanship and weapons training. A warrior's desire for acclaim also motivated frontal attacks, even individual displays, against defensive positions. That happened as mentioned in the Wagon Box Fight and the Hayfield Fight. As a further example of the differences among tribes, this Sioux willingness to attack recklessly is profoundly different from, for example, Apache tactics. An Apache preferred stealth and ambush and almost never risked himself in a direct charge. This suggests that geography had some effect on how native military tactics evolved. Out on the treeless Plains, the Sioux, superb hunters on horseback, were used to cavalry-like tactics and charges. None other than George Custer said that hunting buffalo on horseback was the closest thing to a cavalry charge, both in terms of the skills required and the courage needed to ride pell-mell among a herd of terrified and yet dangerous animals. An Apache, on the other hand, lived in the forested mountains, hunted on foot, stalked his game and survived by being patient and careful. And that was the way he fought, too. Geography is, at least in part, destiny. Or at least, tactics.

Missionaries, like Father Pierre-Jean De Smet, tried to spread the Christian gospel. But the only thing that might have appealed to most of the Sioux about Christianity was the crucifixion, for that was an example of fortitude in action—self-torture and sacrifice as a means to enlightenment and salvation. But they would then wonder why it was left to only one man to endure the sacrifice for all humanity. Their own display of fortitude was the Sun Dance, a form of self-torture that connected the individual warrior to the supernatural. A warrior had his pectoral muscles pierced and then bone skewers inserted in the two wounds. The bones were tied to a cord the other end of which was attached to a pole. While dancing and looking at the sun the warrior pulls against the skewers until they tear free of the flesh. There were variations on this, but the basic idea was the same in all Sun Dances.

The warrior underwent the ritual torture in order to display fortitude and to gain insight and establish a relationship or rapport with the supernatural. The object was not to suffer and die to redeem humankind, but to suffer and live in greater harmony with the supernatural. It was also a sacrifice that was both real and symbolic at the same time. Lakota historian Joseph Marshall explains: "To perform the Sun Dance is to truly give or offer the one gift that is most meaningful: the gift of self, which is all any of us truly has to give."[30]

(As an aside, it is interesting that the Catholics made some inroads into Lakota culture, possibly because the complexity and mysticism of the Catholics appealed to the Lakota imagination and compared favorably with the rather more simple—and practical—notions of the Protestants, who, of course, equated labor with piety. Renowned Lakota holy man Black Elk converted to Catholicism in his later years and actually became a missionary. Then, too, after the tribes were defeated, there was a widespread and despairing yearning for a messiah. That yearning led to the Ghost Dance in some cases and to Christian conversion in some others.)

The Sioux society was as systematically organized as their cosmology. They had regular police societies that kept order, especially on communal hunts. As mentioned, they had councils of elders who advised the people on important matters. Their social mores were equally prescribed and proscribed, including the odd custom of avoidance—the son-in-law must avoid contact with his mother-in-law. Similarly, the new daughter-in-law must avoid looking at or speaking to her father-in-law.[31] This taboo was also practiced by the Apache—and perhaps others—and raises the question of how and why it came about. Two cultures that were so different in most ways must have received this taboo from some common source. But where? Certainly it made life in a communal village a little awkward now and then, especially for a man with more than one wife. On the other hand, perhaps it was a clever way of avoiding common causes of conflict in such a small community.

Boys started their weapons training early, and by the age of eleven they were ready to go on a raid, although their duties were restricted to serving the warriors by doing menial chores around the camp. A raid, therefore, was not only an economic exercise but also a rite of passage for the boys. It was an important cultural event. Viewed that way, it's not difficult to understand why it was impossible for the individual Sioux warriors to stop raiding, despite the piece of paper the elders had agreed to. If you cannot raid, how can you become a man? If you cannot raid, how do you achieve the acclaim of the tribe? How do you acquire wealth that you can then give away and gain additional acclaim? Government and army officers were consistently frustrated by chiefs who said they could not control their young men. But it was true. Not only did a chief generally not have that authority (which white officials could never seem to understand), but warfare and raiding were the essence of a man's identity and his path to advancement—along with success in hunting. "I fight, therefore I am" was the proof of a warrior's reality.

An equally respected career path was to become a shaman, a holy man—although the "office" did not preclude one from also being a warrior. He received his role in a vision or perhaps a dream. Like Christian ministers, he received a "call." The shaman's role was to understand the ways of the gods and to instruct the others in the tribe about their demands and behavior, their powers and the ceremonies necessary to propitiate them. Given the complexity of the Sioux theology, this was a vast responsibility. The gods, for example, had multiple facets. The buffalo, for example— *tatanka*—was the patron of "generosity, industry and fecundity" as well as the guiding spirit of the successful hunter. The bear—*mato*—was patron of medicine and wisdom.[32] "Lakota believed that the power to heal wounds was given to men in visions by the Bear spirit."[33] All these gods required separate ceremonies not only to offer thanks and devotion but also to ward off the potential harm of the evil gods.

The main building block of society was the extended family group, called a *tiyospe*: "individuals banded together under a common leader and often related through descent or marriage to the patriarch . . . [the *tiyospe*] was the ancient and important core of Sioux society."[34] As was common with nomadic hunters, the Sioux traveled in these relatively small family groups much of the year, until it came time for a gathering of the bands, usually for a summer meeting and the communal buffalo hunt in the fall, followed by winter quarters. And there were gatherings for ceremonial events, like the Sun Dance. But the need to travel in smaller groups was dictated by the environment, since it was obviously easier to support a smaller camp by hunting. The typical village consisted of anywhere from twenty to forty tepees, each occupied by a family. Smaller horse herds would not use up the available grazing, so that a village might stay in a productive locale longer than a larger one could. (One of the many ironies of Custer's defeat at the Little Bighorn is that the huge village would have had to break up in another day or so. Had Custer arrived just a little later, he and his troops might have survived the campaign. Of course, the fear that the Indians would scatter— along with the need to maintain the element of surprise—motivated Custer's precipitate attack.) Whether the Sioux lived in small groups or in great gatherings depended on the season. And in winter they gathered along a river or stream that offered high banks and trees and so provided some protection from the wretched weather. Or sometimes bands would retreat to the Black Hills where the topography offered shelter from the storms.

If the straight line might be called a prevailing symbol of a white civilization (of which railroad tracks were the most obvious and important illustration), the circle was the primary symbol of the Sioux culture—and symbols importantly affect the way a culture thinks; the circle was both a visual symbol and a metaphor. A circle has no beginning and no end and so symbolizes not the life of an individual but the life of the universe. The Sioux arranged their camps in circles. The interior of a tepee is a circle (the Lakota word "tipi" means "they live there").[35] They organized many, though not all, of their "winter counts," which were the painted pictographic record of their history, in circles that spiraled out from the center. As Royal Hassrick explains: "The sun, the moon, the earth and the sky are round. The day, the night, the moon and the year circle the sky. The four winds circle the edge of the world. The bodies of animals and the stems of plants are round. Everything in nature, except the rock, is round. Therefore the circle was, for the Sioux, a sacred symbol and could indicate the universe, the sun, time or direction, depending upon its particular form and color."[36] Black Elk referred to the entire Sioux tribe as the "the sacred hoop of the nation." The people were one with their metaphor: "You have noticed that everything an Indian does is in circles, and that is because the Power of the World always works in circles, and everything tries to be round. In the old days, when we were a strong and happy people, all our power came from the sacred hoop of the nation, and so long as the hoop was unbroken, the people flourished. . . . Everything the Power of the World does is in circles."[37]

And the circle was, and is, as different from the cross as the Sioux theology was different from the religion the missionaries believed would transform the Sioux from warriors into farmers. Further, the Sioux mystical number was four, which corresponded to the four cardinal points of the compass. Christians, of course, to the extent that they have a mystical number, embrace the trinity. Generally, it was only after the "sacred hoop of the nation" was broken that more than a handful of Sioux turned to the cross.

Aside from dedication to family and community, very little in the Sioux culture was remotely compatible with the pacifist ideas of the eastern humanitarians who would become so influential in the debates about how best to treat the western tribes (more on this later). Indeed, it is hard to imagine more incompatible sets of values than the Sioux and, for example, the Quakers, and the contrast raises significant questions about any policy process that ignores the culture and history of the adversary and simply assumes that one's own set of values will be more or less immediately acceptable to the counterparty, once carefully explained. To a Sioux warrior, a Quaker pacifist would have been an object of ridicule and scorn. And a laughably easy target. The hard men in the army believed that the only way to solve the problem of the Plains Indians was to destroy their nomadic way of life. Once that was done, the psalm singers and the pacifists might have their turn. But those same hard men had to ask themselves: did they have the means to do what must be done?

THE ARMY

Indian warfare is a distinct and separate species of hostilities, requiring different talent, different materiel, as well as personnel, and different rules of conduct.
—George Armstrong Custer[38]

The Regular Army is composed of bummers, loafers and foreign paupers.
—*New York Sun*[39]

The nation had only recently completed a war of hitherto unimaginable bloodshed, destruction, and cost. Debt was still a crushing burden that affected all aspects of the country's politics and institutions, not least the army. The citizen soldiers of the Civil War had long been mustered out and replaced by a motley collection of immigrants and misfits. In the immediate postwar decade half the enlisted soldiers were immigrants, mostly from Ireland and Germany, although most other European countries were represented. In fairness, some of these immigrants had served in foreign armies and would go on to provide useful service to the United States. They were not all, as the Duke of Wellington described his own troops in a conversation with the Earl of Stanhope, "the mere scum of the earth." But many had joined simply to avoid starvation. Or they wanted a free trip west to the gold fields, at which point they intended to desert. The native-born Americans were no better in the eyes of the army. As Margaret Carrington wrote about the harsh discipline of the frontier: "Drastic measures had to be used in those days. The men, both foreign and domestic were a hard set."[40] Desertion averaged an astounding 33 percent during the postwar period. And given the fact that desertion could be a capital crime, conditions must have been miserable to motivate so many to run away. Or the troops, many of them anyway, were the kind who did not worry about consequences. As a result, new troops were constantly required, which meant that recruiting standards were low, and training well below what was necessary, since even regiments and, more realistically, companies that tried to do a good job in training were typically dealing with raw recruits, many of whom spoke only halting English. Further, eternal congressional parsimony and antipathy meant that training in something as fundamental as marksmanship was limited to what historian Robert Utley describes as a firing off a "handful of cartridges a year."[41] The troops who died at the Fetterman Battle and later at the Little Bighorn sacrificed their lives, at least in some part, to a cheese-paring Congress.

The Seventh Cavalry, like other regiments, was supposed to contain twelve companies of one hundred enlisted men each, including noncommissioned officers—sergeant and corporals.[42] A full colonel commanded, a lieutenant colonel was second, and there were three majors, so that the regiment in combat could be divided into three battalions, as indeed it was at the Little Bighorn. But these tactical command arrangements were rarely possible, because officers were constantly ordered on detached service; the colonel commanding the Seventh at the time of the Black Hills and the Little Bighorn was in his office in St. Paul. And the officer commanding the third battalion at the Little Bighorn was a captain, Frederick W. Benteen. The ranks of the army had been severely reduced to the point that by 1874 the congressional authorization was for twenty-five thousand enlisted men and two thousand officers, though in fact the army rarely even mustered the full complement. The rolls almost never listed more than 19,000 men.[43] Turnover from disease, discharge, and desertion combined to keep the army undermanned.

As mentioned, Custer's Black Hills Expedition included Gatling guns and a three-inch-caliber cannon capable of firing explosive shells. Gatling guns were in theory lethal weapons against massed troops, and there were times in Plains warfare when the Indians were enraged sufficiently to charge en masse. But the Gatlings were unreliable mechanically and tended to foul after a few rounds. Custer took these into the Black Hills, but his experience there may have suggested to him that they were more trouble than they were worth. Significantly, he left them behind at the Little Bighorn. The troopers were armed with .45-caliber breech-loading single-shot carbines. These were generally reliable, although there were loud complaints after the Little Bighorn that the ejectors jammed after a few rounds. Still, they remained the primary cavalry arm well into the 1890s. Conventional wisdom might wonder about issuing troops single-shot weapons. Why not give the men lever-action repeaters? There were at least two schools of thought on this question. First, was there a lever-action rifle that had the hitting power of a .45-caliber rifle? But more importantly, could the officers maintain fire discipline if excited troops could fire off seven or eight rounds in a few seconds? How soon would they run out of ammunition? The US army was not the only one to come down on the side of single-shot rifles. The British were still using single-shot Martini-Henry's in 1879 when they defeated a massive Zulu attack at Rorke's Drift. Armies noted these things. Men with only one shot theoretically aimed more carefully and still could get off something like twelve rounds a minute. But as importantly, single-shot rifles saved money.

The Black Hills Expedition, though, was delayed because "four fifths of our carbines are unserviceable."[44] This was Custer's report to headquarters in St Paul. Custer was referring to the condition of the regiments' existing older-model carbines, which were in the process of being replaced by the newer .45-caliber Springfields. Custer also requests "revolvers for this command, Smith & Wesson or Colt's improved pattern preferred."[45] The .45-caliber revolver was an especially useful weapon for the cavalry. When attacking a village, for example, in close quarters, the chaotic nature of the attack meant that a handgun with multiple shots was essential. The new weapons finally arrived, to Custer's relief. In his final July 1 report he said: "The new arms give great satisfaction."[46]

The troops that Custer would lead were representative of the army at the time. Poorly trained, most were unemployed men who could find no other work in the depression-ravaged economy. Morale was low, too, because of harsh discipline, poor living conditions, low pay, and the remoteness of so many frontier posts. Privates earned thirteen dollars a month; sergeants, twenty-two dollars. And since greenbacks were at a discount against gold, this pay did not go very far if the local sutler, or civilian merchant, demanded gold specie, which was the norm.

The troops were largely unmotivated by anything other than regular food and lodging, such as it was, unlike the volunteer troops of the Civil War, who fought for a cause they believed in (both North and South) and who were therefore willing to tolerate the hardships and dangers of total war. The troops of the 1870s had no such patriotic motives. As reporter William Curtis wrote: "The majority of the enlisted men in the army are simply human driftwood—men who have committed crimes elsewhere and are hiding in the service under assumed names . . . men who are disappointed, disheartened and ambitionless, and find the life of a soldier a relief."[47] Even Custer's wife, Libbie, who usually viewed the regiment through rose-colored glasses, had to admit that many of the men were "fugitives from justice," while others had joined to escape "the scoldings of a turbulent wife."[48]

There were some opinions that differed, however, from Libbie's. German immigrant Private Theodore Ewert wrote in his diary that the majority of officers were drunken louts who cared nothing about the welfare of their men and who knew next to nothing about their business. (Alcoholism was a problem among the frontier officers, although Custer neither smoked nor drank.) Ewert was one of the troops who went with Custer into the Black Hills. According to Ewert, "The officer of the U.S. Army has no respect for a man under his command, though I know men—privates—that were far superior to their company commanders both morally and intellectually."[49] This sort of class consciousness (and class solidarity) was typical of the army at the time—and typical of most armies throughout history. The very fact of hierarchies and discipline created resentment among some soldiers. Few enlisted men ever believe(d) that their officer really knows what he is doing; contempt is an enlisted man's eternal prerogative, to be shared only with his messmates. And the non-coms believe it would all collapse, if it were not for them. But this resentment seems to have been unusually severe among the troops of the Seventh Cavalry. Again Private Ewert had some thoughts on this subject:

> Oh, if only some of our Senators or Representatives, friends of justice, could see with their own eyes how officers lord it over the poor private, how insultingly each word is shouted out to him, how an officer, if out of humor, will, right or wrong, vent his anger on some poor private or non-commissioned officer, how a man, constantly subjected to such treatment will at length lose his manhood and become little more than a cowardly slave! How unjustly, brutally and tyrannically the rank and file are treated! Could they see this and know that an enlisted man cannot get the redress under any circumstance, they would, as honest and justice loving men, take some steps that would ensure us of the rank and file at least such rights as the regulations allows [sic] us and insure us treatment as humans and not as brutes, for we are men and men alike, physically, morally and intellectually, giving the officer simply the advantage of rank and social position.[50]

Military leadership rests on two foundations: knowing your business and looking after your men. In Custer's Seventh, both may have been lacking, according to some (though not all) in the ranks. Custer in fact knew his business, as the upcoming expeditions would show. But whether he looked after his troops properly—and, more to the point, required his officers to do so—is a different question.

The combination of massacres like Sand Creek plus resentment of the cost of maintaining a standing army and the traditional antipathy in some congressional quarters to the very idea of the military meant that the army had to struggle to maintain its fitness for service. As budgets and man-power authorizations were cut, the army had to face increasing responsi-bilities with decreasing assets. Commanding General William T. Sherman lamented that the army was also caught in a political squeeze between eastern politicians and humanitarians who wanted a peace policy and west-erners who wanted more vigorous action against the hostile tribes, as well as the opening of reservation land, like the Black Hills. Then, too, the army's role as an occupation force in Reconstruction meant that the regi-ments were split up and dispersed throughout the South, where they were caught between various squabbling parties—Southern white supremacists, radical Republican politicians in the north, conservative Democrats, and a general population that was growing steadily tired of Reconstruction and the costs of maintaining an army of policemen. The country also had a long history of antipathy toward the very idea of a standing army, regardless of the economic situation. The tradition of the minuteman and the citizen soldier was strong and had ably justified itself in the late war. The Second Amendment might be understood in part as an argument against a standing army: "A well-regulated militia, being necessary to the security of a free state, the right of the people to keep and bear arms, shall not be infringed." In other words, a well-regulated militia was considered preferable to a large standing army.

Maintaining a large (and expensive) professional army was some-thing that despotic European countries did, not something a republic that prided itself on personal freedom could endorse. Professional soldiers with loyal regiments were historically a political risk to liberty. People knew of Caesar's Rubicon and Napoleon's Elba. Besides, the likelihood of future foreign wars seemed small. Indeed, there was a school of thought that posited future wars between nation-states were unlikely because of the growth of international trade. Mutual commercial interests would obviate future conflicts. This quaint notion appeared periodically throughout the years as international trade developed and expanded. In this particular iter-ation, it ran concurrently with the Franco-Prussian War. Writer Ambrose

Bierce had no patience with such notions: "Let us have a little less of 'hands across the sea' and a little more of that elemental distrust that is the security of nations. War loves to come like a thief in the night; professions of eternal amity provide the night."[51] But Bierce's voice was, as usual, in the minority.

In short, even though it was shrinking, the postwar army was not a popular institution with the American public. Besides, the troops that were not involved in Reconstruction police duty were scattered around remote frontier posts; they were mostly out of sight. Their service and value were largely invisible. Staff officers were stationed in Washington, but the line officers and troops were on distant assignments. When the army's activities did make headlines, the news was usually negative—Indian disasters and massacres, Reconstruction disputes, labor riots. Small as the army had become, it was still expensive, and the taxes needed to support it were generated from the far more populous (and unthreatened) east than the west, where the settlers demanded more, not less, activity from the soldiers. But there were far fewer westerners, and their voices fell on mostly deaf ears of the policy makers. There were occasional calls in Congress for abolishing the War Department entirely, and even venerable West Point trembled periodically for its continued existence.

Life in most frontier forts was anything but felicitous. Most forts were small collections of buildings around a parade ground. The troops themselves constructed most of these posts, and they necessarily used local building material—adobe or timber or stone, as the case may be. The results were generally not worthy of a Remington painting. Further, this sort of manual labor, while not foreign to most of the men, seemed a far cry from the expected duty of a soldier. Troops spent more time with a hammer or hoe in their hands than they did with a rifle. Sherman was constantly angry about these conditions, because he understood the devastating effect on morale and desertion and even on the officers' performance of their duties. Describing these posts Sherman said: "Had the southern planters put their negroes in such hovels, a sample would, ere this, have been carried to Boston and exhibited as illustrative of the cruelty and inhumanity of the man masters."[52]

Not all frontier forts were collections of hovels, of course. The larger posts like Leavenworth or Fort Abraham Lincoln boasted well-appointed houses for the officers, livable barracks for the enlisted men, and medical facilities. Libbie Custer described Fort Lincoln:

> Fort Lincoln was built with quarters for six companies. [The other companies of the Seventh were stationed at Fort Rice, twenty-five or so miles to the south.] The barracks for the soldiers were on the side of the parade ground nearest the river, while seven detached houses for officers faced the river opposite. On the left of the parade ground was the long granary and the little military prison called the "guardhouse." Opposite, completing the square, were the quartermaster and commissary storehouses for supplies and the adjutant's office. Outside the garrison proper, near the river, were the stables for six hundred horses. Still further out were the quarters for the laundresses, easily traced by the swinging clotheslines in front and dubbed for this reason "Suds Row." Some distance from there were the log huts of the Indian scouts and their families, while on the same side also was the level plain used for parades and drill. On the left of the post was the sutler's store, with a billiard room attached.[53]

The Fort Abraham Lincoln infantry post was located about mile to the north on a high bluff overlooking the Missouri River. The presence of these soldiers (generally three companies) was of some small reassurance to Libbie and the other women when the cavalry was on the expedition. But they were realistic enough to know that if the Indians attacked in any strength, the infantry would have its hands full defending its post. Further, raiders could attack the depleted cavalry post and depart before the infantry could arrive.

The closer the fort was to a navigable river, the more comfortable it was likely to be, since steamboats could deliver supplies and construction materials. Hence Fort Lincoln's comparative opulence. But navigable rivers were in short supply in the west—the Missouri and the Yellowstone were the primary ones. Sherman's description of the tiny outposts scattered throughout the west was all too accurate. There were one hundred and eleven western forts during the height of the Indian wars.[54] And given the reduced size of the army it was inevitable that only one or two companies could garrison most of these little outposts. There weren't enough men to go around.

As mentioned, most forts were not guarded by exterior walls. Whether that was from contempt for the fighting quality of the Indians or a further example of penny pinching is difficult to say. But in any case, life in most of these little posts was anything but comfortable. The officers were far from home, with no entertainments close by and with few, if any, colleagues of similar military or social position to talk to, they were often tempted to resort to alcohol. And that of course had a terrible effect on an officer's ability to perform even routine duties. "Take a boy of sixteen from his mother's apron strings, shut him up under constant surveillance for four years at West Point, send him out to a two company post upon the frontier where he does little but play seven-up and drink whiskey at the sutler's, and by the time he is forty five he will furnish the most complete illustration of suppressed mental development of which human nature is capable." This was the opinion of Lieutenant General Richard Taylor, CSA.[55] (Seven-up is a card game and a part of another evil afflicting the frontier army—gambling.)

If the troops were infantry, their usefulness against hostile tribes was largely symbolic, if that. Yet to congressional penny pinchers, infantry was preferable, because a foot soldier cost roughly half of what it cost to maintain a cavalryman and his horse. Of course, most senior officers considered cavalry to be the best weapon against the hostile tribes—for obvious reasons. But there were some, like General William B. Hazen, who commanded infantry and who dismissively opined that cavalry horses tended to break down too easily and that even a relatively short operation of a week or so would ultimately find the infantry outpacing the horsemen.[56] But Hazen was a prickly sort, and his opinion was in the minority when the subject came to fighting Indians. And even if he was right, it hardly mattered; the highly mobile Plains tribes could elude any major army force, mounted or otherwise—unless they didn't want to. As a general rule, it was only in the winter, when the Indians were stationary and felt themselves safe from attack, that the army could use infantry or cavalry with any degree of offensive success. Other critics inside and outside the army complained that the cavalry were just infantry on horseback. They dismounted to fight, because they were poorly trained as cavalrymen. Potato farmers from Ireland hardly fit the image of the beau sabreur. And since their carbines were lighter than infantry rifles, they were indifferent infantry, at that. Further, every fourth man had to be detailed as a horse holder during action (his own horse and three others), so by definition the cavalry went into action with their firepower reduced by 25 percent. What's more, the heavy cavalry horses required substantial amounts of grain each day (fourteen pounds, according to Custer).[57] That meant that during operations the troops were reliant on wagon trains (three wagons per company of cavalry),[58] and these in turn greatly restricted the cavalry's range of action and virtually eliminated extensive operations in certain types of terrain. General George Crook's innovative use of pack mules in the Southwest greatly improved his troopers' ability to follow and find the otherwise elusive mountain-dwelling Apache. But Crook was dealing with a much smaller number of Apache, that is, smaller bands of marauders, so his columns could be smaller and could therefore get by using mule trains instead of wagons.

Whether infantry or cavalry, the companies of the various regiments rarely came together, so that whatever esprit de corps existed—if it existed—was associated with the company. (The Seventh Cavalry was reassembled in 1873 to protect the Northern Pacific Railroad survey of the Yellowstone Valley, and the regiment was also together for the Black Hills Expedition the following year. Both assignments underscore the importance the army and the government placed on these missions.) Since most of the frontier forts were garrisoned by just one or two companies, there was little if any identification with the regiment. Their band of brothers was rather small. Further, the junior officers commanding the companies were responsible for training the troops. There is nothing inherently wrong with that, but the junior officers were, like their seniors, a mixed bag in terms of ability, and without regimental oversight, the quality of training was predictably uneven. (A captain commanded a company and had a lieutenant and a second lieutenant as subordinates. And of course there was a first sergeant who prided himself on actually running things, along with sergeants and corporals as his assistants. A company was supposed to muster roughly fifty to one hundred men—the postwar numbers fluctuated greatly as cuts were made—but frontier companies were rarely fully manned, either in terms of enlisted men or officers.) Many regular army captains and lieutenants on the frontier had held much more senior brevet rank from the Civil War, so their relatively humble rank did not automatically imply inexperience. But neither did their brevet rank automatically guarantee motivation and dedication. The isolation of so many of these posts offered an aggressive officer the chance to develop professionally, but only to a point. Remembering his service in a southern Arizona fort, Captain Richard Ewell said he learned everything about handling a company of cavalry and nothing about anything else (Ewell went on to become a lieutenant general in the Confederate army). But as General Taylor pointed out, the isolation could have the opposite effect on a poorly motivated officer, or it could gradually drain away any initial motivation as boredom and loneliness and endless routine made their inroads. And needless to say, these smaller posts did not even have the benefit of the regimental band. They had a sutler, contracted civilian storekeeper who provided whiskey and other such necessities usually in exchange for gold specie, which the soldiers, as mentioned, had to buy in exchange for greenbacks—at a markup amounting sometimes to as much as 100 percent— two greenbacks for one gold dollar.

Ewell's post in southern Arizona, Fort Buchanan, is representative of most frontier army life. A rough collection of *jacales*, Spanish for "shack," basically, the fort's buildings were constructed of local live oak and roofed with brush. During the summer rainy season these roofs were sieves. Dirt floors became mud floors. The log walls were chinked with mud, and when the winds came up from Mexico and the rain came sideways, the mud redoubled. The fort's pigsty added nothing to the quality of the air, and the latrines did not help either. All the troops had a touch, or worse, of malaria because of the proximity of swampy areas known as ciénegas. There was some local supply of food, but the troops also tried to ward off scurvy by planting gardens. And they spent much of their time cutting hay for their animals. In fact, the citizens of Tucson, fifty miles away, complained that the soldiers did little or nothing but support their own existence. This was unfair when the active and professional Ewell and his two companies of cavalry were assigned to the post, but they were replaced in 1861 by two companies of infantry. And it was from this post that the Apache wars started in earnest because of the misjudgments of a junior infantry officer.

Fort Buchanan is typical of the frontier posts so deprecated by a regular army officer who knew what that life was like and advised his daughter against marrying into the army: "How in the world any girl of ordinary sense can think of marrying a line officer I cannot imagine, for they must make up their minds to spend a life of exile, deprivation and poverty."[59] The young woman followed her father's advice and rejected the suitor.

Officers could bring their wives and children to their posts, as Colonel Carrington and several of his subordinates did. And some noncommissioned officers brought along their families. But it was not an easy decision, given the rough nature of the conditions and the danger of both travel and existence in these far-off places. Even the everyday problems of housekeeping were difficult on a frontier post. There were usually laundresses, who were the wives, official or otherwise, of enlisted men. But managing a clean house and educating the children were full-time jobs for the officers' wives. The senior wives also, most of them, felt some sort of responsibility to counsel and support the wives of the younger officers. This was traditional in the armed forces, and still is. The shock to a young wife of army life on the frontier could be emotionally disabling. And destabilizing to the tiny community. It's worth emphasizing the courage of all these women. Not only was the basic work assigned to them difficult because of the conditions, but the fate of a woman captured by the hostiles was well known. Rape was certain, followed, if the women were lucky, by virtual slavery in the village; if they were not lucky, death and mutilation would be their fate. The idea of keeping a last bullet for yourself was not limited to the troops.

Libbie Custer enjoyed her travels with the regiment, but in later years she confessed that she was constantly nervous and at times really fearful: "I do not think the actual fear of death was thought of so much as the all-absorbing terror of capture. Our regiment had rescued some white women from captivity in Kansas, and we never forgot their stories. One of our number became so convinced that their fate awaited us that she called a resolute woman to one side to implore her to promise that, when the Indians came into the post, she would put a bullet through her heart, before she carried out her determination to shoot herself."[60]

While this may seem melodramatic, it was a widely held principle.

And with good reason. When Fort Phil Kearny seemed on the verge of being overwhelmed by the Sioux, Carrington made plans to have the women and children cluster in the powder magazine. If the Indians made it over the walls, he intended to blow up the magazine and spare the women and children the outrages they certainly would have suffered. It's worth remembering that Carrington and his troops had just collected the bodies, such as they were, of William Fetterman and his troops.[61]

Medical facilities at remote outposts were primitive at best, and disease was far more likely to send a soldier to the grave than an Indian arrow or bullet. Each post had a surgeon or assistant surgeon, but given the relatively poor pay and living conditions, the cream of the medical world did not flock to the army as a career. Further, the state of medical knowledge was low, and consisted of disbursing a few pills or binding up wounds. During the Black Hills Expedition, the ever acerbic Private Ewert went to an officer to help him bring the doctor, for one of Ewert's messmates was ill. But the doctor had passed out from drinking. They went to the other doctor, who was also drunk, but he examined the soldier and pronounced him fit. The soldier died that night. "After this day," wrote Ewert, "the title of 'doctor' was dropped by the members of H Company and either one of the two talked about as 'Butcher Allen' or 'Drunken Williams.'"[62]

As wretched as many of these forts were, the settlers appreciated them. For one, they offered some level of protection and a visible symbol of the army's willingness to react to Indian raids against the settlements. Their mere presence was thought to be, and often was, a preventative asset. Farmers and ranchers also looked on the forts as a market for their produce and livestock, and the projected closing of any western outpost, however ramshackle, raised howls of protests from the local civilians, and usually these howls were heard in Washington. Certainly it was less expensive to supply a fort from local producers, less expensive than sending long, slow wagon trains over great distances to remote outposts with the added risk of hostile attacks, as well as the problem of wastage and spoilage. Of course, some supplies such as ammunition, weapons, and uniforms had to be sent from army supply centers. But local food supplies made sense as long as the civilian suppliers did not try to take advantage of their virtual monopolies. Critics said that the settlers tended to exaggerate the danger of Indian attacks so that they would not lose an important market. And, as was usual in most of the complicated questions of Indian policy, this criticism had some merit.

Sometimes there were no settlements close by. Sometimes the forts were the first into the country, as in the case of Forts Phil Kearny and C. F. Smith, so there were no local supplies. And in the fierce Wyoming winter, getting supplies through from Fort Laramie was virtually impossible. Hence the chronic shortage of ammunition, among other necessities, at Phil Kearny. Scurvy was rampant that first winter because of a lack of fruits and vegetables.

It was easy enough for the staff officers in Washington to order a supply train to embark. It was also easy enough in Washington to assume there would be small difficulty in organizing and conducting a supply train through a Wyoming road in winter. Staff officers could be calm about these problems, because they did not have to face, or even understand, a Wyoming winter.

This disconnect between the line officers and the staff was a systemic problem. The staff officers were attached to the War Department, which of course was headed by a civilian political appointee. As with most bureaucratic organizations, there was a maze of regulations, but the central problem was that the staff officers controlled logistics for the line. The staff decided what the troops in the field needed. There were ten staff departments, but the thorniest issues lay with the Quartermaster Department, which was responsible for procuring and transporting most supplies along with the Sustenance Department, which handled procurement and shipment of food. Of course, requests could be submitted, but the ultimate decisions lay with the staff. The staff in Washington had counterparts in the division and departmental offices, so they operated in parallel to the line army, but they were rarely in the field and so could not always accurately assess the needs of the troops. This meant that a great deal of bureaucratic paperwork was required if the commanders in the field were to receive the supplies and materiel that they needed. In short, field commanders had no control over logistics.

General Sherman was appointed to overall command of the army when Grant became president. The trans-Mississippi was separated into two divisions—the Missouri and the Pacific. At the time of Custer's expedition General Philip Sheridan commanded the Missouri Division, which stretched from St. Louis to the Rocky Mountains. Within that division were three departments—the Dakota, the Platte, and the Missouri. The Platte was commanded by General Edward Ord and later by General Crook, who would figure importantly in the Black Hills. General Alfred Terry commanded the Dakota Department, which consisted of Minnesota and most of North and South Dakota and Montana. The division between the Dakotas and the Platte caused problems, because after the Red Cloud War, hostile raiders came south from the reservations and crossed into the department of the Platte because there were more settlements there to attack. But they then retreated to the Dakota reservations and returned to Terry's military jurisdiction. Once again, the army drew lines on a map, and once again the tribesmen ignored them. But it was this sort of problem that motivated Custer's Black Hills Expedition. The proposed new fort would block these excursions. At least that was the hope.

CHAPTER FOUR

THE GILDED AGE

*Why, it is telegraphed all over the country and commented on
as something wonderful if a congressman votes honestly and
unselfishly and refuses to take advantage of his position to
steal from the government.*
— Mark Twain and Charles Dudley Warner,
The Gilded Age, 1873

*Politics: A strife of interests masquerading as a contest of
principles. The conduct of public affairs for private advantage.*
— Ambrose Bierce, *The Devil's Dictionary*

When it comes to graft, few eras in this country's history can
match the years just after the Civil War, the period Mark
Twain labeled the Gilded Age. Washington, DC, was inundated with lob-
byists who represented commercial interests, and the commercial interests were inundated with requests from politicians for financial favors.
Graft and corruption traveled a two-way street. The process had become
so refined and so accepted in both government and private industry that
there arose a clear distinction between honest graft and dishonest graft.[1]
Honest graft was associated with a project, such as a railroad, in which the
project was actually completed more or less as proposed. True, the politicians who had to gain approval for the necessary appropriations were paid
handsomely for their troubles, but the public good did not suffer overly,
because the railroad was delivered on time and with something like the
proposed quality. "Dishonest graft," on the other hand, was associated
with a project that was not delivered as promised, that involved shoddy

materials and workmanship that resulted in failure, such as whole sections of track sinking into swampland that had been certified as suitable for construction. The crudest examples of dishonest graft were the Indian agents (who were all politically appointed) who received funds and supplies to be distributed to the reservation Indians and who skimmed money, sold supplies, and delivered far less than was promised to the Indians—far less in quantity and quality. But of course the only ones who suffered directly from this kind of graft were the tribes. When they became incensed over their treatment and went marauding, however, the white settlers and travelers would be the indirect or secondary victims of the Indian Bureau's "dishonest graft."

Regular bribes were paid to politicians of both parties, generally to grease the skids for major projects and appropriations. As Mark Twain's character in *The Gilded Age* put it: "The fact is . . . the price is raised so high on a United States Senator now that it affects the whole market; you can't get any public improvements through on reasonable terms. Simony is what I call it. Simony."[2] Well, yes. It was rampant, secular simony, and it's instructive to remember that Twain's (co-written with Charles Dudley Warner) novel was published in 1873.

Graft went hand in hand with cronyism in President Ulysses S. Grant's eight years in office. Much of the malfeasance has been laid at Grant's feet, but his troubles are somewhat easy to understand, given his military background. Experience had taught him to delegate action and to let his trusted subordinates carry out the assignment according to their best judgment. That worked in war, where victory and defeat were self-evident results. Commanders who delivered victories could be trusted with further assignments; commanders who suffered defeat could be relieved of their duties. But that management style did not work so well in government, where the opportunities for graft were legion, and the likelihood of getting caught was small and the penalties smaller. Unlike the battlefield, the smoke-filled room yielded no transparency of result. Further, subordinates in the army were expected to, and usually did, follow orders. In politics, subordinates, colleagues, and political allies passed executive directives through a filter of self-interest and followed them, or not, as the occasion demanded.

In fairness to Grant, he and his administration did not invent or initiate the widespread abuse of political power. That had been a mainstay of politics for decades. In fact, it came under the rubric of "patronage" and was widely regarded as the best means for a political party or person to stay in power. As historian Josiah Bunting writes: "By the end of the Civil War more than fifty thousand citizens were employed in the (civilian) federal bureaucracy. . . . Criteria for appointment and promotion were usually unstated, but competence and training beyond a minimum were not usually prerequisites for continued tenure. Rather, federal appointments were used to reward political supporters and contributors small and large."[3] By the time of Custer's Black Hills Expedition, there were more than twice as many federal bureaucrats as soldiers. While the army was shrinking, the army of bureaucrats was flourishing.

No stranger to the sometimes toxic internal politics of the army, the newly inaugurated President Grant was nevertheless harried by the patronage demands of his supporters. As he wrote to his sister: "I scarcely get one moment alone. Office seeking in this country, I regret to say, is getting to be one of the industries of the age. It gives me no peace."[4]

It was the way things were done, though, and the fairest criticism of Grant's administration may be that, although he inherited a system of patronage graft and corruption, he did nothing to change it. Perhaps it would have been impossible, though. Many saw nothing wrong with the system: As Twain wrote in *The Gilded Age*: "To be sure you can buy now and then a Senator or a Representative, but they do not know it is wrong, and so they are not ashamed of it."[5]

Sometimes the bribes were a little more subtle than straight cash. Stock in a new company requesting appropriations or guarantees also changed hands. Relatives of powerful politicians took places at the trough. Grant's wretched brother, Orvil, was involved in the sordid business of selling post traderships on reservations and forts—a scandal that would eventually snare Custer in its political net and almost cost him command of the Seventh Cavalry during the 1876 campaign. (Custer's testimony against the practice of selling traderships aroused political enemies and angered President Grant.)

Grant's brother-in-law, Abel Corbin, was involved in one nefarious scheme with James Fisk and Jay Gould, who were financiers and proto-

typical robber barons. Gould and Fisk were both involved in the Erie Railroad and were close associates of the notorious William "Boss" Tweed
of Tammany Hall, who joined them in scattering bribes to politicians and
judges in order to advance their various financial schemes. In the summer
of 1869 Gould and Fisk devised a plan to manipulate the market in gold.
They began buying up gold at a reasonably low price, and in order to drive
the price higher, they contacted (that is, bribed) Grant's brother-in-law,
Corbin, to urge Grant not to sell Treasury supplies of gold, but rather to
hold it in the Treasury. Lower supply meant higher prices. There was so
little gold in circulation that any new Treasury offerings could affect the
price significantly. (Gould also bribed Assistant Secretary of the Treasury
Daniel Butterfield with $10,000 to alert Gould about upcoming Treasury
gold sales.) Grant, however, wanted the Treasury to sell its gold for greenbacks and thereby take them out of circulation (there was still $376 million
outstanding).[6] Grant refused to curtail gold sales, dumped more on the open
market, and the result was yet another in a line of Black Fridays. Gold
prices plunged, and Gould and Fisk lost money but survived. Fisk physically survived for another couple of years before his amorous adventures
caught up with him, and he was shot dead by a jealous rival. Absurdly,
the woman in dispute was a prostitute. The attempts by Gould and Fisk to
manipulate the gold market resulted in yet another scandal in the Gilded
Age, but they also underscore the fact that gold was very much a part of
the government's economic calculations.

Probably at no point in the nation's history, until then, were government and private industry in such close collaboration—both legitimate and
otherwise. A great deal of this cooperation had to do with the settlement of
the west, which included determining how best to interact with the tribes,
whether they were peaceful, hostile, or both, depending on the season.
The land west of the Mississippi was to a great extent federal property,
acquired first by the Louisiana Purchase and second by the Mexican War.
It was widely understood that transcontinental railroads would have to be
built to connect the two sides of the country. (The telegraph was finished
in 1861 but, obviously, moved only information—and in small doses.
Transcontinental stagecoach lines were only a stopgap measure.) It was
also understood that by stimulating development of towns, ranches, and

farms along the rail lines, the railroads would be a powerful weapon in subduing those tribes that were inclined to hostility. The railroads would also degrade the buffalo environment during construction and by building settlements along and across their normal migratory routes. Simple demographics would sooner or later overwhelm the tribesmen. They would ultimately go to reservations, some willingly, some unwillingly, but they would all ultimately go—the ones who were left alive, that is. Immigration would play a major role in this process, for it was believed the lure of inexpensive (and easily financed) land would attract European farmers and artisans—as in fact it did. (The first of several Homestead Acts was passed in 1862.) Naturally, the railroads would be the logical transportation choice for the new European arrivals. The business strategy for the railroads therefore consisted to a large extent of real estate development. The theory was that when the prosperous towns, farms, and ranches grew up along the routes, eventually their products and produce would be shipped to eastern markets by rail, while necessary goods and equipment from the eastern manufacturers would come by return ticket. The railroads would promote the prosperity of the new settlements by bringing their products to market, quickly and cheaply. And those markets would include not only domestic but also international markets. (Western products included the four million or so buffalo hides that were sent east and in some cases abroad, where they were converted into leather drive belts for British machinery in the textile mills and straps for British army rifles.) Another example: Chicago with its great stockyards and slaughterhouses had, during the Civil War, also become a place where meatpacking and canning grew into major industries. Those industries were initially developed to feed the troops, but after the war some of those same capabilities were applied to the export markets, thereby strengthening the country's trade position. Fast transportation also stimulated the export of wheat— brought east from the midwestern farmers. Wheat was the United States' principal export in the early 1870s.

It all seemed to fit together and make sense. But there were two major problems with the railroads' business strategy: construction was an extremely slow process, and the costs were enormous. Obviously there would be no cash flow from operations until major sections of the line were completed—and only then if the section connected important population and commercial centers. And even that kind of regional business was unlikely to be large enough to support ongoing construction costs for a transcontinental line. The railroad companies, therefore, had two essential needs before they could begin to be viable: land and money. And both of those, in turn, required the cooperation of Congress.

That cooperation came in two important forms: land grants and financing, sometimes directly through appropriations, or indirectly through loan guarantees. Since the land west of the Mississippi was largely federally owned, the railroads needed the government to grant them title to huge swaths of land, not just for a narrow right-of-way, but in some cases for millions of acres along the proposed rail line. Those acres could then be sold or used as collateral to support the railroads' borrowing.

The Union Pacific was the first transcontinental railroad to be chartered, and financed, by Congress. Chartered in 1862 the entire line would be completed in 1869. Along the way enormous amounts of money changed hands, much of it fraudulently.

The Union Pacific followed a model for private and governmental cooperation in a project that was simultaneously designed to promote national interests as well as the private interests of financiers, investors, and corporate insiders. The steps were well known to all concerned parties and observers. A group of entrepreneurs and financiers raised a pool of start-up capital. They used the money to distribute bribes and gratuities to influential congressmen. Thus motivated, the congressmen introduced legislation that would create a new railroad under a federal charter. An accommodating Congress passed the legislation that funded the new enterprise with a combination of cash subsidies, loan guarantees, and land grants. The railroad then surveyed the proposed route and began construction using contractors and subcontractors, some of whom were owned by insiders or their relatives. As each section of track was finished, a government official certified that the track was actually there and operational (the opportunities for bribing inspectors are obvious). Certification led to payment of cash as well as the transfer of land title to the railroad for that section. The railroad, through its real estate arm, then began to sell the land (perhaps after some insider trading) along the route to immigrants and pioneer families. The sale of land would create cash flow to the railroad companies and, in theory, make further construction at least partially self-financing (and there was always the possibility that the land might contain valuable timber or mineral deposits that could be developed or sold off). The railroad would also sell bonds based on the value of the land or the assets of the company or, in some cases, guaranteed by the federal government or, in other cases, backed by nothing at all except the name of the company. Meanwhile the railroad took out advertisements in newspapers around the country—promoting their land and railroad services. The ads were useful in securing the support of the newspapers, which were then expected to write positive articles about the railroad, its bonds, and the allure of land that was in and about the newspaper's circulation area. That would then attract potential immigrants, new subscribers, businesses, and additional advertising. Newspapers in major commercial centers, like New York, were also expected to do their part—in exchange for advertising dollars. The positive articles also helped support the trust and confidence of investors, nationally and internationally. Sophisticated public relations campaigns generated by the railroad marketing staff supplemented paid advertisements. Enemies and rivals of the railroad company, for example, other financiers, also had their relationships with newspapers, so no one could expect unanimous enthusiasm for a project. What's more, politics were ever present, so that if the party in power supported the railroad project, the party out of power and its newspaper allies could be expected to attack the venture. But the key was to have the louder and, if possible, the more respected journalistic and political voices in your corner. This was expensive but came under the category of "a cost of doing business."

It all fit together. But there was a major problem: if you owned a railroad—or, more to the point, a *proposed* railroad—it would be years before you saw any kind of return on your investment (as mentioned, it took seven years to complete the Union Pacific). If you owned a railroad *construction* company, on the other hand, you would get your cash as soon as your work was completed—in fact, as different phases of your work were completed. The best of all possible worlds, therefore, would be to own both, especially if the construction company could then subcontract the actual work and merely make a profit without doing anything, without even having to hire workers other than a few clerks to shuffle invoices. The profit came as a result of the financial spread between the contracted price and the subcontracted price.

This was essentially the idea behind the Crédit Mobilier, which was a dummy corporation secretly owned by the directors of the Union Pacific Railroad in a classic example of conflict of interest and insider trading. The Union Pacific awarded the construction contracts to Crédit Mobilier as though it were an independent construction company. Crédit Mobilier in turn subcontracted the actual work, bought and sold materials to the subcontractors at a profit, and also submitted grossly inflated (i.e., fraudulent) invoices to the Union Pacific, that is, to themselves. The Union Pacific in turn submitted the invoices to the federal government, which had agreed to finance the railroad's construction to the tune of roughly $50 million (the exact dollar amounts are understandably murky) in addition to granting the Union Pacific twenty million acres of land on which to build the line and to sell as real estate. The actual costs incurred in construction were in the neighborhood of $30 million. The difference went into the pockets of Union Pacific directors and insiders. Of course, not all of the $20 or so million stayed in the bank accounts of the Union Pacific insiders. Some of the money went to bribes for influential politicians. These bribes sometimes took the form of Crédit Mobilier stock given gratis or sold at par. The stock could then be sold for an enormous profit, since the market price of the stock was well above the par value. (It reached four times par value.) As Bunting writes:

> One of the principals (of Credit Mobilier), both a director of the company and a Member of the House of Representatives, was Oakes Ames of Massachusetts, who, thinking to forestall adverse action by the Congress, when it was discovered what was going on, passed out shares of Credit Mobilier stock to members of both the House and Senate. . . . In extenuation Ames argued that giving shares to congressmen was "the same thing as going into a business community and interesting the leading men by giving them shares. . . . A member of Congress has the right to own property in anything he chooses to invest in. . . . There is no difficulty in inducing men to look after their own property."[7]

As Mark Twain said: "To be sure you can buy now and then a Senator or a Representative, but they do not know it is wrong, and so they are not ashamed of it."[8]

When the Golden Spike was pounded in, the Union Pacific was joined to the Central Pacific. The Crédit Mobilier graft and fraud were not exposed until three years later, and they attached themselves to Grant's administration. Grant's first vice president was Schuyler Colfax; Colfax had taken Crédit Mobilier bribes and was disgraced and replaced in the 1872 election by Senator Henry Wilson of Massachusetts. Wilson was subsequently accused of taking similar Crédit Mobilier bribes.[9]

When it came to direct appropriations of cash, the government was not always as cooperative as it was with the Union Pacific. In those cases, the railroad companies financed their operations primarily by selling bonds. Sometimes these bonds carried government guarantees, other times, they did not. The investors were in many cases the same institutions and people who earlier bought federal Treasury bonds—banks, both domestic and foreign; investment companies; and individual Americans, wealthy or otherwise. Investors were enthusiastic, in general. Railroads seemed to be a sure bet. After all, they were an essential engine of progress, the government was backing them with land and sometimes guarantees, immigrants were streaming in and would soon turn the empty western regions into a modern Eden. (Transatlantic shipping companies would adopt a business model that was similar to the railroads' plan to transport goods to eastern markets and return with settlers and miners; shipping companies took American exports to Europe and returned with their steerages filled with immigrants. This was especially successful after the 1873 economic troubles in Europe.)

Even unsold, the land could be used to back additional bond sales. Although it was impossible to set a value on empty land along a proposed, that is, nonexistent, rail line, that impossibility did not stop clever Wall Street bond salesmen. They could attach any reasonable-sounding value to empty land, and the lack of any market-making mechanism for the land meant there were not many checks to the salesmen's creativity. As for the bond buyers, many of whom were small investors from Middle America who had successfully invested in Union war bonds, few believed there was any risk. They had the essential ingredients that credit requires: trust and confidence. After all, the railroads were the pet project of the federal government. Besides, there was the army to protect the construction and operation of the lines. None other than General-in-Chief William Tecumseh Sherman said: "It is our duty and it shall be my study to make the progress of construction of the great Pacific railroads . . . as safe as possible."[10] Sherman obviously understood the military uses of railroads. Like nearly everyone else, including the tribes, he understood the implications of the inevitable collision between the railroads and the nomadic, buffalo-dependent culture of the Plains Indians. As Custer wrote in an article for *Galaxy* magazine: "The experience of the past, particularly that of recent years, has shown that no one measure so quickly and effectively frees a country from the horrors and devastations of Indian wars and Indian depredations generally as the building and successful operation of a railroad through the region overrun."[11] At one point Custer even suggested building a railroad through the heart of the west and running from the Canadian border to the Mexican border.

Also, the army had learned during the Civil War that fast transportation of troops and supplies meant more efficient use of both. The Federals and Confederates illustrated their understanding of the strategic value of railroads by spending great efforts to destroy their enemy's rail lines and rolling stock. The experience of building and repairing railroads and equipment during the war provided useful postwar construction expertise. With the postwar army drastically downsized, fast transportation to potential trouble spots was especially important. Fewer troops could be made to go farther, literally, and of course the most likely trouble spots needing army attention were in the west. Furthermore, policing those trouble spots also required forts and occasional campaigns, both of which would need supplies that the proposed railroads could carry faster and more cheaply to the forts than the traditional wagon trains. The combination of railroad and riverboat transportation would extend the army's reach and presence deep into the areas of hostility. Perhaps, the army reasoned, their mere presence would cow the tribes and obviate the need for active warfare. Most professional officers would have welcomed that. As Custer observed in his memoirs, "The first and great interest of the army officer is to preserve peace with the Indians. His home during his life is to be at some military post in Indian country, and aside from the obligations of duty, his own comfort and quiet and the possibility of escaping arduous and harassing field service against Indians at all seasons of the year, accompanied by frequent changes of station, which render it impossible for him to have his family with him, render a state of peace with Indians the most desirable of all things to him."[12] There was of course another side of Custer—one that reveled in the excitement of campaigns and expeditions, especially in the summer. Without the hostility of some of the tribes, those expeditions, with their exhilarating prospect of combat, would be unnecessary. Like a sailor who longs for the shore when he's at sea and longs for the sea when ashore, Custer was restlessly and reliably inconsistent. Then, too, his national reputation and celebrity rested on his exploits as a combat commander and an Indian fighter. It's hard to imagine he would have enjoyed for very long a life of peaceful garrison duty, domestic felicities notwithstanding. There are no headlines—or opportunities—in that sort of life.

Regardless of one's perspective—military, commercial, or political—building railroads, especially transcontinental railroads, made sense to almost everyone in the post–Civil War period. It all hinged, though, on government grants and appropriations. And those did not come cheap. In Twain's *Gilded Age* the president of a fledgling transportation company headquartered on Wall Street explained how it all worked:

A congressional appropriation costs money. Just reflect, for instance. A majority of the House committee, say $10,000 apiece—$40,000; a majority of the Senate Committee, the same each—say, $40,000; a little extra to one or two chairmen of one or two such committees, say $10,000 each—and there's $100,000 gone to begin with. Then seven male lobbyists at $3,000 each—$21,000; one female lobbyist, $10,000; a high moral Congressman or Senator here and there—the high moral ones cost more, because they give tone to a measure—say ten of these at $3,000 each is $30,000; then a lot of small fry country members who won't vote for anything whatever without pay—say twenty at $500 apiece, is $10,000; a lot of dinners for members—say $10,000 altogether. Lot of jimcracks for Congressmen's wives and children—these go a long way—you can't spend too much money in that line—well, these things cost in a lump say $10,000—along there somewhere—and then comes your . . . advertisements in a hundred and fifty papers at ever so much a line—because you've got to keep the papers all right or you are gone up, you know.[13]

The Gilded Age is a novel, of course, but with some allowance for Twain's tendency to exaggerate for humorous effect, there's more than a grain of truth there.[14] Watching Congress line its pockets, Twain's contemporary journalist Ambrose Bierce defined a Representative: "In national politics, a member of the Lower House in this world, and without discernable hope of promotion in the next."[15] To which Twain added: "It could probably be shown by facts and figures that there is no distinctly native American criminal class except Congress."[16]

As Twain pointed out earlier, the newspapers had a stake in this business. Most newspapers, especially in the west, regularly propagandized for their regions, touting their towns as logical way stations on the railroads' path. It was called "booming." Railroads meant immigration, population, more readers, business growth, real estate sales, and even more advertising dollars. Railroads not only created new communities as they crept westward; they bolstered existing towns by bringing settlers in and shipping their produce and products out.

In short, railroads were important elements of the economic, social and military strategies. In fact, it's fair to say that the railroads were viewed as a key strategic answer to most of the major problems—and opportunities—facing the country. Certainly that was the position of the railroad companies, their financiers, and political partners. Looking back over his somewhat checkered career and speaking about his role in the transcontinental railroad he helped finance, the Northern Pacific, Jay Cooke said: "To my mind the enterprise was a legitimate and noble undertaking. . . . Naught but Indians, buffaloes, etc., existed where now stand great cities and villages . . . with thousands of churches and schools. Next to my great financial work during the war I [consider] the successful opening of this grand route from the lakes to the Pacific [my greatest achievement]. . . . As the years have passed on I cannot but feel a great satisfaction in having been the instrument in opening and adding . . . millions of people, so many churches, schools, and colleges . . . wheat fields and mines to our country."[17]

There's no denying the essential accuracy of Cooke's reminiscences. That is what happened, after all. But between the time of his nostalgic glances backward and the beginnings of his vision for his railroad, a great deal of money and a great many lives would be lost. And a different way of life would be virtually eradicated.

CHAPTER FIVE

POLITICS, PHILANTHROPY, AND CORRUPTION

*If you will investigate all the Indian troubles, you will find
that there is something wrong of this nature at the bottom of
all of them, something relating to supplies, or else a tardy and
broken faith on the part of the general government.*
—Brigadier General George Crook[1]

*Wars of extermination are demoralizing and wicked. Our
superiority should make us lenient toward the Indian.*
—President Ulysses S. Grant

The aftermath of the Fetterman Battle revealed, once again, the deep fissures between various parties in the federal government—and in public opinion. Lewis V. Bogy, the Commissioner of Indian Affairs, blamed Henry Carrington for Fetterman's disaster—not for the way he handled the battle but for *provoking* it: "These Indians being in absolute want of guns and ammunition to make their winter hunt were on a friendly visit to the fort, desiring to communicate with the commanding officer . . . so that they might be enabled to procure their winter supply of buffalo."[2] Bogy apparently did not know that the Sioux had been hunting buffalo successfully with bows and arrows for quite a long time. Whether he was being intentionally ignorant is difficult to say, but ignorant his statement certainly was. His view of the fight is so far from the reality that it looks very much like a politically animated version, which, as with most politically contaminated versions of fact, was a distant cousin, if not a total

111

stranger, to the truth. What's more, the idea of issuing arms to people who were actively engaged in attacking soldiers and travelers on the Bozeman Trail was imbecilic. As Custer says in his memoir: "The army declared itself almost unanimously against the issue of arms to the Indians, while the traders who were looking for profits, and others of the Indian Bureau proclaimed loudly in favor of the issue, unlimited and unrestrained."[3] Certain interest groups in Washington may have criticized Custer's opinion as being chauvinistic and inhumane, but those same circles of opinion were not being shot at. Nor had most of them ever seen an Indian warrior.

Despite the army's protest, arms were now and then distributed to the tribes as part of a treaty. Custer describes an encounter with the Cheyenne during his service in General Winfield Scott Hancock's 1867 campaign:

> Most of the Indians were mounted, all were bedecked in their brightest colors, their heads crowned with the brilliant war bonnet, their lances bearing the crimson pennant, their bows strung, and quivers full of barbed arrows. In addition to these weapons, which with the hunting knife and tomahawk are considered as forming the armaments of the warrior, each one was supplied with either a breech loading rifle or revolver, sometimes with both—the latter obtained through the wise foresight and strong love of fair play which prevails in the Indian Department, which, seeing that its wards are determined to fight, is equally determined that there shall be no advantage taken, but that the two sides shall be armed alike; proving too in this manner the wonderful liberality of our government, which is not only able to furnish its soldiers with the latest improved style of breech loaders to defend it and themselves, but is equally able and willing to give the same pattern of arms to their common foe.[4]

Commissioner Bogy's attitude also reflected the long-standing disagreement between the army and the Bureau of Indian Affairs about how best to manage the tribes. Currently the bureau controlled the Indian agencies, which in turn were managed by agents appointed by the government. The agent's job was to distribute the subsidies agreed to by treaty with the various tribes, in exchange for land or an end to hostilities. This system had been in place since well before the Civil War. Before 1849 the bureau was under the jurisdiction of the War Department. But that year the bureau was transferred to the Department of the Interior. By the 1860s this was a very sore subject with the army, which believed that the bureau and its agents were corrupt, that the agents were political appointees who were neither qualified nor honest and who got their positions as payoffs for political support or bribes. Much of that was true. The positions of Indian agent (and licensed post traders) were valuable assets in the patronage business, and the politicians in Washington were not about to relinquish that power. Further, these appointments resulted in more than onetime windfalls to the agents and those who appointed them—regular and ongoing kickbacks were an expected element in the deal. Despite army complaints, the bureau stayed with the Department of the Interior. And under the thumb of politicians.

It was not difficult to get rich as an Indian agent. Since the agent's job was to supervise the distribution of subsidies—food, clothing, blankets, and occasional cash—to the Indians, the opportunities for fraud were legion. For years there was talk of an "Indian Ring," a conspiracy of agents, contractors, and licensed traders getting together to defraud both the government and those Indians who had agreed to move to reservations and live off government subsidies, (although, as in Red Cloud's case, they could still hunt to supplement the rations). But whether there actually was a wide conspiracy or whether the agents were thieves and rascals operating independently is a subject for debate. It didn't matter—the losers were the Indians and the taxpayers. There was very little oversight—one of the army's legitimate criticisms. One of the easiest ways to cheat the tribes was simply to receive a shipment of corn or flour and sell some of it into the civilian market. The Indians had little if any understanding of accounting, and besides, to whom were they going to complain about shortfalls? The agent? Another favorite device was to contract for a herd of cattle with a supplier who would then subcontract the business for a significantly lower amount; the first contractor then split the difference with the agent. In one transaction involving the purchase of eight thousand head of cattle for agencies along the Missouri River, the original contractor made a profit of $250,000—which in today's money is roughly $4.5 million.[5]

Family members were frequently on the agency payrolls. A daughter in one case was paid as the reservation schoolteacher, although she did no teaching. Appropriations for construction of agency buildings were a fertile source of cash. In one instance an agent received $10,000 to build a school; he built a small log cabin for about $200. Invoices and receipts were easy to forge, or, in the case of the Indians who were illiterate, it was simple enough to get one of them to make his mark on a receipt. The census of Indians on the reservation was yet another source of easy money. An agent for the Spotted Tail Agency submitted a census listing 9,170 Indians when in fact there were only 4,775. By virtually doubling the population he thereby received twice the amount of subsidies. And it would not be too far-fetched to assume that, after keeping and selling the one fictional half, he skimmed some of the subsidies actually delivered to the Indians. Shipping companies were paid mileage, and it was easy enough to convert a hundred-mile trip into something significantly longer. Who in Washington knew the wandering roads and distances out on the Plains?[6]

Walter Burleigh, an agent for the Yankton Agency in 1865 before leaving to run (successfully) for Congress, accidentally left behind a document that detailed only one of undoubtedly many similar transactions during his tenure:

W. A. Burleigh received payment in gold, $15,000
W. A. Burleigh sold gold for 100% premium, 30,000
W. A. Burleigh paid per capita $5 to 2,000 persons, 10,000
Amount pocketed by W. A. Burleigh, 20,000
Amount paid to Hon. Sec. of Interior, 10,000
Amount paid to Commissioner of Indian Affairs 5,000
Amount paid by W. A. Burleigh to self, 5,000[7]

Since the greenback was at a significant discount to gold, Burleigh was able to sell the gold for twice the amount of paper dollars, some of which he distributed to the tribes (two thousand persons at $5.00 each), some of which he used to bribe his political bosses, and some of which he kept. (His statement that he paid $10,000 to the "Honorable" Secretary of the Interior is a fine piece of unintentional irony.) Small wonder the politicians in Washington wanted to maintain control of the bureau. Further, like the soldiers, if the Indians needed gold specie to buy from the appointed traders, they would have to rediscount their already discounted greenbacks, so that the value of their contracted subsidy was reduced to a fraction of what they were owed. (The two thousand reservation Indians should each have received $7.50 in gold but ended up with $2.50 in purchasing power. What's more, they had no alternative to the politically appointed trader who could adjust his monopoly prices as he liked—to say nothing of the quality of the goods. As a result the greenbacks the tribe finally received were worth less in purchasing power than those same greenbacks were worth to the politicians who also received them; the politicians and agents operated competitive markets and so could shop around for the best prices. In short, one greenback dollar was worth more to a corrupt politician than to the reservation Indian who received it as part of his promised treaty annuities.)[8]

Speaking of the agency system, Custer says:

> It is a common saying in the west that next to, if not indeed before, the consulship to Liverpool, an Indian agency is the most desirable office in the gift of the Government. Of course, the more treaties an Indian agent can negotiate, the larger the appropriation of money and goods which passes through his hands and the more valuable his office. An Indian war on every other day, with treaty making on intermittent days, would be therefore the condition of affairs most satisfactory to such Indian agents. . . . I repeat then that a condition of peace with the Indians is above all things desirable to the military officer stationed in their country; something very like the reverse to the Indian agent.[9]

This refers to the fact that Indian agents were authorized to negotiate treaties with local bands. The object of these treaties was to "extinguish" the tribes' title to certain areas of their territory in exchange for annuities, which would be administered by the agent.

Custer's viewpoint is significantly different from a conventional eastern political view that painted the army as a collection of homicidal war lovers and the agents of the civilian government as peaceful humanitarians. Certainly that was the opinion of many easterners at the time. Custer may be overstating the case for effect, but it's useful to remember that the army was the institution that had to undergo the hardship and dangers inherent in war. On the scene, he had a clear view of the dangers created by the Indian Bureau's spoils system that resulted in either cheating the Indian or arming him with modern weapons. Or both. And in the end, it was Custer and his troopers who were killed, not the civilian agents.

Custer was not alone in his criticism. In fact, most regular officers decried the infamous corruption of the Indian Bureau. Nearly all regular officers believed that the bureau should be part of the War Department so that the army could manage the tribes and remove the profit motive (and political patronage) from the equation. Looking back, it would probably have been better that way, certainly in comparison to the stench of corruption emanating from the bureau. This is not to suggest that every army officer was pure of heart and free of venality but rather that the army's chain of command allowed for much more efficient oversight and, further, that the army had an incentive to treat the reservation Indians fairly, because as General George Crook said, "A tardy and broken faith on the part of the general government" was the cause of most Indian unrest and hostility. The soldiers who had to fight the formidable tribes were not inclined to dismiss alternatives to warfare. It's impossible to say just how many warriors were infuriated by the Indian agents' graft, but it's certainly reasonable to think that fraud by the Indian agents swelled the numbers of "summer roamers."

THE PEACE POLICY

Just what were these people—the Plains tribes—really? They had no permanent villages or homes, no notion of property law, no real notion of any law, as the whites understood it. They had no actual government. The chiefs spoke for no one and could be deposed or ignored, and the treaties negotiated by those chiefs could also be ignored, and were, routinely. The Indians were an enigma to almost anyone who thought about them.

Of course, the tribes throughout the country were vastly different. Some eastern tribes were considered "civilized," because they operated socially and politically in ways the whites could at least partially understand. Most lived in permanent villages and supplemented their hunting with agriculture. Even the fierce Iroquois farmed and had political systems and alliances that were somewhat familiar to the whites. The Cherokee, some of them, had plantations and black slaves, though that did not save them from the Trail of Tears. But the nomadic Plains Indians offered almost nothing in their culture and economy that was recognizable. They claimed ownership of land, but not as individuals. And none of the tribes had any way or desire to perfect the title to the land they occupied. They said it was their land because they occupied it, which meant by their definition, traveling over it, hunting on it, and protecting it against rivals, Indian or white. They weren't American citizens, and they weren't foreigners, either. They were in some kind of political and legal limbo—from the white perspective. They, of course, knew perfectly well who and what they were and didn't need any help from these strange people from the east to tell them anything. It was the government and the citizenry who worried over these questions.

In 1831 Chief Justice John Marshall tried to answer some of these thorny questions of tribal identity:

> Though the Indians are acknowledged to have an unquestionable, and, heretofore, unquestioned right to the lands they occupy, *until that right shall be extinguished by a voluntary cession to our government*; yet it may well be doubted whether those tribes which reside within the acknowledged boundaries of the United States can, with strict accuracy, be denominated foreign nations. They may, more correctly be denominated *domestic dependent nations*. They occupy a territory to which *we assert a title independent of their will*, which must take effect in point of possession when their right of possession ceases. Meanwhile, they are in a state of pupilage. Their relation to the United States resembles that of a ward to his guardian.
>
> They look to our government for protection; rely upon its kindness and its power; appeal to it for relief to their wants; and address the president as their great father. They and their country are considered by foreign nations, as well as by ourselves, as being so completely under the sovereignty and dominion of the United States, that any attempt to acquire their lands, or to form a political connexion with them, would be considered by all as an invasion of our territory, and an act of hostility.[10]
> (italics added)

So, the Indians had an "unquestioned right to the lands they occupy" until "that right shall be extinguished by a voluntary cession to our government." And although they were not foreign nations, they were "domestic dependent nations," with whom the government could legitimately negotiate treaties—treaties that included matters of trade, war and peace, as well as titles to land (as in the extinguishing of their title in favor of the government). Governments do not negotiate *treaties* with individuals who happen to have banded together in any form. Treaties are negotiated between nation-states and therefore imply sovereignty. But Marshall ruled that the tribes were not sovereign states, and yet they could negotiate and be parties to treaties. They were in a legal twilight land. They owned the land they occupied, but that land existed in the greater context of US territory. A wry tribal perspective might be that all ownership was apparently equal, but some was more equal than others.

This legal definition was perhaps slightly more workable or useful with the eastern Indian tribes, which were generally not nomadic and had occupied certain territories for centuries. (And, in fairness to Marshall, he had not had to address the issue of the Plains Indians, who were at the time of his ruling partly living in what was Mexican northern territory and partly in the empty territory of the Louisiana Purchase. Possibly, the problem of wide-ranging nomads had not occurred to him.) But when the time came, the Marshall precedent was more difficult to apply to the Plains Indians, who traveled in wide arcs and who fought among themselves over the same territory. In fact, they could not really be said to "occupy" anywhere. The land they claimed for their wanderings covered huge swaths of the west, and much of that territory was unoccupied most of the time, as the tribes went here, there, and everywhere and nowhere in particular. This was a prominent complaint of western settlers—the land lay unused most of the time—because of the nomadic culture of the tribes. Even in winter, when they were stationary, the nomads were not in the same places year to year. Of course, their wanderings were linked to the parallel wanderings of the buffalo, but that only explains their travels; it does not remove the legal quandaries facing government policy makers and law givers. To them the very essence of property (and ownership) implied surveys and boundaries and titles to finite parcels. The land the Indians considered theirs was so vast and borderless that the army's principal problem had eternally been simply finding them. And if occupancy was the key to Marshall's understanding of ownership, where exactly did the Plains tribes live? Can nomads be said to occupy anywhere? Is not the essence of nomadism the refusal to occupy any specific place? And when they intermingled, even peacefully, which tribe could claim ownership? These were the kinds of legal questions that troubled the whites; the Sioux and other tribes were not at all bothered by these parliamentary quibbles. The strong owned the territory. The weak went elsewhere.

By defining the tribes as domestic dependent nations and thereby opening the door for treaties with them, the government also encountered the thorny issue of tribal politics. US officials were forever trying to determine just who spoke for the tribe, who was their chief executive. And since that office did not exist, US officials now and then appointed someone who seemed to be a likely leader. Or at least cooperative. Of course, others in the tribe neither wanted a chief executive to negotiate for them nor listened to the appointed one, whose very appointment by the whites often seemed to be a disqualifying act of treachery to the Indians. As a result, treaties signing away ownership of land had no standing with major elements in the tribes. Why should warriors and hunters pay attention to the agreements made by someone else? Someone whom they had not "elected."

There was another school of thought, however, that relates to this question of territory and ownership. Ironically, this school of thought was accepted in both the white and the Indian cultures. It was also based in law—international law, in fact, not that that mattered to the Indians. It was the concept of "right of conquest." It's useful to remember that the nineteenth century was still firmly in the era of colonization and empire building. The idea of conquering another country, whether civilized or otherwise, and then absorbing all or part of it into an empire was not shocking to anyone. (This does not mean that wars of conquest were universally acclaimed, but simply that the concept and precedents of conquest were well understood. After all, it had been going on for centuries, and as recently as the 1870–1871 war between Prussia and France, the victorious Germans had acquired Alsace-Lorraine.) The United States owned most of the Trans-Mississippi because of the Louisiana Purchase from Napoleon, past master of acquisitive conquest, and because of the Mexican War. After a series of vicious battles, the United States defeated Mexico, and the Treaty of Guadalupe Hidalgo ceded California and the southwest to the United States in exchange for $15 million. It was a clear application of the right of conquest. Invasion, victory, occupation, treaty. Seen in that light, it's something of a wonder that the US government and opinion makers of the day ever bothered to worry over details like whether the Indians were sovereign nations or domestic dependent nations or anything else, for that matter. Why not just conquer them and be done with it? Army officers trained at West Point would not have seriously questioned the concept of conquest; it was the way of the world, and their job was to prosecute the doctrine when the government called it into action. (U. S. Grant said that the conquest of Mexican territory was shameful, but he did not resign over the issue; he fought there. What's more, the total number of Mexicans killed is estimated at twenty-five thousand, a number that is most likely close to the number of hostile Plains tribes in toto.) That was part of a professional army's role. So there were many who asked themselves: "Why are we worrying about legal niceties regarding these miserable tribes of savages? We just snatched away half of Mexico." Certainly many western settlers asked that question. The fact that many other military and civilian people did worry about the issues—both the legality and morality of dealing with the tribes—is something to keep in mind when analyzing sweeping generalizations about the settlement of the west and the roles of the various parties.

There is also no little irony in the fact that the Sioux considered the northern Plains their territory *because* they had fought and beaten the Kiowa, the Cheyenne, and the Crow and ejected them from the Black Hills and surrounding territories. (That of course explains the Crow's abiding alliance with the United States and the army. The Kiowa went elsewhere.) Looking back on his contentious relations with the whites, Red Cloud said: "They made us many promises, more than I can remember, but they never kept but one; they promised to take our land, and they took it." It's an eloquent speech; Red Cloud was good at that. But it also conveniently ignores the fact that the Sioux got that same land in much the same way—and without payment or negotiation. The Sioux believed in the right of conquest even more fervently than the Americans who were now encroaching upon them. They didn't need a treaty or international law to make it so; they only needed victories and enemy scalps. And they had won them. They also had the tribal memory of being ejected from their eastern home-lands by the more powerful and better-armed Cree and Ojibwa—a defeat that strengthened Sioux adherence to wars of acquisition. Retreating from their enemies, they needed territory, and they took it. Further, although their code of conduct stressed honesty and integrity among the kindred, treachery and trickery were acknowledged and celebrated tactics against enemies.[11] If the Sioux were deceived in negotiations with the government, they could hardly claim foul, at least tactically. Neither side comes off looking very honorable, but the Sioux were not virgins in the arts of decep-tion. The ambushers became the ambushed. While the despicable criminals who defrauded the tribes remain a blot on the country's honor, the Sioux are not innocent victims. Nor would they appreciate that characterization.

Popular opinion about what to do with the Plains Indians was mixed and unfixed. Western settlers were the most vociferous and bellicose, for two basic reasons: they were the ones who suffered from Indian raids, and they were primarily the ones who coveted the lands the Indians occupied, to say nothing of the natural resources those lands contained. The lure of the Black Hills was irresistible, but their own government was standing in the way and protecting savage tribes who did nothing with the land they only occasionally inhabited, or, from the westerners' perspective, infested.

Custer's view of the Indians, oft quoted, was significantly more sym-pathetic to the Indians: "If I were an Indian I think I would greatly prefer to cast my lot among those of my people who adhered to the free open plains than to submit to the confined limits of a reservation, there to be the recipient of the blessed benefits of civilization, with its views thrown in without stint or measure."[12] The phrase "blessed benefits of civilization" is another bit of Custer irony. He knew what access to whiskey, for example, could do to a band who gave up the roaming life. Of course he admired the free Indians. They were the world's greatest light cavalry; they lived by hunting, one of Custer's passions; they gloried in war and showered honors on individual heroes; they lived out in the open, not in crowded cities; they came and went as they pleased; they saw no difficulty about a man having several wives—something that Custer, with his appreciation of the ladies, might envy. They were individualists unbothered by structure and bureaucracy. They were, in short, living the life that most appealed to Custer's temperament. They were the embodiment of freedom. The fact that they were enemies of his culture did not disqualify them from Custer's admiration.

There was also a strangeness about them that appealed to Custer's romantic imagination: "In him [the Indian] we will find the representative of a race whose origin is, and promises to be, a subject forever wrapped in mystery; a race incapable of being judged by the rules or laws applicable to any other known race of men; one between which and civilization there seems to have existed from time immemorial a determined and unceasing warfare—a hostility so deep-seated and inbred with the Indian character that in exceptional instances when the modes and habits of civilization have been reluctantly adopted, it has been at the sacrifice of power and influence as a tribe and the more serious loss of health, vigor and courage as individuals."[13]

To Custer the Indians were a profoundly different people, admirable in some ways; dangerous, of course; mysterious in their beliefs and customs; unfathomable in most of their ways. They were "The Other" and "a book of unceasing interest."[14] And when they inevitably surrendered to the tide of white civilization, they would cease to be what they had always been and would fall into a kind of cultural and psychological malaise that Custer, as well as many Plains chiefs and warriors, foresaw quite clearly. "In making this change the Indian has to sacrifice all that is dear to his heart; he abandons the only mode of life in which he can be a warrior and win triumphs and honors worthy to be sought after; and in taking up the pursuits of the white man, he does that which he has always been taught from his earliest infancy to regard as degrading to his manhood—to labor, to work for his daily bread, an avocation suitable only for squaws."[15]

In the case of Custer, a part of him regretted the inevitable conclusion. In the case of the Indians, who saw the same result, they felt, in addition to anger, quite rightly a sense of impending doom and despair. Interestingly, that reaction was the desired object of Sherman's concept of war—to demoralize the enemy by demonstrating that the old ways were gone, and gone forever. That way there would be nothing left to defend. Sherman took no particular joy in the strategy; he had ruined much of the South during the war in the idea that defeating the enemy's morale and economic base was more important than killing its soldiers—or wasting his own. He was a practical and unsentimental man. He knew that "war is hell." And he was right. Even so, he had some sympathy for the Indian hostiles: "The poor Indian finds himself hemmed in, and so the poor devil naturally wriggles against his doom."[16] He knew what was coming; indeed, everyone knew what was coming. It was only a matter of how it would come, and when.

The government had established in 1867 a Peace Commission consisting of Generals Sherman, Alfred Terry, and William Harney, and a number of civilians, notably Indian Commissioner Nathaniel Taylor. Their assignment was to come up with recommendations for establishing peace with the hostile tribes. Their principal recommendation was to create two reservations—one in the north (which would ultimately be established as a result of the Red Cloud War) and one in the south. The object was to clear the corridor of western emigrant trails and the transcontinental railroads, both the Union Pacific and the Kansas Pacific (which would in fact terminate at Denver and connect with the Denver Pacific, which went north to the Union Pacific at Cheyenne, Wyoming.) Two treaties were the result— the Medicine Lodge Treaty of 1867 established the southern reservation in Indian Territory. It would be the home of the Kiowa, the Comanche, and the Southern Cheyenne. The 1868 Treaty of Fort Laramie ended the Red Cloud War.[17] Neither of these treaties put an end to hostilities.

Transferring the Indian Bureau to the War Department was the army's primary objective, but, not surprisingly, the bureau and the Department of the Interior were against that proposal. The idea had some support in Congress, though not yet enough to secure passage. The army had renewed optimism, however, because in 1868 Ulysses S. Grant was elected president. Grant supported the idea and also could be expected to approve of a more aggressive approach to handling the Plains tribes. The Fetterman Battle still bitterly resonated with the army, which is hardly surprising. Moreover the battle at Beecher's Island[18] and raids against the settlements and emigrant trails proved to the army that the southern tribes had no sincere desire for peace and were merely using the reservation as a sanctuary and source of supplies.

In January of 1869 a committee of Quakers fresh from their national conference called on Grant, who had not yet been inaugurated. They came to advocate a more peaceful approach to the problem of the Indians, particularly the Plains tribes. The contrast between Sherman's attitude and the Quakers' could hardly have been more different. Perhaps both understood that war was hell, but Sherman's idea was to prosecute war as vigorously as possible and so get it over with, whereas the Quakers' notion was to avoid war at all costs. No doubt Sherman thought that the Quakers were naive. No doubt in some ways they were. But they became a strong voice in the political debate about how to deal with the warlike Plains tribes.

The Quakers naturally abhorred the casualties caused by combat with the tribes. The massacre at Sand Creek was particularly appalling, and not just to the Quakers. Eastern opinion was loud in denouncing the atrocity. Few made the distinction between Chivington's volunteer Colorado militia and the regular army. If they did, to them it was another distinction without a difference. The volunteers wore blue uniforms, after all. Besides, the army had its own black marks. Custer's 1868 attack at the Washita River was not universally applauded. Not only did he abandon Major Joel Elliott and his seventeen men to their fate, but he made an attack that critics said was uncalled for and resulted in noncombatant casualties. Indeed, Cheyenne Indian agent Edward W. Wynkoop resigned in protest over the attack and went east to make his criticisms public in the eastern press.

To the surprise of almost everyone, no doubt including the Quakers, their recommendations for a peaceful policy with the Indians found a receptive audience in president-elect Grant. After listening to their presentation Grant said, "Let us have peace,"[19] once again demonstrating the unpredictable quality that one of his former officers called "unpronounceable."[20]

The elements of what came to be called Grant's Peace Policy developed over time, but the basic ideas were that the tribes would of course be moved to reservations where they would become self-sufficient through agriculture. Their farms would by definition introduce them to the concept of "severalty," which meant individual ownership of property. It would be hard to overstate how radical a change this idea would introduce. A concept that the white culture took for granted—private property—was alien to everything the Lakota believed about their land. The earth was a mother, not a platted parcel. And taken to its logical extreme, severalty meant the reservation would gradually cease to be, since it would be divided into farms owned by individual Indian farmers. The government would provide the Indians with the tools and training they would need to become successful farmers, as well as regular food and clothing while they were getting established. And while white culture at the time believed that a move from nomadic hunting to agriculture was a positive step toward civilization, modern views are less certain. The estimable historian John Keegan writes: "Pastoralism and agriculture are not, as we congratulate ourselves, self-evident advances for human beings. Their development marks both a desperate necessity and a regression. The life of a nomad was probably healthier by far than that of a farmer, happier too, and as long as wildlife remained plentiful, more prosperous also."[21] Of course, civilizing the tribes was not an end in itself for most whites (excepting, perhaps, the missionaries); it was a means to removing the troublesome people who were standing in the way of further western development. So, the question of whether agricultural life was less healthy and prosperous than nomadic hunting was academic and, therefore, essentially irrelevant.

In addition to learning agriculture, the tribes would be introduced to the verities of Christianity, though exactly which specific verities would become a matter of dispute among the various Christian sects. Protestantism, though, would be the prevailing theme, much to the disgust of the Catholics, who felt they should have a role in this process. (After all, Jesuit missionary Pierre-Jean De Smet was probably the most well-known and influential of the western missionaries.) There would be schools for the Indian children taught by enlightened white teachers. Episcopal bishop William H. Hare advocated boarding schools with the obvious intent of separating the Indian children from the influence of family and tribe.[22] He said of the Indian problem:

> I soon came to look upon everything as provisional. . . . *All reservations*, whether the reserving of land from the ordinary laws of settlement, or the *reserving* of the Indian nationality from absorption into ours, or the reserving of old tribal superstitions and notions and habits from the natural process of decadence, or the *reserving* of the Indian language from extinction, *are only necessary evils [and just] temporary*

expedients. . . . The Indians are not an insulated people, like some of the islanders of the South Sea. Our work is not that of building up a National Indian Church with a national liturgy in the Indian tongue. It is rather that of resolving the Indian structure and preparing its parts for being taken up into the great whole in Church and State.[23]

In short, the reservations were only a temporary measure while the tribesmen became prepared for absorption into the wider society, that is, once they had moved to the next level of cultural development: civilization.

Under the Peace Policy, the tribes would no longer be viewed as domestic dependent nations, which meant there would be no more treaties made with them (although existing treaties would be honored). The fundamental idea was to transform a pagan culture that had no concept of law and property ownership and whose members lived communally and existed by nomadic hunting into a collection of Christian individuals who stayed in one place and lived by the sweat of their brow and enjoyed the fruits of their labor on their own land—and so got off the government's payroll as soon as possible. The deadline for that was ten years. The tribe qua tribe would gradually cease to exist and become instead a collection of individuals who shared the same racial characteristics but who owed allegiance only to their immediate families and the laws of the nation. And, most importantly, the warriors would stop attacking settlements and other tribes. They would stop being warriors.

Anyone who thought this could work knew very little about the Plains Indian culture. Interestingly, Grant fell into this group. His experience with Indians was very limited, unlike his immediate subordinates Sherman and General Philip Sheridan, and perhaps he believed the Plains tribes could become farmers. But the principal, if not the only, crops that would thrive on the reservations were anger and resentment. It's well to remember Custer's comment: "In taking up the pursuits of the white man, he does that which he has always been taught from his earliest infancy to regard as degrading to his manhood—to labor, to work for his daily bread, an avocation suitable only for squaws."[24] Custer had obvious flaws, but he knew what he was talking about here. It would be difficult to imagine a less likely candidate for a sturdy plowman than a nineteenth-century Plains Indian warrior. (Some of the less nomadic tribes such as the Mandan and Arikara did a little farming because they lived in more or less permanent villages and used them as a base for their hunting. No doubt the women did much of the actual work. But the Lakota never farmed, nor did they want to.)

As for sending reservation children to school, the Sioux wanted nothing to do with that plan. They understood the motivation behind the idea. They also understood that the fastest way to destroy a culture is to forbid the use of its language and that children sent away to boarding schools would gradually forget their native tongue, religion, and customs. The Sioux steadfastly held to their traditional method of education in which an elder, usually grandparents, taught the children the Sioux ways and beliefs, while a boy's father taught him the skills of hunting and war, and a girl's mother taught her the domestic arts. They neither needed nor wanted white schoolteachers who knew nothing of life on the Plains or life as a Sioux man or woman.

The experience of the tiny bands of Christian missionaries should have suggested the failure of the policy, for although they did make some inroads into the tribes living to the east of the Lakota, their results were scanty. Although sincere and dedicated, they were greatly hampered not only by cultural differences but also by the earlier contacts the natives had with the whites. The first white men the Indians met were hardly Sunday school teachers. As one chief said to Bishop Hare when Hare first arrived: "All the white men that came before you said that they had come to do us good, but they stole our goods and corrupted our women; and how are we to know that you are different?"[25]

In short, the western white settlers were more or less correct when they predicted the failure of the peace policy. Their reasons for that had little or nothing to do with understanding the Sioux culture and everything to do with experience of Sioux depredations. Still, they had a better understanding of the way of the world than did the pious, well-meaning eastern parsons and their allies in the Quakers. The wonder is not that the parsons were utterly (and predictably) wrong because of essential ethnocentrism but that Grant, an experienced soldier and therefore someone who understood man's capacity for violence, went along with the religious innocents. Perhaps he had had enough of blood. Or perhaps it was good politics.

Grant's Peace Policy had other problems to address. There was the widely criticized corruption of the Indian Bureau. Initially he wanted to replace the civilian agents with army officers, but Congress was jealous of its patronage and quickly passed a law that barred army personnel from holding civilian posts. Grant then turned to his Quaker advisors and offered to let them select agents. They agreed. The other denominations wanted some of this business, too, and by 1872 seventy-three agents had been appointed by boards consisting of the multiple Protestant religions.[26] Meanwhile Grant had appointed a former Civil War army colleague, Ely S. Parker, to be the new Commissioner of Indian Affairs. Parker was a full-blooded Seneca who had successfully acculturated himself into white society and who believed in the merits of the Peace Policy. (And perhaps he also demonstrated the huge and fundamental differences that existed among the various tribes. The Seneca were part of the Iroquois Confederacy; between the Iroquois and the Plains Indians the only common denominator was a history of conquest and ferocity, though for the Iroquois that was ancient history. Ironically, the Ojibwa who named the Sioux "little snakes" referred to the Iroquois as "big snakes," in other words, the more dangerous enemy.) Parker believed that the Peace Policy could raise the Indians "toward that healthy Christian civilization in which are embraced the elements of material wealth and intellectual and moral development."[27]

Grant also appointed a Board of Indian Commissioners, successful businessmen with humanitarian impulses. These men would serve without pay and would provide some oversight on the activities of the Indian Bureau. So the agents would be appointed by parsons and the bureau would be watched over by humanitarians. Corruption would be a thing of the past. Peace would reign.

Anyone who thought *this* would work knew very little about Washington, DC. Corrupt agents and creatures of patronage still slipped through the gossamer filters of the well-meaning churchmen. Then, too, even the well-intentioned could succumb to the temptations of profit. Custer met with a Sioux warrior called Running Antelope who called at Fort Lincoln to complain about shortages in rations. Libbie Custer recalled the scene: "The General interrupted and asked the interpreter to say that the Great Father selected agents from among good men before sending them out from Washington. Running Antelope quickly responded, "They may be good men when they leave the Great Father, but they get to be desperate cheats by the time they reach us."[28] Custer did not believe what he said about "good men," for he knew as well as anyone how corrupt most agents and traders were. But he was also well aware of the good intentions of the Peace Policy and was therefore mouthing the party line. As for peace—the years of the Peace Policy saw the worst of the Indian wars, including, most famously, the Little Bighorn and its aftermath.

Then, in 1870, there was another public relations disaster for the army—and a terrible event for the Indians. Major Eugene Baker and two squadrons of cavalry surprised and attacked a Piegan village in Montana. In the fight 173 Piegan were killed—120 men and 53 women and children.[29] Additionally, 140 women and children were taken prisoner. These were released shortly after, perhaps because many were suffering from smallpox. The army defended Baker's action, saying that the Piegan were unquestionably guilty of attacks against the settlements. But there was no escaping the toll of innocent deaths, and there was no use in explaining that when cavalry attack a village, noncombatant casualties were inevitable. In the heat of the fight, amid the dust and confusion and the helter-skelter of close-in combat, with bullets flying and people running everywhere, these things will happen. It was more like being in the middle of a riot than a conventional battle. Then, too, no doubt some of the soldiers shot at anything they saw, whether or not they recognized the target as a warrior. Some did it out of malice or hatred, some out of fear, some out of confusion. Some Piegan undoubtedly were killed by accident, from stray shots. But, said the army in extenuation, there were 140 captives, so the village was not annihilated.

None of these rationalizations had any effect on public opinion in the east. Corpses were corpses. And the army stood accused of "unspeakable barbarism."[30] The event and subsequent reaction was a death blow to the army's hopes of transferring the Indian Bureau to the War Department.

CHAPTER SIX

THE NORTHERN
PACIFIC RAILROAD

*The Indians will be hostile to an extreme degree, yet I think
our interest is to favor the undertaking of the [Northern Pacific
Railroad], as it will help to bring the Indian problem to a final
solution.*

—General Sherman letter to
General Sheridan, 1872[1]

From the perspective of the post-Holocaust world, Sherman's use of
the term "final solution" has a chilling connotation. And Sherman
has been called genocidal, based on a letter written to General Ulysses S.
Grant in 1867: "We are not going to let a few thriving, ragged Indians stop
progress. We must act with vindictive earnestness against the Sioux even
to their extermination—men, women and children."[2] That is certainly plain
enough. Sherman wrote that just after the Fetterman Battle, and he was still
fuming. But neither Sherman nor most of the professional soldiers favored
literal extermination of the Indians.[3] If they had, there would never have
been prisoners taken in battle. General James Carleton—one-time military
governor of New Mexico and as stormy a petrel as Sherman, himself—
issued written orders that women and children were not to be killed. Sherman's letter reflects his frustration with the intransigent Sioux rather than a
blanket indictment of all the tribes. "Genocide" means extermination of an
entire race of people, and no one seriously proposed that. Many tribes, after
all, were not only friendly but also were active allies in the fight against the
Sioux, Cheyenne, and Arapaho hostiles. And many of the fellow tribesmen

of the hostiles, such as Red Cloud and Spotted Tail, were settled on reservations. Whether they were happy about it is another matter, but at least they were not on the warpath. And their surrender was not the result of personal pacifism; both had been terrifying warriors in their younger days. Spotted Tail was reported to have taken over a hundred scalps by the time he was thirty. But by the 1870s he and his band and Red Cloud and his band were alive and living on government rations. And if their rations were substandard in quality or delivery, it was the fault of corrupt individuals, not the result of a sinister or murderous army plot. So despite his plain speaking, Sherman was not advocating "genocide"; he was looking for a final solution in the strictest possible meaning of the term—a solution that would end the vexing problem of Sioux and their allies' raids against western expansion. He certainly did advocate attacking and killing hostile Sioux and their allies. Killing is the business of war. His strategy of "total war," developed in the Civil War, was also designed to generate the surrender of the enemy by destroying infrastructure and economy. As military historian B. H. Liddell-Hart wrote of Sherman: "To interrupt the ordinary life of the people and quench hope of its resumption is more effective than any military result short of the complete destruction of the armies."[4] In the case of the hostiles, "ordinary life" meant nomadic hunting, and their economy meant horse herds, tepees, and foodstuffs stored for winter use—and, of course, the buffalo. But those who surrendered were not then shipped to a concentration camp and murdered. Their nomadic culture was destroyed, but not the people who gave up their arms. So no matter what Sherman felt in a moment of frustration—no matter, really, if he actually meant what he said—the fact remains that the Sioux were not exterminated. To use the term "genocide" is to conflate the treatment received by the Sioux with the Nazi murder of the Jews and is dubious at best.[5] Red Cloud and Spotted Tail were brought to Washington; Spotted Tail and a dozen of his tribesmen were entertained by financier Jay Cooke at his mansion outside Philadelphia in 1872. Red Cloud actually made a speech at the Cooper Union in New York City. Sitting Bull appeared in Buffalo Bill's Wild West Show—hardly a program of genocide. As historian Robert Utley writes: "Many officers believed that extinction was the Indian's ordained fate, but few advocated or attempted to bring it about by war. Rather it was an impulse to civilize the Indian that dominated military attitudes as it dominated public sentiment and government policy—and that belies the charge that the United States pursued a policy of genocide. Nor was genocide the result."[6]

Adherents of the broad genocide theory of course will point to the tragic ravages of disease that wiped out whole villages. These diseases, primarily smallpox, hit hardest on the friendly tribes like the Mandan and Arikara, who were not nomadic and lived in permanent villages along the Missouri River, a primary trade route. The Sioux were strengthened in their power by the reduction of the formerly powerful Arikara, who were deadly enemies of the Sioux. The Mandan virtually ceased to exist, and the Arikara lost half their people. But nomadism did not completely protect the Sioux. One winter count calls the years 1818 and 1850 "Smallpox."

The western civilians, on the other hand, were a somewhat different story. As mentioned, some of the worst atrocities committed against Indians were the work of civilian mobs or volunteer militiamen led by officers appointed by the civilian governments. Editorial writers often responded to Indian raids with calls for extermination. In Colorado the *Rocky Mountain News* called for "a few weeks of active extermination against the red devils," and the *Denver Commonwealth* for the perpetrators of "such unnatural brutal butchery to be hunted to the farthest bounds of these broad plains and burned at the stake alive."[7] These editorials were in response to a series of raids on ranches and stage stops that resulted in the butchery of men, women, and children, some of whose mangled corpses were taken to Denver and put on public display to enflame popular outrage. Col. John Chivington's attack at Sand Creek followed soon thereafter.

Here again it's important to note the difference between western attitudes and those of the eastern politicians and press. It was in the east that Grant's Peace Policy was constructed, and eastern politicians and clergymen were the prime movers of the policy. So, Sherman had a political problem on his hands. He and the Regular Army were caught in the middle of a regional dispute over fundamental issues of nationhood, national morality, national expansion, and economic growth. It's not difficult to understand both points of view. Westerners scorned the easterners who exercised their philanthropy at a safe distance from the warlike tribes; easterners were outraged by the bloodthirstiness of the western politicians and editorialists, and they were properly outraged by the mindless and sadistic slaughter at Sand Creek in Colorado territory and Camp Grant in Arizona.

As he mulled over military policy, Sherman understood there would be no single solution to the problem of Indian hostility; it would be a combination of immigration, land development, mining, army presence, negotiations, and, when necessary, active campaigning and combat. In combination these forces would inevitably "interrupt the ordinary life of the people and quench hope of its resumption."[8] Helping to tie those elements together were the railroads.

When the golden spike was hammered in at Promontory Point, Utah, the nation had its first transcontinental railway system. The western-most section was a central route running from Omaha, Nebraska, to Sacramento, California. The act authorizing the railroad, signed by Abraham Lincoln in 1862, named two companies, the Union Pacific and the Central Pacific, to build the railroad with government subsidies and a large grant of land along the line. The Central Pacific would build east, while the Union Pacific built west. The two came together in 1869—after many delays, payoffs, and frauds, most notably the Crédit Mobilier scheme. (In an action that foreshadowed the Northern Pacific transcontinental project, the Union Pacific construction crews were attacked and harassed by Plains tribesmen who perfectly understood the dire significance of a railroad running through their hunting grounds. No doubt, too, they appreciated the opportunities for plunder and personal glory.) In his memoirs Sherman called the completion of the rail line: "One of the greatest and most beneficent achievements of man on earth."[9]

Seeing the success of the Union Pacific, both in terms of actual railroad construction and insider trading and fraud, other entrepreneurs decided it would be a good idea to propose another transcontinental line, this time a northern route—one that would run from Duluth, Minnesota (the port city on Lake Superior), to the Puget Sound in Washington. Initially, the idea sparked little, if any, interest in Congress. There was a slim argument to be made for the line—the port facilities of Duluth could deliver western produce south to Chicago or east to Boston and New York via the Great Lakes and various canals. (Advocates actually touted the miserable winter weather in Duluth as an advantage—perishable foods could be stored there without fear of spoilage.) On the other hand, opponents described it as a road from nowhere to nowhere. But in 1862 gold was discovered in Montana, and suddenly a northern route that passed through and serviced the gold fields seemed to make a little more sense. Even a politician with his hand out needed at least some credible rationale for his support, and the gold strike seemed to fit the bill. The legislation was helped along by some political allies, like Speaker of the House Thaddeus Stevens, whose enthusiasm for the project went suspiciously beyond concern for the national interests.[10]

In 1864 Lincoln signed legislation to create the Northern Pacific Railroad. Unlike the Union Pacific deal, however, there were no cash subsidies included, although Congress did grant the NPRR almost fifty million acres of public land between Duluth, Minnesota, and the Pacific. Obviously, 1864 was a critical period of the Civil War. Money was tight, the national debt was ballooning, and, aside from connecting to the gold fields, there seemed to be no vital national interest to be served by a second and northern transcontinental. On the other hand, the land grants cost the government nothing—at least, no cash—and the vast majority of the proposed route was uninhabited, except by various Indian tribes. The only possible benefit to the nation was the well-understood impact of a railroad on the hostile tribes—along with the rather tenuous benefit of connection to the gold fields of Montana, tenuous because there were other routes to move the gold to commercial centers (after all, they had been mining there since 1862). In any case, Congress could and did ignore arguments for subsidies, legitimate or otherwise. At the moment the government had more important matters to deal with. There was a war on.

For the first years of its existence, things did not go smoothly for the infant railroad. Short of cash and struggling to meet deadlines imposed by the legislation, the NPRR was on the verge of extinction by 1870 when Jay Cooke became interested and agreed to undertake the NPRR's financing.

For reasons that certainly included the money others made with the Union Pacific and his own experience in earlier transportation finance, Cooke decided that the Northern Pacific was a viable commercial possibility. His natural nose for profit combined with his patriotic belief in the value of the project (as a means of civilizing the west) told him that the NPRR was a good deal for Jay Cooke & Company and for the expanding nation. Further, Cooke knew where the levers of power were, and he understood how to operate them. His plan was to go back to his friends in Congress and renegotiate a more favorable financial arrangement. Historian M. John Lubetkin describes Cooke's methods: "Cooke in the back of his mind expected Congress to give the Northern Pacific both land grants and, if not cash upon track certification, at least bond guarantees. It was no more than what had been done for the Union Pacific and the Central Pacific, and he anticipated that Congress would give the NP a direct money subsidy [west of] the Red River or would guarantee its bonds as it had for the central line." But the mood of Congress had changed. Cooke was forced to scale back his proposals. "Ultimately Cooke asked Congress to amend the Northern Pacific's charter to let him sell bonds, secured by property mortgages. . . . Even this was difficult, but when it came to distributing cash, stock, jobs, consultancies, waivers of debt and other gratuities, Cooke never hesitated. His financial wand touched senators, congressmen, governors, and the vice president."[11]

Cooke got his amendments, although no cash and no guarantees. But at least he was now able to sell Northern Pacific bonds. He intended to market them to many of the same customers who had earlier bought Treasury bonds from his firm—speculators, banks, and the small investors of Middle America. The bonds were denominated in gold, had a maturity of thirty years and paid 7.3 percent interest. And now that the Civil War was over, he thought he could expand his reach to foreign banks and investors. His target was $100 million, and he was confident his excellent record as a banker would get the fledgling Northern Pacific up and building. His reputation did indeed inspire confidence and trust. If there was a slight odor of scandal surrounding him, it was overlooked, for it was widely understood that he was just operating according to the rules of the time—and he was operating more successfully than some of his bitter rivals, such as J. Pierpont Morgan. In short, his odor was less pungent than some of his competition. Besides, the small investor didn't know, and probably didn't care, what went on behind the scenes. Railroad finance was like law and sausages in Bismarck's (apocryphal) observation. The investor only wanted to know that he would get the interest on the railroad bonds he bought, and that when the bonds matured, he would get his principle. And, if for some reason the investor needed or wanted to sell his bonds on the open market, he trusted that he would be able to do that without taking a loss. There was even the possibility of speculative profit. Investors assumed that Jay Cooke's name would be a sufficient guarantee of all of that.

The small investor would become increasingly important as Cooke ran into difficulty when he tried selling his bonds to British and European banks. Cooke opened an office in London but was unsuccessful selling NPRR bonds there, primarily because of a sudden rash of negative articles about the NPRR that were instigated by competitor J. P. Morgan (Morgan had his journalistic connections, too). Then in 1871 a committee of bankers from Vienna came to the United States to investigate the NPRR's commercial viability and investment potential. Cooke entertained them lavishly. But, after dining well and often, they returned home and issued a negative report, much to Cooke's disgust. Meanwhile, the French and the Prussians were winding up a war and were uninterested in American investments. What's more, the reparations the French had to pay to the Prussians at the war's conclusion in 1871 were denominated in gold: "With so much French gold flowing into Berlin, German speaking Vienna quickly became a target for land speculation. Building and loan associations, which had existed for a dozen years or so in central Europe, built up more capital than they knew what to do with. Thousands of Viennese builders could obtain mortgages."[12] The explosion of bank credit lessened interest in American investments and also led to a bubble that would burst two years later. (The NPRR even changed the name of its western-most location to "Bismarck" in an attempt to flatter the Iron Chancellor into investing some of the newly unified German empire's wealth into NPRR bonds. Otto von Bismarck sent a polite thank you note, but no gold.)

The name "Bismarck" was also designed to attract not only German gold but also German immigrants. Certainly that was a major part of Cooke's strategy for the NPRR. He sent teams of promoters to Sweden, Norway, Denmark, Germany, and Great Britain. He reasoned that the sturdy yeomen of these countries could adapt to the sometimes difficult weather along the northern line.[13] Despite these efforts, the surge of hoped-for immigration did not occur. It would come, but largely because of the depression that hit

Europe in 1873. But by then it would be too late for Jay Cooke & Company and the first incarnation of the Northern Pacific Railroad.

Poor management and shady dealings of the NPRR's senior officials, especially J. Gregory Smith, added to Cooke's travails. Smith also had a large stake in the Vermont Central Railroad. Northern Pacific funds that passed through Smith's hands disappeared somehow. Most likely Smith used the money to prop up his shaky Vermont operation, although undoubtedly some remained in his pocket. Further, Smith was suspected of insider trading in land sales through the Lake Superior and Puget Sound Land Company—a real estate operation affiliated with the NPRR and run by one of Smith's cronies. It's fair to wonder how these shenanigans could have happened under Cooke's nose, but he was not an active manager of the railroad. He was running Jay Cooke & Company and was financing the NPRR with an eye to substantial equity. He believed he had enough on his hands—raising the money—without dealing with the day-to-day management of the fledgling railroad. Perhaps he was like President Grant in his willingness to rely on associates and subordinates—to the ultimate chagrin of both.

Still, Cooke was able to raise funds to get the NPRR up and building. Once under way, the construction of the railroad from Duluth encountered extreme difficulties associated with the many Minnesota lakes and wetlands along the route. Contractors were paid as they completed each mile and so were more concerned with speed than with quality or structural integrity. Track laid in boggy areas simply disappeared and had to be rebuilt using extensive amounts of gravel for fill. The opportunities for fraud were legion. For example, the brother-in-law of a chief engineer received the subcontract for bridging the streams and bogs of northern Minnesota. The fact that the engineer liked long sections of straight track meant that a great many bridges had to be built, even though some of those crossings could have been avoided by simply going around them.[14] Unlike the blatant cheating of the Crédit Mobilier, this kind of fraud was harder to detect and might even be successfully defended by the principals. After all, who was on-site and qualified to argue with the route laid out by the chief engineer?

Despite these setbacks, Cooke was able to sell his bonds, and construction continued. True, one engine transiting a newly laid section of track collapsed the track and sank into the bog, and, true, a railroad bridge built over the Mississippi would stand for only two years before collapsing.[15] But even with all these troubles and more, by 1873 the railroad had reached Bismarck, Dakota Territory. The little settlement was on the east bank of the Missouri River. On the other bank, about four miles away, was the new army post called Fort Abraham Lincoln, soon to be home of the Seventh Cavalry. Immediately across the river from the fort was the usual collection of rustic bars and brothels. These washed away, periodically, along with some of the barkeeps, gamblers, and prostitutes, when the river ice broke up and the river flooded. But new entrepreneurs always took the place of the departed.

From Bismarck, the next phase of the NPRR required a survey of the Yellowstone Valley. There had been a survey in 1871, but it had reached only to the Yellowstone where Glendive Creek enters. An 1872 survey was intended to finish the job by having two sets of surveying parties, one from Fort Rice (twenty-five or so miles south of Bismarck) working west, the other from Fort Ellis (near Bozeman, Montana) working east. The two parties were to meet where the Powder River joins the Yellowstone. But attacks against the crew and the army guarding the Fort Ellis expedition aroused some trepidation among the commanders and NPRR engineers and caused them to call a halt to the work before they reached the Powder and the other surveying team. Approximately three hundred Sioux and Cheyenne led by Sitting Bull and war chief Gall—both of whom who would play significant roles at the Little Bighorn—made the attack. One civilian and one sergeant were killed in the fighting, and three enlisted men were badly wounded. As a fight, it was hardly even a skirmish, especially to officers who had seen service in the Civil War. What's more, the Indians retreated from the field, apparently defeated. As usual, their losses, if any, were difficult to assess. But the episode made the surveyors nervous, and the army commander, who preferred staying in camp with a whiskey jug, was content to turn around and go back. When the army decided to turn back without completing their mission, they handed the Sioux a victory they had not won on the battlefield. Moreover, newspaper reports sensationalized the battle and exaggerated the number of expedition casualties—the *Sioux City Daily Journal* reported forty killed and wounded.[16] Eastern newspapers reprinted the report.

The eastern survey ran into similar trouble. Several troops including two officers were ambushed, killed, and mutilated by the very same Gall and his Hunkpapa warriors. Having been repulsed by the western survey team, they had turned east and attacked the team that had come out from Fort Rice. One of those killed was Lt. Louis Dent Adair, a cousin of the First Lady, Julia Dent Grant. And in that engagement Thomas Rosser, the chief engineer of the Fort Rice expedition, very nearly was trapped and killed along with Adair. He managed to fight his way out, killing one Indian, but it was, as the Duke of Wellington said about Waterloo, "the nearest run thing."

The reports of Indian fighting during the 1872 survey made many potential and current investors in NPRR bonds more than a little nervous. Investor confidence began to ebb. Worse, Cooke was counting on large commissions from a new issue of Treasury bonds. He had every reason to believe that he would be the exclusive agent for the sale, but opposition from J. P. Morgan and his partner, Anthony J. Drexel, in the form of newspaper articles spreading rumors about Jay Cooke & Company's difficulties in selling NPRR bonds in Europe, blocked Cooke's appointment as exclusive sales agent. An important source of commission revenue to the bank was lost.

As public confidence in the NPRR project sagged, the price of the NPRR bonds on the open market—bonds that had been purchased and were now offered for resale—also began to sag. Cooke therefore had to prop his bond prices up in order to support future bond sales. No one would want a 7 percent bond at par if he could get an earlier NPRR bond at a discount and thereby earn a higher yield. Or, if the NPRR bonds were suffering significant open-market depreciation, no one would want them—or the new issues—at all. That meant Jay Cooke & Company now and then had to buy back NPRR bonds on the open market to keep their price from falling. Or he had to find other investors who would oblige him. Economist Scott Reynolds Nelson writes: "As construction slowed and financing proved difficult [Cooke] used his brother's position as a board member of the federally sponsored Freedmen's Savings and Trust Company to pump up his faltering Northern Pacific bonds. On behalf of thousands of newly freed slaves who had invested their savings in the bank, Cooke's brother invested in his brother's Northern Pacific bonds at the top of the market. These unbacked gilt edged bonds did well. At first."[17]

Regardless of the bad news from the Yellowstone, which Cooke no doubt regarded as a temporary setback, he was undaunted. There would have to be another survey the following summer—one that would require an increased level of protection from the army. The unthinkable alternative was simply to stop construction and leave the western terminus at Bismarck. To Cooke, the only conceivable way to maintain the viability of the railroad was to finish it to the West Coast. A line from Duluth to Bismarck was indeed a line from nowhere to nowhere. Worse, such an admission of defeat, even if only temporary, would devastate the NPRR's bond values as nervous investors dumped their holdings, making it nearly impossible to sell new bonds at anything like a reasonable interest rate. There was simply no choice but to go on.

Some in the NPRR management hierarchy were secretly in favor of halting at Bismarck, thinking that Indian hostility and aggressiveness made going any farther virtually impossible. Until the Indian problem was solved, they reasoned, any attempt to extend the line looked like a waste of dwindling assets. And solving the Indian problem was the army's responsibility, a responsibility that would require an aggressive offensive, not a passive role doing guard duty for the surveyors. As major stockholders in the NPRR they were beginning to get as edgy as Wall Street and Main Street about the project's ultimate completion and commercial viability. And many of these insiders would find a private way to divest themselves of their holdings before the news got really bad for the NPRR and Jay Cooke.

In the summer of 1873 there would be another survey, and this time there would be no problems with manpower or with marginal leadership, for in addition to the essentially defensive role of the infantry, the Seventh Cavalry would add offensive punch. And commanding the Seventh would be George Armstrong Custer.

CHAPTER SEVEN

CUSTER AGONISTES

Oh, but could you have seen some of the charges that were made!
While thinking of them I cannot but exclaim "Glorious War!"
—George Armstrong Custer[1]

I should never associate with him on terms of any intimacy
and why? Simply because of his recent unfeeling treatment
of enlisted men of this command and shameful discourtesy to
officers, he has proved himself unworthy of the respect of all
right-minded men.
—Captain Albert Barnitz, Seventh Cavalry,
on George Custer[2]

Just after the end of the Civil War something happened to Custer. The Boy General who was legitimately admired by his troops (witness their copying his red scarf and flamboyant manner) changed into an often cruel martinet. The sudden transition from a wartime leader reveling in the acclaim of a nation and in the affection of his troops (most of them, since no commander is universally loved or admired) was apparently a shock to his system. Volunteer troops who had faithfully followed him into battle were glad the war was over, happy and perhaps surprised to be in one piece. They wanted to go home. They were citizen soldiers in the best American tradition. The entire mood of the army seems to have changed, and Custer did not understand it. For him, the army was his life; for almost everyone else the army was something to leave as soon as possible.

Ordered to organize a division consisting of volunteer regiments from the Midwest—war veterans whose enlistments had not expired yet but who had checked out psychologically from the army—he was faced with two difficult situations. First, he had lost his fundamental vocation—combat—and, second, he was ordered to lead volunteer troops from Louisiana into Texas—troops who had volunteered to fight for the Union, but who were now ready to go home, not to Texas. The troops were in a surly mood, and Custer, by virtue of his command position and his efforts to impose his will, found himself thoroughly detested by many of the men. It's not difficult to imagine his confusion. Used to the accolades of his men, used to their enthusiasm as he led them into harm's way, he could not recognize or comprehend their attitudes now. He loved the army. They did not and were heartily sick of the whole business. They had done their duty; they had won the war. Now home fires beckoned, as well as neglected farms and shops. Desertion became a problem—one that he had not faced during the war. His response did him no credit. In one significant incident, he court-martialed a popular sergeant who had an outstanding war record. The crime was circulating a petition for the removal of an unpopular officer. Technically, this was mutiny and the court-martial sentenced the sergeant to the firing squad. Custer had the entire division assembled to watch the execution and gave the "Ready" and "Aim" commands while the condemned man and a convicted deserter sat on their coffins. Before ordering "Fire," Custer had the sergeant led away and then executed the deserter. By any standard, that was inexcusable.

This grotesque and sadistic display was intended as an object lesson to the troops, but the only thing they learned was that Custer was deeply flawed. He would never again achieve the virtually unanimous acclaim and loyalty from his officers and troops that he'd enjoyed during the Civil War. From this point on his command (both officers and men) would be split into factions—factions that would contribute to Custer's ultimate destruction.

Custer's mission in Texas was ostensibly to protect and advance the process of Reconstruction—a job that meant overawing and sometimes arresting Texans who had not yet come to terms with defeat and with the emancipation of the slaves. Custer was a Democrat, which meant he was not quite so keen on the Radical Republican plans for Reconstruction. "He did not favor crushing the South. Ever since West Point, even during the war, he had found Southerners personally agreeable. He believed in elevating blacks but not at the expense of whites. He decried recruitment of blacks into the military, judging shovels and hoes more fitting for them than muskets. As for black suffrage, a key plank in the Radical platform, "I should as soon think of elevating an Indian chief to the Popedom of Rome."[3] Custer's politics led him into hot water more than once. He accompanied President Andrew Johnson, who would be impeached essentially for his policies on Reconstruction, in Johnson's "Swing Around the Circle"—a speaking tour of northern states designed to bolster his political supporters. Custer's position would therefore be well established and glaringly unpopular with the Radical Republicans who would tighten their grip on Reconstruction policies when Ulysses S. Grant was elected in 1868 and then again in 1872, only to lose control of the House in 1874. Given this attitude, Custer got along reasonably well with the plantation owners and former rebels in Texas. He had fought them because of secession, not because of slavery—and because the battlefield was his milieu and combat his métier. He would never find anything that could take the place of either.

Custer was in Texas for another reason, too. It was the army's version of gunboat diplomacy. The French had installed an Austrian archduke, Maximilian, as a puppet emperor in Mexico after overthrowing the elected government of Benito Juárez. As mentioned earlier, the French action was in response to unpaid loans from the Mexican government, and they sent an invading army while the United States was fighting the Civil War and was in no condition to raise issues of the Monroe Doctrine. After Appomattox, the war in Mexico between the French and the Juaristas was still going on, and in fact Joseph "Jo" Shelby, a diehard Confederate who refused to surrender, had led his troops to Mexico and fought with Maximilian's Frenchmen against Juárez. The Juaristas had offered Custer a command, but his superiors refused him permission for a year's leave of absence for fear of irritating the French. Sending the army to Texas was one thing; having regular officers, and famous ones at that, fighting for the Juaristas was something else. (The French pulled their army out in 1866. The Juaristas would ultimately defeat the Mexican remains of Maximilian's army, capture Maximilian and stand him before a firing squad. In Maximilian's case, there was no last-minute reprieve.)

When the Seventh Cavalry was formed in 1867 Custer was appointed Lieutenant Colonel (in the regular army) and second-in-command. The commanding officers of the Seventh were, from then on, older and more sedentary officers, so that the operations of the regiment were essentially Custer's to command.

Custer and the Seventh participated in General Winfield Hancock's futile 1867 campaign against the Plains tribes in Oklahoma and then, more successfully in 1868, against the Cheyenne at the Washita River. That battle established Custer's reputation as an Indian fighter but caused controversy within the army over the loss of Major Joel Elliott and his entire unit. Elliott was Custer's second-in-command, and he and his troops were cut off during the attack. Custer left the field without looking for Elliott and his seventeen men, who were subsequently found dead, to a man. A subsequent autopsy on Elliott detailed the extent of his mutilation: "Two bullet holes in the head, one in the left cheek, right hand cut off, left foot almost cut off . . . deep gash in right groin, deep gashes in calves of both legs, little finger of left hand cut off, and throat cut." His men had similar wounds. (A small irony worth mentioning: Elliott was raised as a Quaker.)

It was between those two campaigns that Custer left his command without leave and traveled across Kansas to see his wife, Libbie. He was court-martialed and suspended for a year without pay, but he was called back to active duty by his patron, General Philip Sheridan, who had assumed command of the entire Division of the Missouri, which included all of the Plains.

After the Washita campaign Custer took long periods of leave and went to New York, where he enjoyed the social whirl and used his considerable fame and contacts to dabble in investments in mining and railroads, but these were not successful. He also tried, unsuccessfully, to sell stock in a mining operation. Indeed, Custer's forays into the worlds of business and finance were invariably failures, but his attempts to generate a fortune through speculation were hardly unique during the Gilded Age. He also used his time and contacts to lobby for promotion—a tactic that was endemic in the army at the time because there were too many officers and not enough positions. Consequently, men who had served in the Civil War with exalted brevet ranks were reduced to their regular army commissions, like Frederick Benteen, a brevet colonel in the war now reduced to his regular rank: captain and company commander in Custer's Seventh. He was also an inveterate and vitriolic Custer critic. (Custer, too, had been reduced to his regular prewar rank of captain, but he was promoted to lieutenant colonel when assigned to the Seventh, so the suggestion that he was demoted after the war is incorrect. He was in fact promoted and even lifted above others in seniority.)

After the campaigns against the southern Plains tribes, the Seventh was broken up and scattered throughout the South on more Reconstruction duties—which meant essentially keeping a lid on white supremacists and the Ku Klux Klan (as an example of the assignment, army units in South Carolina alone arrested some three thousand Klansmen).[4] Custer and two companies were sent to Kentucky, where he fought boredom by racing horses and writing articles for the magazine *Turf, Field and Farm*.

Custer was a competent writer, and his articles display some humor and a talent for self-deprecation, but underlying it all is the sense that he wrote to keep his name in the limelight and to generate a little extra income. While in Kentucky he worked on his memoir *My Life on the Plains*, a readable book that his critics, such as Captain Benteen, called "My Lie on the Plains," explicitly charging that the book was short on facts and long on self-promotion (but when it comes to Custer, Benteen is hardly a reliable source).

Custer's writing style does reflect his romantic self-image (no doubt reinforced by his wife's view of him). He used the passive voice a little too freely, and if there was an opportunity to use "steed" instead of "horse," he often took it. In describing a buffalo hunt in one of his articles he wrote: "Two well-directed shots had been fired, already, the speed of the buffalo was diminishing, and the blood rushing from his mouth and nose told me my aim had reached a vital spot." Custer hunted buffalo on horseback with a pistol. He thought it was the closest thing to a cavalry combat. Part of the appeal was the danger. Buffalo were not passive targets. They ran, but they also were capable of turning and charging, and their strength was such that they could throw a horse and rider to the ground and gore either or both. And in the thick of the race accidents happened. On one occasion Custer killed his own horse and on two others shot and wounded his mounts. The death of that first horse left him stranded alone on the Plains in hostile territory, and it was only through sheer luck ("Custer's luck") that his troopers found him. He was forever wandering away. Small wonder that he admired the Plains Indians and small wonder that his pen name for his articles was "Nomad."

Custer was not the only professional soldier who wrote decent, and better, prose. Both Grant and Gen. Sherman wrote their memoirs, and Grant's in particular reflects his ability to express himself clearly and without rhetorical or stylistic flourishes. Like his orders, his writing is clear and concise. Sherman's memoirs are similarly readable, if a notch below Grant's in a style that modern readers would appreciate. Other officers, less famous but equally worth the time, were John Gregory Bourke, who soldiered with George Crook, and wrote not only his own memoirs but also several useful ethnographic studies of various Indian tribes, including the Moqui (or Hopi) of the Southwest. Army Captain John Cremony wrote a very good book called *Life among the Apaches*. Not all the frontier officers were idle intellectually. And many maintained diaries that are still available today and worth looking into. In comparison to these other writers, Custer's prose is a trifle more florid, which is as much a reflection of his personality as an attempt to imitate popular nineteenth-century styles. His writing drifts into contrivance when he is trying to strike a pose, but when he is describing events he is certainly competent.

Even with his writing, though, Custer's duty in Kentucky was dull. He had a few weeks of entertainment in early 1872 when the third son of the czar of Russia, Grand Duke Alexei, visited the United States. General Sheridan organized a western hunting trip because the young Russian wanted to shoot a buffalo or two. Sheridan invited Custer and Buffalo Bill Cody to come along. Another unlikely guest was Spotted Tail, who joined the hunt with some of his fellow Brulé and who were treated to a lavish dinner complete with champagne. Sheridan is famously quoted as saying, "The only good Indians I knew were dead" which is not quite the more dramatic version of the quote. Sheridan denied saying it. But regardless of whether or not he did, it does not square very well with inviting a headman of the Brulé and his fellow chiefs and family to a champagne dinner also attended by Russian royalty and his gorgeously attired staff. Also attending the dinner was Spotted Tail's daughter, who made a great hit with the Russian archduke and with Custer, both of whom had a well-developed eye for the ladies. The invitation to the hunt and to the regal dinner suggests that relations between the army commanders and various bands of Indians and their leaders were more nuanced than some would like to acknowledge. Spotted Tail had his own motives for coming—he wanted competition at his reservation trading post in order to avoid the monopolistic pricing of the corrupt post trader. He may have understood that Sheridan had a political problem addressing that issue. But Spotted Tail at least wanted to make the effort.[5] Later, when there was discussion about the sale of reservation lands, Spotted Tail was quoted during negotiations as wanting to be able to live on the interest of his money. Perhaps his dinner with Jay Cooke introduced him to the way things worked in the white world of finance.

The 1872 hunting excursion was a great success and was widely reported, so that Custer's name was back in the headlines again. Apparently Custer and the young nobleman got along famously, because the Grand Duke invited him and Libbie to join him later in New Orleans. But after that it was back to Kentucky.

By 1873 the nation was growing tired of the costs and political turmoil associated with Reconstruction. The proof of this sentiment was the congressional election of 1874 when the conservative Democrats gained overwhelming control of the House, thereby signaling the end of aggressive Reconstruction policies. The economic difficulties and the Grant administration scandals also contributed to the victory for the Democrats. People were skeptical about maintaining a standing army in order to protect the rights of people who, only a few years before, had been bought and sold like cattle, and who, many believed, were hardly better. There were other important assignments for the army, such as it was; it was time for the freedmen to look after themselves. Hostile Indians were attacking surveying crews of important economic institutions, in which many Middle Americans had invested. Travel routes and settlements in the west were also being attacked. Given the choice between the complexities of Reconstruction and the protection of the blacks on the one hand, and the completion of a transcontinental railroad and the development of the west on the other, the answer was obvious. After all, which course was more in the national interest: settlement of the west with its vast mineral and agricultural resources, or the social and political development of the former slaves? Which course would contribute to the growth of the country and its material wealth? What's more, the frontier towns and cities, their newspapers and political representatives, were calling for greater action against the marauding Indians. The divide between the attitudes of the westerners versus those in the east was a never-ending theme, fueled by the westerners' continuing hatred of the peace policies that turned hundreds of thousands of western acres over to primitive hunter-gatherers who did nothing productive with the land. It was an offense against the Protestant work ethic and, in their view, common sense. Also, it would be naive to overlook the political influence of the railroads in general and Jay Cooke in particular—and the fact that not a few politicians had an economic interest in these projects. Given those pressures, the issues of Reconstruction and the rights of former slaves were destined for second place. That was fine with most army officers. Few professional soldiers relished the police work involved in Reconstruction. In fairness, soldiers like Grant and Sherman had suffered four years of war in the cause of emancipation. They could very well tell themselves they had done enough. (Although in truth many, if not most, had fought more for the idea of Union and less for the emancipation of the slaves. General-in-Chief Henry Halleck, in correspondence with Sherman as he was marching to the sea, referred to the blacks as "the inevitable sambos." Freed slaves were a problem, not a symbol of moral victory or a cause for rejoicing.) But this kind of duty in which regiments were broken up and troops scattered throughout the south doing nothing of a military nature was distasteful to most regular officers.

Some might argue that western development versus Reconstruction was a false dichotomy, since both projects could have been advanced simultaneously. But the key to the dilemma was the army. The army was required for both efforts, and the army was shrinking. Regardless of the army commanders' attitude toward Reconstruction, ex-slaves, or the Indian problems, the army they had been left with was too small to do even one of the jobs it had been assigned, much less more than that. Certainly, penny-pinching by Congress had something to do with the still-overhanging burden of the national debt. Paying troops to do police work in the South, where there was civilian government in place, while Indians were attacking travel routes, settlements, and railroad surveyors, seemed to many like a misuse of limited assets. Let the civilians look after civilian police work and let the army take care of the hostile Indians. While Grant remained a steadfast supporter of the policies of Reconstruction, many in his own Republican Party began to grow weary of the process and to worry about their political futures, as their constituents grew increasingly uneasy and restless about the nation's course. The Republican politicians had good reason to worry, as the election of 1874 demonstrated, when the Democrats won control of the House and rang the death knell of the aggressive Radical Republican Reconstruction policies. Conventional wisdom says that this shift helped to reestablish white supremacy in the South, where it would remain in place until the Civil Rights movement initiated change. And in this case, conventional wisdom appears to be correct. On the other hand, it's fair to wonder if, had the two-to-one ratio of bureaucrats to soldiers been reversed, the army would have been able to do both jobs successfully. Undoubtedly, a thirteen-dollar-a-month private was far less expensive than the lowliest federal clerk. In that light, it seems fair to say that the Republican Congress helped defeat its own most cherished policy; it's one thing to establish the end, but quite another to select and provide the necessary means.

The 1874 reductions in the army made it nearly impossible for the troops to achieve their three postwar assignments: guarding the nation's coastlines, protecting the western frontier, and policing the South during Reconstruction. The cuts also brought promotion for officers and noncommissioned officers to a virtual standstill. That, in turn, hurt morale and fostered a climate of jealousy among the officers and a climate of political favor seeking, since without political and senior officer patronage, an officer could expect to languish in grade for the foreseeable future, if not permanently. While most promotion was by seniority, it was not always the case, as in, for example, Custer's promotion from captain to lieutenant colonel. And those ambitious enough to want a brigadier's star knew that promotion to general was the prerogative of the president. He could and did on occasion bypass seniority. In one sense, that was a good thing, since merit might lift a worthy officer above lesser men, as in the case of George

Crook being promoted to brigadier after his successes against the Apache. In another sense, it meant that officers without access to or influence with the highest levels of army and civilian power had little hope for a star. Similarly frustrated would be officers who had no opportunity to distinguish themselves against the only enemies the country was facing at the moment—the hostile tribes. Like many other officers, Custer understood that his primary hope for further promotion lay in outstanding successes in the field. His friendship with Sheridan would help, but it would probably not be enough to lead to further promotion. And unlike Sheridan, Custer had little or no appetite for the army's role in Reconstruction. Not only was the work a dead end as far as promotion was concerned, but it was also fundamentally distasteful to him. As a conservative Democrat, Custer was temperamentally and politically opposed to the Radical Republican policies regarding Reconstruction and, by extension, the army's role in it. Custer would go even further when he rejoiced in the 1874 victory of the Democrats: "But for the glorious results of the last election, I would feel that men had good cause to have their faith shaken in the permanency of free popular government."[6]

As difficulties with the Indians accelerated to the point that they interrupted important work such as the NPRR's Yellowstone survey, commanding general William T. Sherman was presented with a dilemma and a decision. He had a limited number of troops available, many of which were distributed around the South doing police work. The Seventh Cavalry was one of these. Reconstruction duties were important, especially to the Radical Republicans in Congress—and, perhaps to a slightly lesser extent, President Grant himself. On the other hand, the NPRR was an important national project for a variety of commercial, political, and military reasons. The project was currently stymied in Bismarck by Sioux and Cheyenne enmity and aggressiveness. A new survey of the Yellowstone Valley was the essential next step. Previous army support for the surveys had been inadequate. The army guard would have to be increased, and cavalry would have to be added to the mix in order to provide some offensive power against aggressive adversaries, since infantry troops were useless against the tribesmen for anything other than defensive action. Infantry would guard the wagon trains and the necessarily slow-moving surveyors.

But cavalry would be necessary to fight the well-mounted hostiles, and there was only so much cavalry to go around. Custer and the Seventh were the logical choice for the cavalry arm, since among cavalry officers Custer had one of the shiniest reputations as an Indian fighter. And along with Colonel Ranald Mackenzie in Texas, Custer was Sheridan's favorite officer. Besides, it was possible that the Seventh Cavalry could strike a blow against the hostiles and put an end to their depredations and convince the remaining recalcitrant chiefs to agree to the reservation. Moreover, the Seventh was not the only regiment stationed in small units across the South, so the army was not completely abandoning Reconstruction duties. But the removal of the ten companies of the Seventh reduced the army's presence significantly. As such, the army was to some extent abrogating the rights of the freedmen (who, ironically and unknowingly, were financing some of the Northern Pacific). As usual, there was no perfect choice. Nevertheless, General Sherman made his decision, no doubt after consultation with the president and the War Department. The various companies of the Seventh that were scattered throughout the South were ordered to reassemble and move to the frontier.

When the call came to reassemble the Seventh, Custer welcomed the opportunity for active campaigning again. As his wife wrote: "[Duty in Kentucky] seemed an unsoldierly life, and it was certainly uncongenial, for a true cavalryman feels that life in the saddle on the free open plain is his legitimate existence."[7] Libbie Custer, then and always, saw army life through her own romantic lens, or (more likely) if she had a more realistic view, she kept it to herself. Of course, there were some less ambitious officers who would probably have been perfectly content to serve out their time doing nothing in a civilized environment, far from the possibility of combat, now and then chasing a few Klansmen and breaking up moonshine stills.[8] Not everyone wanted to fight Indians—or anyone, for that matter. Not everyone wanted a brigadier's star—or thought it a realistic possibility. But Libbie knew her husband. He was ready for active service, ready for something less tame. War was his métier. It's fair to say he was not unique in that regard, but he was unusually enthusiastic. And the only possibility of combat was in the west. His activities at the Washita River had made his reputation as an Indian fighter. Now there would be other opportunities. To him, a soldier's job was to fight, not shuffle papers or chase hooded criminals. Besides, it was the path to a star.

The reunited Seventh would be initially stationed at Fort Rice, which was just south of Bismarck on the opposite shore of the Missouri River. Custer was second-in-command of the Seventh. Though his official rank was lieutenant colonel, it was common among all the officers and their families to refer to an officer's Civil War brevet (honorary) rank. Hence Custer was addressed as "General" (having been a Major General of Volunteers and subsequently granted a brevet as major general in the regular army). As mentioned, after the war Custer, like all regular officers, had reverted to his regular army rank—captain. His elevation to lieutenant colonel was therefore a significant reward and expression of senior approval.[9]

The commanding officer of the Seventh was Colonel Samuel Sturgis, who was on detached duty in St. Paul and would not take the field with the troops. Sturgis had reached the stage of his career when an office in a city was more congenial than a tent on the Plains. And he generally approved of Custer; Sturgis's son would join the Seventh as a fresh lieutenant. The elder Sturgis's opinion of Custer would change when his son was among those killed at the Little Bighorn. But that was in the future; for the 1873 expedition into the Yellowstone Valley, Custer would lead the regiment with Sturgis's and General Sheridan's warm approval.

CHAPTER EIGHT

THE YELLOWSTONE EXPEDITION

We encountered the most violent hailstorm which I ever witnessed which stampeded all of our horses and mules, broke our wagons, wounded the men and placed our entire detachment hors de combat.

—Thomas Rosser, Chief Engineer,
Northern Pacific Railroad, 1873[1]

T he companies of the Seventh Cavalry had been scattered among nine southern states. Custer had been separated from most of his troops for two years. He could not know many of the men he would be commanding. He could not know their abilities; they could not know his. Could they ride? Could they shoot? Did they have dash and courage? Did they have esprit or were they sullen and prone to desertion? Had they grown soft or stale during their Reconstruction duties? There had been turnover, naturally. As Robert Utley writes: "Each year death, desertion and discharge claimed from twenty-five to forty percent of the enlisted force."[2] Some of the veterans remained. But what of the others? More importantly, arresting white supremacists and breaking up illegal stills was a far different business from fighting Sioux or Cheyenne warriors— or fighting anyone, for that matter. Further, company commanders who had been used to a life of independent command would have to readjust to life in a regimental structure. Not all would find that to their liking. In addition, many had achieved much higher (brevet) rank in the Civil War and disliked being reduced to regular army status. Custer's evolved—and harsher—leadership style would make matters worse.

Elements of the Seventh, including Custer and his wife, Libbie, traveled by train as far as Yankton, in what is now South Dakota. Capital of the Dakota Territory, the town sat beside the Missouri River; riverboats could therefore support the expedition as it headed upstream for Fort Rice. Some supplies and dependents stayed aboard the steamer. But Libbie decided to join her husband on the march along the river rather than travel with the other wives on the steamboat. She had been an active campaigner before and no doubt preferred the company of her husband to that of the other wives, even if it meant living under canvas. As Lt. Charles W. Larned slyly wrote about the other ladies: "They have all more or less been sick, cooped up in the small cabin of a rear wheeled boat, living on the most atrocious boat fare. . . . During that time they have succeeded in discovering each other's failings with astonishing distinctness, and from all I hear, have made the atmosphere pretty warm."[3] Most army wives, like the emigrant wives, were a hardy breed, psychologically, not just physically. But that doesn't mean they always got along.

Larned, another army writer, was supplementing his pay by submitting articles about the expedition for the *Chicago Inter Ocean*—a newspaper that had a lively interest in stories about the army's various campaigns against the Indians. The article he wrote about the Seventh's upcoming brush with the Sioux would influence—along with Custer's official report—the future of the Northern Pacific Railroad and of Jay Cooke & Company and, by extension, the future of the US economy.

Greeted by a blizzard at Yankton, Libbie and the Seventh went into camp and suffered through Dakota weather, which she described as "eight months of winter and four months of late fall."[4] (She would amend this opinion after suffering the summer heat at Fort Lincoln.) The troops, who had only recently been accustomed to the clemency of the Southern weather, grew ill, many of them. Their animals suffered equally. Libbie Custer writes:

> After that we understood why the frontiersman builds his stables near the house; we also comprehended then when they told us that they did not dare to cross in a blizzard from the house to the stable door without

keeping hold of a rope tied fast to the latch as a guide to their safe return when the stock was fed. Afterwards when even our cool headed soldiers lost their way and wandered aimlessly near their quarters, and when found were dazed in speech and look, the remembrance of the first storm, with the density of the down-coming snow, was a solution to us of their bewilderment.[5]

And this was in April.

The march to Fort Rice consumed more than a month. To some extent, the long march gave Custer the opportunity to assess his troops and officers, and it hardened the men for the tasks that lay ahead. The Seventh arrived at Fort Rice on June 9, 1873, untroubled by any Indian attacks, although, as Larned wrote: "tawdry cavalcades of the rascals, mounted on their little ponies, decked in comical assortments of skins and rags, tin plates, feathers, neckties, beads, earrings and stovepipe hats, have thronged our camp semi-occasionally affording gratification to a mutual but quickly satisfied curiosity."[6] The Seventh would join with the Infantry under the command of Colonel David Stanley, a veteran of the 1872 campaign (Fort Rice wing) and a generally well-regarded officer, although there had been grumblings about his handling of the earlier expedition and also about his drinking. Stanley was far from unique in that failing. (Custer, as mentioned, was entirely abstemious.) Alcoholism, or at least alcohol abuse, was rife within the army among both officers and enlisted men. Long weeks and months in lonesome, uncomfortable, often shabby frontier posts, isolated from civilization and, quite often, from their families, frustrated by the improbability of promotion—all these factors plus the usual human failings tempted more than one soldier to look for escape or relief in the bottle. The difference between the two—officers and men—was that officers usually could get away with prolonged periods of intemperance, whereas enlisted men were subject to quick punishment. One enlisted diarist, Private Murphy, who had been stationed at Fort Phil Kearny, described the punishment of an enlisted man who had drunk too much on the Fourth of July: "At the guard tent four stakes were driven into the ground and the drunken soldier was stretched out full length and tied to them. This was called 'Spread Eagle.' The sun was beating down on him when I saw him, and I thought he was dead. Flies were eating him up and were running in and out of his mouth, ears and nose. It was reported that he died, but in the army one can hear all kinds of reports."[7] Discipline was harsh in the frontier army. Clearly the level of discipline and excessive punishment had something to do with the epidemic of desertion. But it was also true that many soldiers joined the army as a cheap way of getting to the west, especially to the gold fields—or as simply as way of staving off starvation for a time, until better opportunities presented themselves. Many were not dedicated soldiers and looked to escape army life as soon as possible. And when they did they usually took their army-issued weapons and horses with them. Custer was at the time criticized for his harshness. It is a fair criticism, but he was hardly unique in his methods. Even so, Custer's treatment of the "mutinous" sergeant in Texas reads like something out of Dostoyevsky.

The observant Lt. Larned had something to say about Custer's leadership style during the Yellowstone expedition:

> Custer . . . wears the men out by ceaseless and unnecessary labor. The police of the camp, stables twice a day, water call (involving a five mile ride) twice—mounted guard mounting (a guard of 65 men) drills twice, and dress parade composes an exhaustive routine. We all fear that such ill-advised and useless impositions will result in large desertions when the command is paid off, as it will be tomorrow morning. Custer is not belying his reputation—which is that of a man selfishly indifferent to others, and ruthlessly determined to make himself conspicuous at all hazards.[8]

Such attention to detail may reveal a commander who is out of practice and therefore uncomfortable with delegation and unsure about some of his subordinate officers. Or it may indicate that the Seventh's two years of detached service had allowed the men to become lazy or inefficient. Worse, there was the turnover from veterans to new recruits of doubtful motivation. It's also possible that Larned's comments reveal something about a young officer who resents not being a part of the commander's inner circle of relatives and close friends among the officers. The army, and indeed any fairly large unit of the armed forces, is a complicated family containing people who are variously motivated, variously ambitious, and variously adept. Put them together in very close quarters and mix in the usual human affinities and hatreds, and you have a brew that requires deft command management. Deft personnel management was not one of Custer's talents.

In this case, Larned's letter was not written for publication. (The term "police" has nothing to do with law enforcement and refers to keeping the camp clean and orderly—busy work that is usually necessary but often resented by the men having to do it.)

Stanley outranked Custer and would be in overall command of the expedition, but he was generally willing to let Custer handle the cavalry—which in Custer's mind was only correct and also meant going ahead, "cutting loose," often with a relatively small escort, to find the best route for the heavily laden wagon trains. It was the kind of independent service Custer reveled in. After all, he was "Nomad."

On June 20, 1873, ten companies of the Seventh Cavalry and nineteen companies of Stanley's Twenty-Second Infantry left Fort Rice with the intention of rendezvousing with the civilian surveying crew who were leaving from Fort Lincoln.

Larned described the expedition: "We make an imposing show on these rolling prairies—1500 men, 250 teamsters, 40 scouts, 250 wagons, 800 horses, 600 head of cattle and 1500 mules; too imposing, in fact, for the Indians who have not as yet put in an appearance. The marches have been short and somewhat tedious, on account of the difficulty of moving so large and heavy a train."[9] Along with the fifteen hundred men were two English lords on a sightseeing and hunting lark. Libbie and the other wives left the expedition at this point. They took the Northern Pacific east from Bismarck to their various homes.

It is difficult in the modern era to imagine the level of planning necessary to get such an expedition under way—and manage to keep it going. Or, to put it another way, modern military planning, no less complex, is so very different, because everything in that time relied on animals for transportation. Of course, this is obvious, but it greatly complicated military movements. The horses and mules, unlike Indian ponies, did not thrive for long on prairie grasses and needed supplemental corn and oats or risked breaking down. Twenty-three hundred horses and mules requiring fourteen or so pounds of grain a day meant enormous wagon trains assigned to their needs alone.[10] Cavalry horses and mules also required spare shoes, which required farriers and blacksmiths with portable forges and kegs of nails. Veterinary surgeons and their assistants had to be there to look after the animals. There would be a remuda of spare horses and mules—a tempting target for raiders and another headache to manage and guard. And with large herds of grazing animals, the grass at any campsite would very quickly be eaten down to nothing; lengthy stays in any spot, no matter how attractive or useful otherwise, were impossible, because grass was an essential supplement to the animals' diet. Without it, the expedition would soon run through its stores of grain.

Spare wheels and iron tires were needed to replace wooden wheels that had either cracked or shrunk or wrecked—more work for the black-smiths and the wheelwrights. Leather harnesses would wear and break and have to be replaced or repaired. There were no roads, so the damage to the rolling stock was a constant problem. Each company had a blacksmith, farrier, and saddler assigned to it.

The men, of course, had to be fed, too, hence the six hundred head of cattle—cattle that had to be managed by hired civilian drovers. And anyone with any experience of campaigning in Indian country knew that this form of food on the hoof was an easy and attractive target for hostile raiders. (The troops at Fort Phil Kearny lost several hundred of their herd to Sioux raiders and were reduced to short commons for the winter.) Then there were the wagons loaded with hardtack and bacon and beans—the three essentials, along with coffee. These were driven by civilian teamsters whose notions of discipline often differed from the army's. Ammunition, of course, was vital, both for the men's small arms and for the artillery. The column had two three-inch-caliber guns capable of firing explosive shells. The Indians called these "wagon guns" and feared the explosive shells that "fired twice." These guns would see some action in the coming weeks.

Then there were the sutlers—civilian contractors who sold goods the army did not provide, most notably alcohol, tobacco, and other items nec-essary to a soldier's sense of well-being. The sutlers traveled along in their own wagons which, in camp, could become storefronts. (Soldiers who bought liquor were required to drink it at the sutler's wagon.)

Also along was the "scientific corps," civilians skilled in geology, mineralogy, botany, paleontology. These academics, known to the troops as "bug hunters," could be relied on to find fossils and the like but could hardly be expected to look after their own safety. They were therefore provided with a guard unit, along with two mule-drawn wagons, a cook, and some officers' tents.[11] And this being a Custer operation against the hostiles, newspapermen were inevitable—Samuel June Barrows of the *New York Tribune* and William Phelps, a middle-aged former teacher who wrote for the *St. Paul Daily Pioneer*. Custer was always good copy, and when he was around there was a very good chance of action of one kind or another. Not to be outdone, though, Custer would file his own stories. The *New York Tribune* and the *Army and Navy Journal* would reprint his official report.[12] There was one sure way for Custer to control the content of any story about his exploits: write it himself. As Winston Churchill would later say, "Controversy could be left to History but [I intend] to be one of the historians."[13] Custer would later write an article about this expedition for *Galaxy* magazine.[14]

Illness and accidents invariably attended the march, so ambulances and medical teams were vital. And of course there was every expectation of hostile attacks and the subsequent need to attend to wounded troopers or civilians.

Infantry troops needed extra shoes to replace the cheaply made government issues. (Stanley complained that the infantrymen's shoes had insoles made of pressed paper. Reservation Indians were not the only ones who were cheated by government procurement graft.)[15] Shoddily made felt hats fell apart in rainstorms. Heavy flannel uniforms were uncomfortable in the summer heat and much too absorbent during the frequent rainstorms. Tents for the officers and enlisted men, flimsy though they might have been, were essential in the unpredictable weather of the Plains.

Scouts, both friendly Indians (mostly Arikara and Crow), or garrulous or taciturn frontiersmen (such as "Lonesome" Charley Reynolds), were required to keep a sharp eye for hostiles as well as to help find the best trail for the wagon trains. Custer's favorite scout, Bloody Knife, an Arikara and a bitter and inveterate enemy of the Sioux, was at Custer's side. Interpreters were necessary to conduct parlays and negotiations. Most times those parlays were conducted in scraps of words and phrases augmented by the universal sign language of the Plains—a formula for misunderstanding and a metaphor for the relationship between the different peoples who were colliding with each other in an atmosphere of violence and mistrust. An officer conducting a parlay had no way of knowing whether his interpreter was conveying his message accurately. And nuance was impossible. So, too, legalisms and legal language. (All of which renders the various treaty negotiations and agreements as more than a little questionable, almost laughable, even to those tribesmen who wanted to agree and comply.)

Dakota weather was a continual adversary. The prairie soil quickly turned to sticky mud after a rainstorm, effectively immobilizing the heavy wagons of both the army and the surveyors. Rainstorms swelled streams that otherwise would have been fordable but afterward required bridging. Sometimes the army's pontoons were equal to the job, but other times the army engineers had to improvise, even in some cases sending swimmers across with ropes, which could then be joined to heavier cables, which in turn would be attached to an improvised wagon bed that would act as a ferry. An even more elaborate improvisation involved tying water kegs to the beds of stripped-down wagons and using them as pontoons (western rivers, especially in spate, are nothing to take lightly). For the enlisted man on an expedition like this one, the days were long and the work heavy. It's no wonder that Private Theodore Ewert was cranky. No doubt he was not the only one.

Stanley recorded that it rained fourteen out of the first seventeen days on the march. These rainstorms on the Plains were not gentle showers but rather were violent lightning storms capable of stampeding the stock. Terrified by lightning, beef herds could run off to be gathered up by watchful Sioux warriors who were constantly in the area keeping an eye on the expedition. Frightened mules that were hitched to their wagons were fully capable of running off and smashing the equipment. Bad weather added a new dimension to a mule's natural unpredictability. More than one civilian teamster in these kinds of expeditions was killed from falling under the wheels of his wagon.

Drinking water, of course, was critical, although much of the march would parallel the rivers; still there would be long stretches where water was not available and the men and animals would suffer alike. Not all the western rivers were pristine "gin clear" habitat for trout. Some were bitter and alkaline, others muddy to the point of being undrinkable. Some dried up in the summer months. These dry riverbeds made especially dangerous courses for flash floods. In a heavy storm a flooded river would simply rise and overflow the banks, which was bad enough. But a flash flood would roar down a dry watercourse with astonishing speed and sweep away anything in its path, men or animals. (Drucker Canyon in southern Arizona is named for an officer who was drowned in just that kind of flash flood.) Heat and drought seemed to alternate with rainstorms and mud.

Wind was a nearly constant irritant, making animals fractious and nervous and in some cases blowing down the flimsy tents of the troops in camp. Stanley himself noted that the army's tents were of such poor quality that "there is very little difference in [being] in a tent [or] out of it."[16] (Interestingly, during the subsequent 1874 Black Hills Expedition, Custer's rather more comfortable tent was supplied by the Northern Pacific Railroad—an indication that the relationship with the company was at the very least cordial.)

The treeless prairie meant that wood for campfires would be scarce, although the cottonwood groves that lined the streams and rivers provided some essential, if inefficient, fuel. Cottonwood is a soft wood, burns quickly, and gives off relatively less heat than hardwoods, meaning more work for the wood-cutting parties.[17] Once the sun went down on the Plains, the campfires were important for more than just cooking.

But it was not all misery and danger. For entertainment, the Seventh brought along the regimental band. Some Custer critics point to the band and its signature tune, "Garryowen," as another example of Custer's vainglory. But officers and men alike throughout the army almost unanimously appreciated their regimental bands. In the isolated forts there was little or no other entertainment, except cards and whiskey, unless there was a town nearby where there were more cards and whiskey with the added attraction of "soiled doves." Even the unlucky Colonel Henry Carrington of Fort Phil Kearny brought along his regimental band, and when the war department started looking toward the musicians as a way of cutting costs, regimental officers and men protested vigorously. Further, Carrington was the opposite of Custer in terms of style; he was anything but flamboyant and most of his officers, not least Captain William Fetterman, held him in contempt for being overly cautious. But all regarded the band as a useful, indeed essential, ingredient in the morale of the troops, not only in garrison but also in battle. When Custer attacked Chief Black Kettle's village on the Washita River, he announced the charge by having the band play "Garryowen." How the horn players were able to coax out a tune in those freezing conditions is hard to imagine, but apparently they did make some sort of effort. Band members were not musical specialists, however. They carried arms, too. As mentioned, Carrington's Fort Phil Kearny bandsmen were armed with Spencer seven-shot carbines.

So it was no surprise or cause for comment when the Seventh brought their band on the Yellowstone expedition. As the Seventh left Fort Rice on the way to meet the surveying party, the band struck up the usual martial tunes, no doubt including "Garryowen" and "The Girl I Left Behind Me." "The *New York Tribune's* Samuel June Barrows, who was covering the Yellowstone expedition, called the music 'a little rough, but whatever its deficiencies [it] has the tonic effect on the mind, which soothes the nerves and strengthens the muscles.'"[18] The Yellowstone Valley would soon be treated to another hearty rendition of "Garryowen," accompanied by rifle fire and the war cries of the Sioux.

The amount of planning required to stage such an expedition and to anticipate contingencies in a largely unknown country filled with tribesmen who had already demonstrated their hostility (which required the large expedition in the first place) arouses some admiration for the officers and men who organized and conducted the campaign. Life in the frontier army was a much more complicated business than just shouldering arms or saddling up and heading west. Fortunately, the expedition would be generally near navigable rivers, the Yellowstone most obviously. Steamboats could therefore provide transportation of additional supplies as well as communication with the base and evacuation of the sick and wounded. Both the *Key West* and the *Josephine* were chartered to steam up the Yellowstone and support the troops.[19] And of course no one in the expedition knew exactly where they were going. The object of the survey, after all, was to find the best route for a railroad. That required a lot of searching, false trails, backtracking and decisions between two or more imperfect choices with the nagging feeling that there might still be a better way, a shorter way, or an easier way for construction crews who would come later.

As the cavalry and infantry were leaving Fort Rice, the NPRR surveyors and engineers were heading west from Fort Lincoln. (Fort Lincoln had originally been established as an infantry base, called Fort McKeen, and was undergoing extensive renovations to accommodate the Seventh Cavalry, too. But it wasn't ready yet.) No more than an hour after these surveyors and their infantry guard left their camp, they were attacked by upward of one hundred Sioux, most likely Hunkpapa. The infantry killed two of the attackers and drove off the rest. The dead Sioux were scalped and mutilated by the army's Indian scouts. It was a small fight, but hardly a good omen.

A few days later, these same surveyors encountered a violent hailstorm that literally wrecked wagons and inflicted painful bruises, and worse, on the men and animals. The Chief Engineer of the Northern Pacific, Thomas Rosser, in letter to his wife, wrote: "Many of the officers and men were knocked down by the ice and badly hurt; we had a large dog that was killed by the hail and the prairie is covered with antelope that were killed by the hail stones."[20]

Not surprisingly Stanley's infantry lagged behind the Seventh, which managed to cross the flooded Big Muddy Creek with a pontoon bridge and connect with Rosser's surveyors. When Stanley's column finally rendezvoused with Custer and Rosser, friction between the leaders of the expedition that had been kept beneath the surface started to become more pronounced. Thomas Rosser, as it turned out, had been one of Custer's close friends at West Point. Rosser had gone on to fight for the Confederacy and had risen to the rank of brigadier general. The two former comrades had even faced each other in battle in the Shenandoah Valley, but there were no hard feelings now. In fact, Custer was delighted to see his old friend again. As the leader of the NPRR's part of the expedition, Rosser became one of Custer's inner circle, which rankled Stanley. It was the same story of factionalism in the postwar army, but factionalism that was especially pronounced in Custer's outfit. There seemed to be only two categories of officers: those Custer liked, and those he didn't. There was not much middle ground in his affections (in fact, there was not much middle ground in any aspect of Custer's character; moderation was not his style). Likewise, there were few officers who were ambivalent about Custer. Larned referred to Custer's inner circle as "the royal family."[21] But Custer was not alone in making critical judgments about colleagues. Young Lt. Larned thought well of Stanley, but not of his officers: "The infantry officers I have met have not impressed me favorably. They appear to belong to a very inferior class of society."[22] Just three years out of West Point, Larned's contempt for the infantry reflected the bias he acquired at the Academy, where the infantry was generally lowest on the totem pole of officer assignments, well below engineers, topographical engineers, artillery, and cavalry, in that general order. More than likely, some of Stanley's officers were hold-overs from the war and had not even graduated from the Point, which would lower their status even more. (Of all the branches of the service, the infantry had the highest percentage of officers who were not West Point graduates.) Of course, Custer's dismal record at the Academy (famously finishing last, in part because of demerits for behavior) did not hamper his assignments, but then there was a war on, a war that allowed him to rise on merit and render his academic record irrelevant. New graduates who fared badly academically were most likely to be assigned to the infantry.

Custer disliked and resented Stanley on principle grounds—because he resented having Stanley in command—and on practical grounds—because of Stanley's habitual drinking. For his part, Stanley returned Custer's disapproval with interest. Writing to his wife Stanley said: "I have had no trouble with Custer and will try to avoid any, but I have seen enough of him to convince me that he is a cold blooded, untruthful, and unprincipled man. He is universally despised by all the officers of his regiment excepting his relatives and one or two sycophants. . . . As I said I will try, but I am not sure I can avoid trouble with him."[23]

In fact Custer's "royal family" was quite a bit larger than Stanley indicated. It included Custer's younger brother, Tom, now a first lieutenant but brevet lieutenant colonel and, if possible, an even more ardent and aggressive soldier than his brother—he won two Congressional Medals of Honor in the war. There was also James Calhoun, Custer's brother-in-law, William W. Cooke (no relation to Jay Cooke), Miles Keogh, George Yates, Algernon "Fresh" Smith, and Myles Moylan—all Custer partisans and, except for Moylan, all names that would appear on the killed-in-action list at the Little Bighorn. Fred Grant, the president's son and an officer, was also along, and although he was not as partisan as the others, he was well liked and good company. He had no command responsibility but went along as part of Custer's entourage. (As an indication of the value of connections and patronage, Fred Grant, just two years out of West Point, was promoted to Brevet Lieutenant Colonel and assigned to Sheridan's staff; he was joining Custer on temporary duty.) And Custer brought Mary Adams, his cook. A former slave, Mary was adept around the campfire, especially with game.

Aside from factionalism, though, there were other reasons for the friction between the officers. Stanley had been slow in following Custer to Rosser's camp and as a result was delayed by a rapidly rising river (Big Muddy Creek) that carried away the army's bridging equipment and required some of the improvisations mentioned above. Custer and his clique blamed the delay on Stanley's drunkenness. The cavalry had arrived in time to build the pontoon bridge across the river, but Stanley's much-delayed departure that morning meant that the river had risen and carried away the pontoons before Stanley got there. Many of Custer's officers regarded Stanley's drinking as a significant danger to the expedition. They had no doubt heard similar stories about Stanley when he led the 1872 Yellowstone expedition. Disapproval of Stanley's drinking did not stop others in the royal family from indulging. But they could tell themselves they were not in command. And there was some truth in that, although not much.

With the raging Big Muddy Creek, the West once again displayed the unforgiving nature of its geography. Suddenly rising rivers could easily become barriers to military movements. Of course, that has been true throughout history, but although it was common for an army encumbered with wagons to be stymied by swollen rivers, the same rivers posed much less of a challenge to mounted Sioux warriors encumbered by nothing more than a rifle and mounted on a pony experienced in swimming. Even when the Indians were moving camp with their families, lodge poles and equipage, horses and dogs, their knowledge of the country and places to cross rivers, and their skill in doing so, meant their mobility was far less circumscribed than the army that often was operating in terra incognita, even with the advice of scouts. In a matter of weeks the Yellowstone would prove a barrier to Custer's operations and at the same time provide an avenue for the Sioux to outflank Custer's troops. Throughout the Western wars against native tribes, the army's reliance on supply wagons hampered their ability to find or follow their enemy; it was generally just during a winter campaign, when the tribes went into more or less permanent camp, that the army could surprise and attack with any degree of success. (Of course, if the Indians did not care about being found, because they were offensively minded and ready to give battle, they were not at all hard to find.) When the cavalry could cut loose from the supply trains, they had a chance to close in on the enemy, although they could only carry enough food, forage, and ammunition to last about two weeks—on his last patrol, Custer took enough for fifteen days. (General Crook perfected the use of pack mules instead of wagon trains, and, along with his use of Apache scouts, he had success against the elusive hostiles in Arizona; hence his promotion to brigadier over more senior officers. But Crook was dealing with much smaller units of troops and smaller numbers of hostiles.) Infantry was virtually hopeless against the mounted Plains tribes—unless the Indians were foolish enough to attack a defended position. Infantry was useful primarily for garrison duty or guarding supply dumps or the supply trains, as they did on the Yellowstone expeditions. True, infantry could operate in winter when the tribes were more or less stationary, as General Miles proved after Custer's defeat, but winter campaigning on the Plains was an arduous and bitter ordeal with no guarantee of success and a very good possibility of disaster. Blizzards and subzero temperatures could quickly reduce troops to frostbitten statues. And since the majority of the army was composed of infantry, because it was a less expensive arm to maintain, cavalry was a comparatively scarce asset, which meant that full-scale offensive operations against the Indians was a difficult, rather infrequent, and often unsuccessful proposition. That, in turn, explains why aggressive army officers, like Custer, were so keen to attack hostiles whenever possible. Finding them was a rare event, and the great fear was that they would scatter to the winds before the army could come to grips with them. Also, surprise attacks had proved to be an effective tactic. Robert Utley writes: "In such circumstances Indians usually panicked. Suddenly confronted with soldiers among their tipis, each man turned instinctively to the safety of his family. Thus distracted the fighting force could not offer organized resistance, and the village exploded into fleeing family groups. This could be expected to happen even when the Indians enjoyed superi-

Custer; his wife, Libbie; and his brother, Tom. *Photo courtesy of Paul Horsted/dakotaphoto.com.*

Red Cloud, the victor in the war along the Bozeman Trail, which led to the 1868 Treaty of Fort Laramie. *Photo courtesy of Paul Horsted/dakotaphoto.com.*

Spotted Tail, the Brulé chief who said, "I want to live on the interest of my money." *Photo courtesy of Paul Horsted/dakotaphoto.com.*

Across the Plains. *Photograph by William H. Illingworth. Photo courtesy of Paul Horsted/dakotaphoto.com.*

Custer's camp in the Black Hills. *Photograph by William H. Illingworth. Photo courtesy of Paul Horsted/dakotaphoto.com.*

On the march through the Black Hills. *Photograph by William H. Illingworth. Photo courtesy of Paul Horsted/dakotaphoto.com.*

Panning for gold—the opposite of industrial mining—required only a strong back, the ability to identify gold specks, and a willingness to risk one's scalp. *Photo courtesy of Paul Horsted/dakotaphoto.com.*

Single-file column threading through a narrow Black Hills canyon. The wagon train would have been two miles long. *Photograph by William H. Illingworth. Photo courtesy of Paul Horsted/dakotaphoto.com.*

Custer with his grizzly along with Bloody Knife, Colonel Ludlow (standing to Custer's left), and Private Noonan (standing behind). *Photo courtesy of Paul Horsted/dakotaphoto.com.*

Custer outside his tent. Note the NPRR markings—an indication of the cordial relationship between Custer in particular, the army in general, and the struggling railroad. Custer's hounds are taking their ease after chasing and not catching pronghorn antelope. *Photo courtesy of Paul Horsted/dakotaphoto.com.*

Officers' champagne party hosted by Custer's second-in-command, Major Tilford. The glowering white-haired officer in the rear is Captain Benteen. The party was held while Custer was away exploring Harney Peak. *Photo courtesy of Paul Horsted/dakotaphoto.com.*

Deadwood, Dakota Territory. This is the earliest known photo of the nascent mining camp. *Photo courtesy of Paul Horsted/dakotaphoto.com.*

Deadwood at the height of the gold rush—Wild Bill's last stop. *Photo courtesy of Paul Horsted/dakotaphoto.com.*

Industrial mining came into the Hills after the Lakota title was extinguished. *Photo courtesy of Paul Horsted/dakotaphoto.com.*

Another view of the environmental impact of industrial gold mining—one of the very many things the Lakota feared would happen once Custer's expedition opened the Black Hills. *Photo courtesy of Paul Horsted/dakotaphoto.com.*

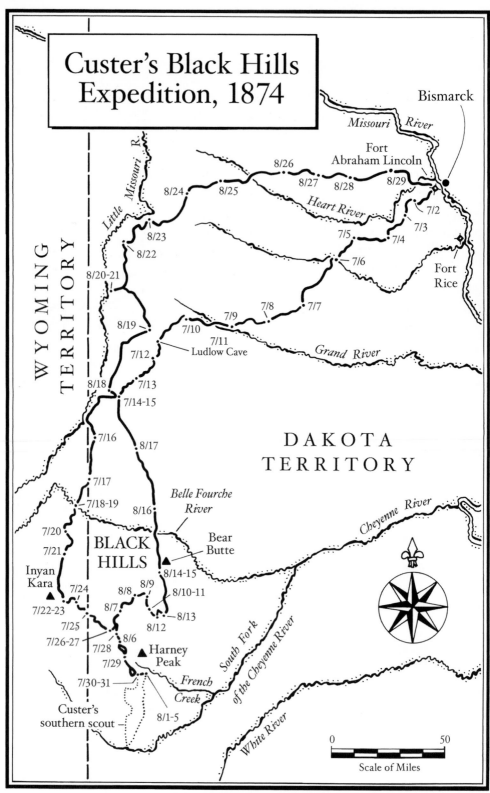

Map illustrated by Rick Britton.

ority of numbers."[24] The need to maintain secrecy and surprise and the fear that the Indians would scatter and escape could easily tempt a commander into a precipitate attack, as it did Custer at the Little Bighorn and, arguably, at the Washita.

These ideas about Indian warfare were more or less accepted throughout the frontier army, that is, when you find them, pitch into them or else they'll escape. But Custer's mission during the 1873 Yellowstone expedition was to protect the survey by extending the army's reach, scouting far ahead with smaller units to prevent surprise attacks, while deploying other cavalry units around the plodding wagon trains and surveyors. His primary mission was not to go off searching for unknown villages to attack. Besides, if he wanted a fight, he had every reason to believe that the Indians were in an aggressive mood. As such, he was more likely to be attacked than to attack. And so it proved.

CHAPTER NINE

THE YELLOWSTONE BATTLES

*Everything being in readiness for a general advance, the
charge was ordered, and the squadrons took the gallop to the
tune of Garryowen, the band being posted immediately in the
rear of the skirmish line.*

—George Armstrong Custer,
1873 Official Report[1]

The animosity between Colonel David Stanley and Custer boiled over during the march west. Stanley was a capable officer when sober, but when drunk he was abrasive and abusive. He made the mistake of arresting Custer over some trivial matter.[2] That meant Custer had to march at the rear of the column for two days. Not only was this an insult, and meant to be, but it was a very dusty and uncomfortable position in the line of march. The air was not very good back there. When he sobered up, Stanley realized he had more than overreacted and asked for Custer's pardon, which Custer granted, no doubt still smarting but also enjoying what amounted to victory over an abject and remorseful Stanley. From that point on Custer would have his way. As inveterate Custer antagonist and all-purpose griper Frederick Benteen said: "Stanley was stupidly drunk and that is how Custer got away with him."[3] And getting away meant going ahead not only to scout the best possible trail for the trains but also to search around a little for Indians.

Having passed through the Dakota Badlands into the more congenial environment of the Yellowstone Valley, the expedition did turn into the "big picnic"[4] that new departmental commander Brigadier General Alfred

171

Terry predicted it would. Custer now had the freedom not only to scout ahead on his own initiative but also to indulge in his passion for hunting. The Yellowstone Valley was rich in game, which, to state the obvious, is one reason the Sioux were so desperate to keep the railroad, the army, every other white person—and enemy tribes—out of it. Custer routinely took a squad of twenty or so riflemen out to scour the environs of the march, hunting primarily for antelope, deer, and elk. He and his party provided a useful amount of meat to supplement the regular rations for himself and his royal family and for the messes of the men. He turned his share of the game over to Mary Adams, who concocted something far better than normal army fare. Custer also made good use of his association with the "bug hunters." From them he learned the craft of taxidermy, and he spent many of his off-duty hours preparing the heads and skins of game animals he'd shot. He also indulged in a little fossil hunting of his own. West Point's scientific curriculum instilled in its graduates an interest in all the sciences of the day—topography, geology, chemistry, biology. Even Custer acquired and maintained that interest, despite his indifferent academic record.

But as the column penetrated deeper into the Yellowstone Valley, as it passed the mouth of the Powder River and headed farther into Sioux country, Custer needed to change his focus from hunting game and fossils to scouting for hostiles. At the beginning of August he led a detachment of two companies—about ninety men—forward of the column to the point where the Tongue River empties into the Yellowstone. This was hostile country. They were traveling on the northern bank of the Yellowstone, as in fact the entire expedition was doing. It was August fourth, and the sun was beating down on the men and animals. So around eleven in the morning they found a grove of trees on the river opposite the Tongue and stopped for a rest and siesta. (Reveille was typically around three o'clock a.m., so by eleven o'clock the troops and their animals had earned a rest.) All along the Yellowstone in both directions were groves of trees, mostly cottonwoods. But from Custer's chosen rest stop the riverbanks were clear for a mile or so in both directions. That gave him a clear view of the surrounding country. After watering their horses and picketing them to graze, Custer posted a half dozen men "on the open plane beyond"[5] to guard against surprise attack. Then he and the rest of the troopers took off their boots and stretched out in the shade.

"How long we slept I scarcely know—perhaps an hour, when the cry of 'Indians! Indians!' quickly followed by the crack of the pickets' carbines, aroused and brought us—officers, men and horses—to our feet. There was neither time nor occasion for questions to be asked or answered. Catching up my rifle, and without waiting to don hat or boots, I glanced through the open plain or valley beyond, and saw a small party of Indians bearing down toward us as fast as their ponies could carry them."[6]

There were six of them, and their object was apparently to run off Custer's horses. The pickets' carbine fire turned them away, though, while Custer and his men saddled up and gave chase. Custer was in the lead followed by his brother and a squad of twenty men. Miles Moylan led the rest of the troopers but stayed somewhat behind the Custer brothers: "We could only see half a dozen Sioux warriors galloping up and down our front, boldly challenging us by their manner to attempt their capture or death. Of course it was an easy matter to drive them away, but as we advanced it became noticeable that they retired, and when we halted or diminished our speed they did likewise."[7]

By this time Custer was familiar with the decoy tactic. In his official report of the fighting Custer even refers to the Fort Phil Kearny disaster[8] as an example of the ploy, although it's fair to wonder how anyone knew exactly how the Sioux decoyed Fetterman and his troops, since none of the troopers survived to tell the tale. But Fetterman aside, the decoy tactic was typical of the Sioux, and no doubt Bloody Knife or any of the scouts might have warned Custer about it, either in this action or prior to it. Whatever the reason, Custer's failure to fall for the trick indicates that the army had reason to trust in his ability as an Indian fighter, certainly in comparison to officers like Fetterman, who had too much confidence in their own troops and not enough knowledge of Indian tactics.

In fairness to the unlucky officers like Fetterman and other veterans of the Civil War or recent graduates of West Point, they learned nothing about Indian warfare at the Academy. The subject was not in the curriculum, for the long-tenured professors at the Academy were certain that their mission was to prepare officers for the next war against nation-states, not to fight a collection of undisciplined savages. And if that war did not materialize, their second mission was to train engineering officers to build the country's public infrastructure and defenses and to explore and map the country's huge western territories. Those officers who did not qualify for these attractive assignments were sent to the frontier to learn the craft of Indian fighting on their own, often through bitter and sometimes bloody experience. The handful of officers like Custer, who did have firsthand— and successful—experience were therefore all the more valuable to the army's high command.

Custer would prove his mettle once again that August 4. Halting his brother's twenty-man squad, Custer and his orderly advanced toward the six Indians. On his left there was another grove of trees. The six Sioux ahead suddenly stopped, as did Custer, who signaled a halt to the troops following him at a few hundred yards.

I then made a sign to the latter [the six Sioux] for a parlay, which was done simply by riding my horse in a circle. To this the savages only responded by looking on in silence for a few moments, as if to say, "Catch us if you can." My suspicions were more than ever aroused, and I sent my orderly back to tell Colonel Custer [i.e., Tom; Lieutenant Colonel was his brevet rank] to keep a sharp eye upon the heavy bushes on our left and scarcely three hundred yards distant from where I sat on my horse. The orderly had delivered the message, and had almost rejoined me, when, judging from our halt that we intended to pursue no further, the real design and purpose of the savages was made evident. The small party in front had faced toward us and were advancing as if to attack. I could scarcely credit the evidence of my eyes, but my astonishment had only begun when turning to the wood on my left I beheld bursting from their concealment between three and four hundred Sioux warriors mounted and caparisoned with all the flaming adornments of paint and feathers which go to make up the Indian war costume.[9]

Custer wheeled his horse around and dashed back toward Tom, who dismounted his troopers, since it is obviously easier to aim and fire a carbine on foot than on horseback. Following standard cavalry procedure, one in four of the troopers was assigned to hold his own and three other horses while his comrades pitched down on the ground to prepare a volley fire. Custer dashed through the line barely ahead of the pursuing warriors, who were then met by a volley from Tom's troopers, and then a second and a third. The fire halted and then dispersed the attackers. Custer reported that several warriors were seen to reel in their saddles, and a number of ponies were hit and spilled their riders onto the grass.

By this time Moylan and his men had reached the fight, so that it was ninety troopers against three hundred to four hundred Sioux. Custer determined that the best course of action was to fight a gradual retreat to their original grove of trees, where the horses would be safe and the men could use a natural embankment as an embrasure from which to fire.

Slowly in a semicircle the troopers fought their way back to the grove. Once there, they secured the horses in the trees, and since there was sufficient cover, Custer could assign one trooper to hold eight horses while the rest of his men spread out along the embankment in a semicircle. It was a good defensive position and frustrated the attackers, who, after making several charges, withdrew from range, dismounted, and then began crawling toward the cavalry line. They tried to set the grass on fire, but it was still too green and the flames did not take very well, although they did raise some thick smoke. The fight went on for three hours, and the troopers' ammunition was running low. Excited troopers, many in their first engagement of any kind, fired too quickly once ordered to fire at will. (As mentioned, this was one of the standard army arguments against supplying the men with repeating rifles, which obviously could fire even faster than breech-loading single shots.) Moreover, the Sioux who had dismounted and tried to set the fires made difficult targets, moving stealthily through the tall grass.

The Sioux tried an encircling movement by sending riders downstream to the pebbly banks of the Yellowstone, so that from there they could work their way back upstream behind the grove where the cavalry horses were kept. Obviously, that would have placed them in the rear of the defenders—a formula for disaster to the troops. But troopers on the left of the line detected some movement and fired on one of the warriors, and that discouraged the others. Custer's comments on this maneuver reveal his assessment of the Indian's fighting mettle: "Had they been willing, as white men would have been, to assume greater risks, their success would have been assured."[10] In other words, Custer's Last Stand might well have occurred three years earlier.

Custer then sent men back to the grove to collect ammunition from the horse holders, who had not been engaged. By three o'clock the troopers were growing anxious. Their ammunition was dangerously low, and the Sioux were showing no sign of wanting to break off the fight.

Then suddenly "we observed an unusual commotion in the ranks of our adversaries."[11] The Sioux were beginning to retreat. Custer and his men could see a cloud of dust on the bluffs to the right of his position. It was the rest of the column. "All eyes were turned to the bluffs in the distance, and there were to be seen, coming almost with the speed of wind, four squadrons of Uncle Sam's best cavalry, with banners flying, horses manes and tails floating on the breeze, and comrades spurring forward in generous emulation as to which squadron should land its colors first in the fight. It was a grand and welcome sight."[12] (A "squadron" is two companies.)

Not to be outdone, Custer ordered his troops to mount and join the charge, and the Seventh Cavalry chased the Sioux for several miles down the valley before halting. Custer later claimed that "the number of Indians and ponies killed and wounded in this engagement, as shown by their subsequent admission, almost equaled that of half our entire force engaged."[13] Perhaps, but estimates of Indian casualties in these engagements were always difficult to make with any accuracy, since the warriors made great efforts to rescue their wounded and to retrieve their dead. Custer was more or less left with counting dead and wounded Indian ponies. Custer's own loss was just one man wounded along with two horses.[14]

The Sioux, however, did not leave without inflicting serious damage. The regimental veterinarian, Dr. John Honsinger, and the sutler, Augustus Baliran, along with two enlisted men were trying to catch up to Custer's troops and were ambushed by the Sioux. One of the enlisted men escaped to tell the tale, but the other three were killed.[15]

Despite these casualties the fight definitely was a victory for Custer and his men. They had held off at least three times their number, perhaps more, and had, with the eventual help of the rest of his troopers, driven the

Sioux from the field after inflicting some casualties, albeit an unknown number. Custer's behavior and leadership were cool and professional.

His official report, however, which was dated August 18, 1873, differed rather significantly from the article he later wrote for the *Galaxy* magazine. In his report he does not mention the arrival of the relief forces. Instead he says:

> The fight began at 1130 AM and was waged without cessation until near three o'clock all efforts of the Indians to dislodge us proving unsuccessful. The Indians had become extremely weary, and had almost discontinued their offensive movements, when my ammunition ran low. I decided to mount the squadron and charge the Indians, with the intention of driving them from the field.
>
> Captain Moylan promptly had his men in the saddle, and throwing forward twenty mounted skirmishers under Lieutenant Varnum, the entire squadron moved forward at a trot. No sooner did the Indians discern our intentions than, despite their superiority in numbers, they cowardly prepared for flight, in which preparation they were greatly hastened when Captain Moylan's squadron charged them and drove them "pell-mell" for three miles.[16]

No mention of the relief force.

Which way was it? There are many variations of the story, and by the time the *Galaxy* article was published, Custer was past commenting, having met his destiny at the Little Bighorn. It seems most likely that Custer's troops saw the dust of the relief column, possibly saw some of the horsemen and took the opportunity to charge the Sioux, who were unnerved by the sight of the relief column and tired of the fight, in any event. Custer's charge provided the denouement to the battle. His later remembrance of the fluttering guidons and banners and the gallant, galloping rescuers may well have been the way he saw it in his mind's eye, the way it should have looked—something like what Frederic Remington would someday paint—and the way his readers would expect and appreciate it. On the other hand, maybe his initial reaction, when he wrote his official report and did not mention the relief column, was to enhance his own stature as a combat leader cum gallant warrior. It's a somewhat more romantic image than that of a beleaguered leader fighting a defensive battle and holding out for help, although perhaps on later consideration he realized that a little modesty would not do his reputation any harm and might, in fact, enhance it.

In any event, it was a victory, albeit small, and there was more fighting to come.

When the cavalry was reunited with the infantry and the rest of the expedition, Stanley and Custer conferred and agreed that Custer should follow the trail of the warriors who had attacked him. This time, with his full complement of troops, he might be able to strike a stinging blow against the hostiles. Examining the trail with Bloody Knife, Custer estimated the village as nearly five hundred lodges, which suggested that summer roamers had joined Sitting Bull. Stanley and the infantry would continue the march, watch over the surveyors, and be ready to support Custer in the event of action.

"On the 8th instant we discovered the trail of a large village to which the party that attacked us belonged. . . . Leaving all tents and wagons behind and taking with us rations for seven days, we started in pursuit at ten o'clock on the night of the 8th."[17]

The trail led to the Yellowstone River, and it was clear that the hostile village had crossed the river at this point, which Custer estimated to be "about six hundred yards wide."[18] Custer tried to follow, first sending a raft across with a jury-rigged cable, but the raft was swept downstream. Next a swimmer tried to haul the cable but was for some reason not able to find a way to connect the cable to the shore. Custer next ordered two of the bullocks slaughtered and skinned to make bull boats—a hide-covered bowl design favored by the tribes of the upper Missouri. (Why Custer had brought some of the cattle herd along is an open question, since he had seven days of rations. Perhaps the cattle were included in the seven-day supply.) But while this was going on, a small party of Sioux arrived on the opposite bank, discovered the troops, and then dashed away. All possibility of surprise was lost, and Custer abandoned the attempt to cross, perhaps chagrined that his troops could not do what a complete village of Sioux—men, women, children, and animals—had apparently done without much difficulty.

"At early dawn the next day (the 11th instant) the Indians appeared in strong force on the river bank opposite us, and opened a brisk fire upon us from their rifles."[19] Custer posted some sharpshooters to return the fire, and one, Private John Tuttle, managed to drop three warriors before being shot in the head and killed. "In the meantime strong parties of Indians were reported by our pickets to be crossing the river below and above us, their ponies themselves being so accustomed to the river as to render this operation quite practicable for them."[20] Custer was being flanked by means of the same river that had halted his advance. Worse, on the bluffs above the river opposite many hundreds of Sioux—men, women, and children—gathered as if to watch the coming battle; Sitting Bull himself was reportedly among them.

Custer organized his defenses to block the crossing upriver. Meanwhile Stanley arrived with the main column of infantry and artillery to a position on Custer's left (downstream). Custer assembled his remaining six cavalry companies and with the band playing "Garryowen" charged to his right (upstream) and dispersed the Sioux. Ultimately the cavalry chased the warriors eight or nine miles, while Stanley fired a few explosive shells at the spectators across the river and scattered them. The Indians did not like being the target of artillery fire. Of course, neither does anyone else.

Custer's losses were "one officer badly wounded, four men killed, and three wounded; four horses killed and four wounded."[21] Given the numbers of combatants the casualties were extremely light. Custer had roughly 450 cavalrymen. "The number of Indians opposed to us has been estimated by the various officers engaged as from eight hundred to a thousand."[22] Custer also estimated that the Sioux suffered forty casualties in the two days of fighting—the fourth and the eleventh—although, as usual, there is no way of determining whether that figure was accurate. Estimates of enemy casualties have a way of being on the high side when there are no bodies to count.

In his official report, which he no doubt understood would be reprinted in the civilian press, Custer minced no words about the government policies that armed the very warriors who had attacked him:

> The arms with which they fought us (several of which were captured) were
> of the latest improved patterns of breech-loading repeating rifles, and their

supply of metallic rifle cartridges seemed unlimited, as they were anything but sparing in their use. [Another bit of conventional army wisdom was that Indians tended to be poor shots because ammunition was hard to come by, and they did not waste it on practice; Custer is observing that, apparently, things had changed.] So amply have they been supplied with breech loading rifles and ammunition that neither bows nor arrows were employed against us. As evidence that these Indians, or at least many of them, were recently from the Missouri River agencies, we found provisions, such as coffee, in their abandoned camps, and cooking and other domestic utensils, such as only reservation Indians are supplied with.[23]

Summer roamers.

Custer was surely justified in expressing the outrage that all frontier soldiers felt at being shot at by rifles provided through the "imbecilic" peace policies of their own government. Worse, the Indian rifles were far better than the ones provided to the troops. The question had been hotly debated for years. It will be recalled that in his memoir, *My Life on the Plains*, Custer wrote: "The army declared itself almost unanimously against the issue of arms to the Indians, while the traders, who were looking to the profits, and others of the Indian Bureau, proclaimed loudly in favor of the issue, unlimited and unrestrained."[24]

Custer's complete report of the two Yellowstone battles was published by the *New York Tribune* and the *Army and Navy Journal*. Further, the reports of the newspaper correspondents accompanying the expedition also detailed the fighting. Custer no doubt approved of Samuel Barrows's story in the *New York Tribune*: "Strike up *Garryowen*" said [Custer] to the leader of the band. The familiar notes of that stirring Irish air acted like magic. If the commander had had a galvanic battery connecting with the solar plexus of every man in the field, he could hardly have electrified them more thoroughly. What matter of the cornet played a faltering note and the alto horn was a little husky? There was no mistaking the tune and its meaning."[25]

But was Barrows there? His report sounds like something written after the fact.

As usual, Custer was good copy, but the newspaper story and Custer's official report had unintended consequences, as did Lt. Charles Larned's report of the fight to the *Chicago Inter Ocean*. Larned did not overdramatize the action, but he did not need to. The simple facts conveyed the significance without the need for embellishment or interpretation, and the public's understanding of all the reports was clear: the Sioux were not taking this railroad project lying down. If the 1872 expedition aroused some nervousness about the viability of the Northern Pacific, the 1873 Sioux attack on the country's most renowned—and most publicized—Indian fighter ensured that the problem of hostile Indians would return to the nation's consciousness, front and center. The country might applaud Custer's victory, but the fact that there was *any* sort of fighting was the real cause for worry. And although the story of Custer's outnumbered troops defeating hundreds of hostiles in one sense burnished his public image, the fact that he *was* outnumbered and nearly surrounded told anyone who thought about it—and many investors did—that the Sioux were not only in an evil temper; they were aggressive, and they were numerous. There was no doubt that these primitives would eventually be defeated, but "eventually" is not a word that most investors usually like. What about the here and now? And what could go wrong from this point?

To investors—and potential investors—in the NPRR bonds, the risk-reward ratio began to look very much out of balance. Perhaps the NPRR would be finished eventually, but how long would it take? How long before the sturdy yeomen emigrating from northern and central Europe would feel comfortable buying property from the NPRR and settling along the railway to build farms and villages? And then how long would they take to clear the land and create the produce that the railroad would ship to eastern markets? How many months and years would have to pass before the line could begin generating freight and passenger revenue—the revenue necessary to pay the interest and principle on the bonds that continued to come on the market? What if other nervous investors started selling their NPRR bonds? What would that do to the principle value? What if the NPRR was never able to finish the line? What would the bonds be worth then? The whole concept—of the NPRR, so rational at the start—began to look like a fantasy. Many began to ask themselves—should I get out now?

The survey continued without further incident, and the NPRR engineers were happy and relieved to find the stakes left by the Fort Ellis surveyors the summer before. The NPRR engineers and the army could therefore turn around and head back to Bismarck. But the reports of the fighting preceded them—sent by couriers—and while this meant that Custer's and the Seventh's reputation was again in the ascendant, trust and confidence in the Northern Pacific's viability was ebbing. Not only were people drawing their own conclusions about the significance of the Indian attacks; other commentators were beginning to question the NPRR's financial structure and its exaggerated claims about the land the NPRR was offering—not only for sale but as backing for their bonds. E. L. Godkin was the editor of the magazine *The Nation*, and in the fall of 1872 (perhaps significantly after the difficulties and failures of the previous Yellowstone expedition) he wrote: "Unless we are greatly deceived, within the next few years a great many handsomely engraved railroad bonds will go to protest, and certificates of stock by the million will find their way into the hands of the trunk makers."[26] In other words, railroad securities would soon be useful only as a lining for suitcases and trunks. In the world that depended on trust and confidence to uphold stock and bond values, this kind of pronouncement bordered on a self-fulfilling prophecy.

Another skeptic was General William B. Hazen. Hazen was stationed at the remote Fort Buford, which sat at the juncture of the Yellowstone and Missouri Rivers, along the border between today's Montana and North Dakota.

Robert Utley explains:

Jay Cooke's promotional literature [which rhapsodically described the northern Plains as a "fruitful garden"] incensed Hazen, who had endured enough of Fort Buford to have a pessimistic view of the country's agricultural future. He set his opinions to paper and mailed them to The New York Tribune. "WORTHLESS RAILROAD LAND," headlined the Tribune in its issue of February 7, 1874. In the article Hazen scored the Northern Pacific for "shameless falsehoods" and characterized the railroad's so called "Northern Tropic Belt" as an arid waste, sunblasted in summer, frozen in winter, that on its own merits could not command a "penny an acre."[27]

The struggling Northern Pacific turned to its close ally, George Custer, and asked him to write a rebuttal to Hazen's claims—which he did. His article was published in the *Minneapolis Tribune* and, with Custer's characteristic enthusiasm, contradicted Hazen's gloomy assessments.

Hazen was partially correct about the land west of the Missouri but wrong about the country east of the river, as subsequent development would prove. To the east, farms and villages would spring up just as Jay Cooke had envisioned. The land to the west, however, averaged only eighteen inches of rainfall and would not be arable until more modern irrigation methods could be applied. The water table was very deep and required extensive drilling to find it, but it was there and could, and would eventually, be raised using windmills. The drilling and piping and assorted equipment were expensive, though, and were beyond the immediate means of most immigrant families. On the other hand, the land was covered with nutritious grasses that had supported vast buffalo herds and would support cattle in large numbers. So although the western lands were hardly a "fruitful garden," they were far from being an "arid waste."[28] But it needed ranchmen, not plowmen.

Hazen had always been an irascible character and an adversary of Custer and, worse, of his boss, General Philip Sheridan. His quarrels with Sheridan probably explain his exile to Fort Buford. But Hazen's report did not fall on deaf ears in New York. It was, however, merely an extraneous nail in the coffin, because five months before, in September 1873, the financial markets had crashed, and the country's worst economic depression in its short history was well and truly under way.[29]

CHAPTER TEN

ANATOMY OF A CRASH

Beautiful credit! The foundation of modern society. Who shall say this is not the golden age of mutual trust, of unlimited reliance upon human promises? That is a peculiar condition of society which enables a whole nation to instantly recognize point and meaning in the familiar newspaper anecdote which puts into the mouth of a distinguished speculator in lands and mines this remark—"I wasn't worth a cent two years ago, and now I owe two millions of dollars."

> —Mark Twain and Charles Dudley Warner,
> *The Gilded Age*, 1873

Then an event—perhaps a change in government policy, an unexplained failure of a firm previously thought to have been successful—occurs that leads to a pause in the increase in asset prices. Soon, some of the investors who had financed most of their purchases with borrowed money become distress sellers of the real estate or stocks because the interest payments on the money borrowed to finance their purchases are larger than the investment income on the assets. The prices of these assets decline below their purchase price and now the assets are "under water"—the amount owed on the money borrowed to finance the purchase of these assets is larger than their current market value. Their distress sales lead to sharp declines in the prices of the assets and a crash and panic may follow.

> —Charles P. Kindleberger and Robert Aliber,
> *Manias, Panics, and Crashes*, 2005

What caused the Depression of 1873? Doubtless there were many factors. But there was one overarching reason, and it was more or less the same thing that caused every other economic crash throughout history: broken promises.

Readers of Victorian novels, especially those of Anthony Trollope, will recognize one form of finance in particular. Chronically short of money, a feckless hero issues short-term notes—generically called "acceptances" or "bills." These were nothing more than IOUs, a promise to pay the face value at some specified point in the future. He would then take them to a bank or money lender in "The City" and exchange the bill for the face value in cash minus a discount. When the "IOU" matured, usually in three to six months, the bank would present it to the issuer and collect the full face value. The bank's profit would be the difference between the discounted amount it advanced three months or so prior and the full face value it collected at maturity. Many of Trollope's insouciant young heroes got into trouble by issuing these kinds of notes, or worse, endorsing (essentially cosigning) someone else's note and therefore becoming responsible to pay the lender at maturity, when the original (and usually worthless) borrower was unable or unwilling to pay. It was possible, of course, to continue issuing bills, paying off one by signing and discounting a new bill, but that approach led to increasing indebtedness, since the discounted value of each new note had to equal the full face value of the maturing note. And at some point the bank would want to retrieve its principle, as the credit worthiness of the borrower became increasingly dubious. Worse, the bank might—and probably would—sell off the notes to some other investor or some other firm. That firm was not always as lenient or gentlemanly, and the youthful hero—or sometimes the aging roué—would then find himself in legal difficulties.

In short, this kind of credit rested on the name of the borrower (or sometimes the cosigner) and worked especially well when the name was that of an aristocratic or wealthy family. There was no other security, but the banker generally assumed that he could get his money back by selling the bill to another investor or by going to the hero's disgusted family to collect full payment, whereupon the hero would receive a stern lecture from his exasperated father or guardian.[1]

Speaking of feckless heroes who used their famous name for financial leverage, George Custer fell into that category whenever he stepped out of his natural milieu—the army and the battlefield—and entered alien territory, whether politics or business. He was virtually hopeless in both, although like many similar characters he did not realize it. He was a celebrity because of his Civil War exploits and subsequent successes against the hostile tribes, and he enjoyed the acclaim. He spent long leaves in New York being wined and dined by the financial and political elites of the city and, without Libbie, flirting with the ladies of fashion. He had become involved with a Colorado gold mine speculation and used his name to try to sell stock to financiers such as Jay Gould and James Fisk—hardly a pair of moral philosophers. The prospectus stated that Custer himself had pledged thirty-five thousand dollars to the enterprise, although certainly he did not have anything like that amount of money and was therefore lending his name to attract additional investors who might be gullible enough to believe that the names Custer, Gould, and Fisk were automatic guarantors of a successful speculation. Possibly Custer assumed that he would be able to come up with his pledged thirty-five thousand when the mine paid off. Or maybe he saw nothing wrong with the process, much like the congressmen and bureaucrats who did as much and more. It was the way of the world, then. As Trollope says in *The Way We Live Now*: "Nevertheless a certain class of dishonesty, dishonesty magnificent in its proportions, and climbing into high places, has become at the same time so rampant and so splendid that there seems to be reason for fearing that men and women will be taught to feel that dishonesty, if it can become splendid, will cease to be abominable. If dishonesty can live in a gorgeous palace with pictures on all its walls, and gems in all its cupboards, with marble and ivory in all its corners, and can give Apician dinners, and get into Parliament, and deal in millions, then dishonesty is not disgraceful, and the man dishonest after such a fashion is not a low scoundrel."[2] In Trollope's world, a pickpocket was hanged, while a clever but unscrupulous financier could dream of a knighthood.

The mine speculation collapsed several years later.[3] Custer was involved in another questionable transaction, this time a stock speculation in 1875. By early 1876 he had lost something like $8,500 for which he issued a note (feckless hero!) that was endorsed (essentially cosigned) by the notorious Ben Holladay, an entrepreneur who, like many of his ilk, had a consistent odor of fraud hovering around him. Holladay had long been involved in projects associated with the development of the west, mostly with transportation companies such as stagecoach lines. Custer's association with the likes of Holladay, Fisk, and Gould does him no credit, but it is entirely possible, and likely, that they were attracted by Custer's celebrity and saw an opportunity to leverage his name and fame to further their own schemes. No doubt they saw him for what he was; they may have been rascals and frauds, but they were not stupid. And it also seems likely that Custer was easily flattered and at the same time drawn to the possibility of fortune to go along with his fame. If so, he was his own version of "fortune's fool." In the context of Gilded Age venality, Custer's attempts to cash in on his celebrity are pebble splashes, but they do not reflect positively on his character or judgment. Other rumors involved his selection of the unfortunate Augustus Baliran as sutler to the 1873 Yellowstone expedition in exchange for $1,100. (Baliran was one of the three killed by the Sioux.) This accusation, however, was made by Captain Frederick Benteen, who hated Custer bitterly; his claims should be understood in that context. Still, according to the lax standards and practices of the time, such an arrangement is certainly possible.[4] Balancing Custer's ethical account, however, is his testimony against the fraudulent practices of Secretary of War William Belknap and his graft-ridden administration. Had Custer himself been involved in similar kickback schemes, would he have the temerity to testify against Belknap and the whole rotten system of post-tradership fraud? Could he have been so immune to irony and hypocrisy? Politics—the Democrats and the Democratic press combined with Custer's own political sympathies—were also part of his motivation to testify. But perhaps Custer saw no irony or hypocrisy. Or perhaps he, too, drew a distinction between honest graft and dishonest graft and understood that cheating the soldiers was not only wrong but also a formula for discontent among the troops, who had to pay inflated prices to the monopolistic post trader or sutler, just as similar fraud on the reservations led understandably to outrage followed by attacks on the railroads and settlements. That sort of fraud on a grand scale was certainly "dishonest graft." On the other hand, taking a "commission" from a sutler was nothing more than a normal business arrangement. From his point of view there was no harm in it, although he surely understood that the sutler would recoup his payment through the prices he charged the troops. In this case the distinction between honest graft and dishonest graft seems pretty thin—another distinction without much of a difference. But apparently Custer was not troubled by it; it was, after all, the way things were often done. And there is always the possibility that Benteen's accusation was itself fraudulent, and intentionally so. Besides, these were minor issues in the wider world, where things were beginning to unravel.

In September of 1873 Jay Cooke & Company was struggling. The NPRR bonds were not selling as they had in the past. Cooke was having to use his bank's money to prop up bond values. He was also borrowing short term to fund his long-term investments. But short-term interest rates were rising, and things began to look bleak for the NPRR and its bond holders. How did it all happen? Surely a handful or even several hundred hostile Indians could not have started a financial panic, could they? Had Custer's report of the Yellowstone fights, along with Lt. Charles Larned's, rattled the market's nerves? Well, no, not entirely, although the Sioux attacks against the Yellowstone surveyors and the army didn't help things. But the economic difficulties that would soon engulf Cooke and the rest of the nation actually started in Europe among bankers who had never heard of Sitting Bull and could not have located Dakota Territory or the Yellowstone Valley on any map of the Northern Hemisphere.

RUSSIAN WHEAT

> *In the nineteenth century, most financial crises came after an omnipresent commodity suddenly became cheap.*
> —Scott Reynolds Nelson,
> *A Nation of Deadbeats*, 2012

When analyzing various nineteenth-century financial panics, British economist R. C. O. Mathews wrote that it was "futile to try to draw any hard and fast line assigning to [any country] causal primacy in the cycle as a whole or in its individual parts."[5]

In other words, it's complicated. It's not easy or even possible some-times to identify a single cause of economic panics and crashes. Human emotion and fear don't always have legitimate causes; sometimes they make no sense. Other times, there is good reason to be afraid. But with the caveat that financial panics have multiple causes, some of them murky, and that once under way they generate their own manic momentum that borders on hysteria, maybe the place to start looking for causation is in Mathews's own country, perfidious Albion—or as the Austrians of the day might have called it, "Das Perfide Albion."

In the 1870s Britain was the world's largest importer of wheat. Its primary sources were the Russian estates in what is now Ukraine and the farms of Austria Hungary. Like farmers the world over, the Russians and their Austrian counterparts depended on credit. They borrowed in order to plant, grow, and harvest and then repaid when the wheat was sold, presumably at a profit. As long as prices were relatively predictable and stable, it was possible to balance the cost of borrowing versus the revenue from the sale of the wheat. Of course, there would be fluctuations in market prices from time to time, but as long as Britain kept buying, these fluctuations could be managed, primarily through bank credit. Inefficient or inept farm managers might lose money here and there and perhaps even lose their farms, but those who knew what they were doing could operate in the credit and commodities markets successfully.

But suddenly and unexpectedly there was a fundamental change in the markets. In the years after the Civil War the United States began exporting its excess agricultural products, both the raw wheat and the packaged and prepared foods, such as canned fruits, vegetables, and meats. The war had given (northern) food industries the markets and capital to develop both their products and their distribution systems, so it was no great stretch of imagination to extend these capabilities to the export markets. Existing railroads brought products to eastern ports quickly and cheaply. Mean-while, new railroads were under construction both to carry settlers west and to bring their produce east and then to Europe. The superabundance of US agricultural products and the new technologies of packaging, plus the availability of inexpensive land and sea transportation, meant that US agri-cultural products flooded into Europe and drastically undercut the prices that had traditionally been charged.

Hardest hit were the Russian wheat plantations. These farms were in the great estates of the nobility. The well-known and respected noble names, combined with the relatively lax credit standards of the Russian banks, made borrowing far too easy for the aristocrats. The nobles mortgaged their farms as one source of cash. If you were writing a novel about this situation, you would have the young aristocratic hero preening at the court in Saint Petersburg while his man of business, his factor, managed the estates and an army of moujiks and serfs planted and harvested the grain and then went home at night to wretched hovels. Further, like the "feckless heroes" in Trollope, the Russian noblemen issued and discounted short-term notes for immediate cash and no doubt rolled them over as each bill matured, thereby putting off repayment of principle, sometimes, even often, for years. They were therefore borrowing both long term and short term—using mortgages and bills. There is nothing inherently wrong with that, as long as the revenue from the farms was sufficient to pay all the interest and to retire the principle over time. The names of the nobility encouraged bankers to lend short-term money against a mere signature: "Every nobleman signed the bills of his neighbors as a guarantee against default. If the noble families appeared overextended, they might get their coachman to sign their bills."[6] This observation about coachmen came from Richard Clayton Webster, England's representative in Russia at the time. There may be a whiff of condescension in his remark, but it underscores how lax the Russian credit standards were. A novelist might suggest that the bankers, as members of the commercial class, were eager to ingratiate themselves with the nobility, hence their accommodating credit standards. Unfortunately, like Aesop's carefree grasshopper, the Russian nobles and their bankers soon faced a difficult reckoning: failure.

The Russian banks failed because their noble clients defaulted on their loans, and the noble clients defaulted on their loans because they could no longer sell their wheat at previously high prices. Great Britain, the biggest importer of wheat, switched to the cheaper American wheat—wheat that had been grown and harvested in part by immigrant farmers (ironically, some of them Russians) and shipped cheaply to eastern ports by the newly built railways that connected the Midwest to the east. Upward of six thousand mortgaged Russian estates ultimately came up for foreclosure sale, but there were few, if any, buyers.[7] The Russian banks held mortgages to remote land that was worthless for anything other than growing wheat, and the market for Russian wheat had disappeared. And like banks everywhere, the Russians did not have nearly enough capital to repay their own borrowings—loans they had taken out to fund their mortgages. Other international banks had no interest in rushing in to support the Russian banks—sending good money after bad never appeals to a prudent banker. The Russian banks collapsed.

Austria Hungary was the next to suffer the sudden shock of foreign competition. As Scott Reynolds Nelson writes: "By 1872 kerosene and manufactured food were rocketing out of America's heartland, undermining prices for rapeseed, flour and beef, Austria Hungary's biggest exports. Europeans would later call this the American 'Commercial Invasion.'"[8] The credit bubble stimulated in part by the influx of gold from French reparations via the German Empire meant that many Viennese institutions had made questionable mortgage and commercial loans. Defaults added to the general sense of unease. Meanwhile the much-ballyhooed Vienna Exposition—an event that the Austrians were hoping would significantly boost the sale of their products globally and in which they invested heavily, using borrowed money—did not live up to inflated expectations. Nor did the exposition attract the expected swarms of visitors. In fact, fewer than a third of the anticipated visitors arrived. Even worse, on May 9, 1873, the Vienna Stock Exchange announced that the holdings of over one hundred investors would be sold to pay off their debts—debts incurred when speculators borrowed money to buy securities. That afternoon the stock market crashed. Panicky investors unloaded the shares at distressed prices, and as usual the negative momentum accelerated as more and more securities were dumped on the market. The telegraph quickly spread the stories of the crash, adding to the sense of panic. Bankers in London heard stories of Viennese securities traders shooting themselves. The Atlantic cable (laid in 1858) brought the news to America.

Suddenly nervous about the goings-on in Central Europe, the Bank of England began raising its interest rates, gradually at first (from 4 percent) and finally coming to rest a few months later at 9 percent—the highest point in the nineteenth century. As the leading interbank lender in the world, the Bank of England set the rates for other banks and businesses to borrow. The rate increase essentially dried up the availability of credit and likewise the demand for credit. Things came to a halt.

The common denominator in both the Russian and Austrian panics was, initially, the expansion of credit—and poor credit analysis, meaning that the banks did a shoddy job of evaluating the creditworthiness of their borrowers. Too many people and institutions were borrowing too much money with not enough income or wealth to support it (or the "wealth" that was pledged turned out to be worthless land). Frightened of the ill-defined possibilities, the Bank of England raised rates and thereby essentially turned off the credit spigot. Suddenly there was not enough credit available, and even the most creditworthy and prudent firms could not afford to borrow. The industrious ants were cut off from credit along with the improvident grasshoppers. It was a concertina effect—first an expansion and then a contraction. Too much, then too little. The influx of cheap American wheat triggered the panic, but the bursting of the credit bubble was the fundamental cause of the depression. The Great Depression of 1873 was under way in Europe; its contagion would soon spread to the United States, where it would last five years.

Banks in the United States borrowed from the Bank of England, and when the Bank of England raised its rates to 9 percent, that translated into short-term rates in the United States of 18 percent, since the American banks had to think in terms not only of making a profit and repaying the accelerating Bank of England interest but also of the exchange rates between the dollar and the pound sterling. (If the dollar declined in value, it would take more dollars to buy the same amount of sterling—or the same amount of gold required to acquire sterling—which amounts to the same thing. Great Britain had adopted the gold standard in 1821.) Corporate borrowers, such as railroads, that needed to tap London capital markets faced the same dilemma: "As long as the United States was still off the gold standard, railroads that marketed their bonds in England had to denominate their bonds in pounds sterling and pay back their lenders in gold," in other words, the gold equivalent of the sterling bond obligation.[9] A one-thousand-pound-sterling bond was worth a reliable amount of gold; a one-thousand-US-dollar bond was worth an unpredictable (and often declining) amount of gold. As a result, bonds denominated in US dollars were not attractive to European investors. Since the United States had not yet returned to the gold standard, the greenback, backed by nothing, fluctuated dramatically against the price of gold and against other currencies. Says Nelson: "As long as the value of the dollar was in doubt, it would be prone to European interest rate shocks. Only a return to the gold standard would prevent it."[10]

Not only was the cost of money accelerating rapidly; many railroads, like the Northern Pacific, were not generating sufficient revenue to pay their obligations and were relying on issuing new bonds to pay their debt obligations. Economist Hyman Minsky postulated that there are three categories of finance:

> Hedge finance, speculative finance, and Ponzi finance—on the basis of the relation between the operating income and the debt service payments of the individual borrowers. A firm is in the hedge finance group if its anticipated operating income is more than sufficient to pay both the interest and the scheduled reduction in its indebtedness. A firm is in the speculative finance group if its anticipated operating income is sufficient so it can pay the interest on its indebtedness; however the firm must use cash from new loans to repay part or all of the amounts due on maturing loans. A firm is in the Ponzi group if its anticipated operating income is not sufficiently large to pay all of the interest on its indebtedness on the scheduled due dates; to get the cash the firm must either increase its indebtedness or sell some assets.[11]

The Northern Pacific had no government subsidies and no guarantees for its bonds. As it built west its operating income must necessarily have been scanty, since a line between Duluth and Bismarck could hardly generate enough freight and passenger income to cover the massive costs of construction and the interest on the bonds that Jay Cooke & Company were selling. The NPRR's plan all along was to sell its primary asset— land along the line, which more or less meant that the entire scheme started off in the Ponzi finance category. Today the term "Ponzi scheme" has a more than foul stench about it, in the sense that such schemes are primarily designed to enrich the plan insiders (primarily because investors who get in early and get out quickly may actually make money). In that light it's difficult not to think that the very idea behind the Northern Pacific, its fundamental financial structure, pretty closely fit Minsky's Ponzi category.

But it wasn't only the credit crunch and European bank failures that triggered the Depression of 1873 in the United States. In September 1873 Jay Cooke & Company collapsed and closed its doors. Cooke had been borrowing short term to cover purchases of NPRR bonds designed to prop up the prices and also to finance ongoing construction. But given the spike in interest rates, he could no longer meet his debt obligations—loans from other banks and investors. Had Cooke been able to weather the storm of rising interest rates, the American economy might have muddled through, albeit badly damaged. But it was the shock of Cooke's failure that sent the US economy into its tailspin. It was the classic "unexplained failure of a firm previously thought to have been successful." The bank that had financed the Union cause, and the man who had done as much as almost anyone to save the Union, had somehow gone under. Trust and confidence, not only in Jay Cooke but in the entire financial system, suddenly evaporated. Financial markets crashed. (Of course, it was more complicated than that—it always is—but the failure of Cooke was the major factor in panicking the markets.)

When US interest rates rose as a result of international turmoil, it became harder for anyone to borrow at anything like a manageable rate. The NPRR was not alone. Few businesses could or wanted to support the sudden increase in short-term interest. Some closed their doors, others laid off their workers. Unemployment surged in major cities. There were one hundred thousand unemployed in New York City alone, where the unemployment rate reached 25 percent.[12] Nationwide the rate was 14 percent (at best an estimate, since labor statistics were not carefully kept). Eighteen thousand businesses failed, and one-fourth of the nation's railroads also failed. The NPRR was apparently not the only railroad that had questionable financial arrangements.[13] But even well-managed companies could not support the increases in interest rates, and they either shut down or cut back, laying off workers and biding their time.

To make matters worse, immigrants hoping to escape the economic troubles in Europe began to stream into the United States. In a piece of bitter irony, they were crammed into the steerages of ships that had carried cheap American commodities to Europe and in many ways caused the economic troubles that forced the immigrants to leave their homes. Arriving in the United States they congregated in teeming slums of the major cities. Unable to find work, many of the immigrant men joined the army. As mentioned earlier, more than half the troops in the army were recent arrivals. (Students of the Little Bighorn battle will remember that Custer's last message to Captain Frederick Benteen to come to his aid was delivered by Giovanni Martini, an Italian immigrant who spoke very broken English and who had come to the United States in 1873. Fortunately, Martini delivered a note hurriedly written in English. Unfortunately for Custer, Benteen essentially ignored it.)

The value of NPRR bonds—as well as the values of all securities on Wall Street—plunged. The NPRR went into receivership. The western terminus would remain at Bismarck until 1879, when the railroad was reorganized and restarted its slow construction toward the Pacific. Eventually it would reach the West Coast more or less as planned (the final spike was hammered on September 8, 1883) but not in time to rescue Cooke or his bank. Jay Cooke & Company had closed for good, and investors and depositors lost their money. Other banks tumbled, too, including the unfortunate Freedman Savings and Trust Company. "Hundreds of US banks failed" during the three years following Cooke's collapse.[14] Interbank loans, bad commercial loans, poor investments, and the credit crunch toppled the dominos. And the businesses that depended on those banks for commercial credit went to the wall. It would be at least four to five years before the nation began to recover its trust and confidence in the financial system and before the financial system was in a position to deliver the credit the nation required.

The holders of NPRR bonds watched the value of their investments tumble to less than half their par value. But the NPRR management came up with a clever plan to prop up their reputation—and perhaps lay the groundwork for survival:

> In October 1873, a scant month after Cooke's bankruptcy triggered the financial panic, [NPRR's chief land agent] announced that the company would accept its own bonds from investors at par value in exchange for

railroad land. Because of the panic Northern Pacific bonds had dropped
to less than forty cents on the dollar. Speculators and bond holders leapt
at the chance, and over the next year [the NPRR] disposed of nearly half
a million acres of railroad land. The problem was that most of the pur-
chasers were eastern capitalists, anxious to recover their investment in
railroad bonds; few had any intention of taking up farming in the west.[15]

By buying back its own bonds at a cost of land provided gratis by the government, the NPRR managed to relieve some interest payment pressure.
They bought some time at the cost of their primary assets, which sounds
very much like Minsky's description of Ponzi finance.

The sturdy yeoman and his strong back, on which the concept of the
NPRR more or less rested, would immigrate to the west eventually. As
mentioned, economic hardship in Europe would send many to the United
States in search of cheap land and real opportunity. But years would
have to pass before the hoped-for rural development would occur. Some
of the huge tracts of land exchanged for railroad bonds would be turned
into factory farms using hired immigrant labor. Other immigrants would
buy smaller parcels or take up federal land under the Homestead Acts.
But before any of that could be accomplished in any degree of complete-
ness, the bitter enmity of the Sioux and their allies would have to be extinguished—extinguished along with their titles to much of their land.

Once the Depression had gotten its grip on the nation, rumors and
stories of gold in the Black Hills took on renewed importance. Pressures
mounted to do something about resources lying fallow. Westerners never
could see the logic in setting aside valuable land for bands of hostile Indians,
whose depredations were protected by the government against the interests
and welfare of the country's legitimate citizens and whose sustenance and
armament were provided by what the westerners characterized as wrong-
headed government policies. Putting it that way, as western politicians and
editors certainly did, made it difficult for the government to justify, much
less maintain, its current position regarding reservation lands, generally,
and the Black Hills, specifically. What's more, western businessmen knew
that a gold rush yielded far more than gold. Miners needed equipment and
transportation, food and pack animals, weapons and guidance, camping
equipment and lumber for towns and miner's shacks, medical equipment

and even life insurance. A gold rush yielded much more wealth than just what the miners could find.

As stories of gold in the Black Hills continued to circulate along with news about Custer's planned expedition into the Hills, the editors of the *Bismarck Tribune* spoke for the majority of westerners in their June 14, 1874, issue:

> The American people need the country the Indians now occupy; many of our people are out of employment; the masses need some new excitement. The war is over, and the railroad building has been brought to a termination by the greed of the capitalists. . . . And the depression prevails on every side. An Indian war would do no harm, for it must come sooner or later. Who does not recognize the necessity of our people? They must have something to do. Our cities are crowded with men out of employment, our factories are closed, our rolling mills idle—the industries of our country are paralyzed. Custer's expedition may be the pebble which dropped in at an opportune moment will set the mighty sea of American thought in Motion.[16]

Not every soldier agreed that an Indian war "would do no harm," since they would be the ones who would have to fight it. But civilians and soldiers were pretty generally agreed that the possibility of gold in the Black Hills could not be ignored any longer. Far away Washington had its doubts, but those doubts would soon be overcome. There were simply too many factors pushing Washington toward the expedition, factors that were both legitimate, and less so. The national debt was denominated in gold, yet the Treasury did not have nearly enough even to begin to make substantial inroads into the debt. In plain language the Treasury needed more gold. Also, most agreed that the country needed to return to the gold standard and retire the weak greenback, which was so subject to severe inflationary pressures. Then there was the depression and unemployment, and the very real possibility that a gold strike would have the usual trickle-down effect on the economy and on western settlement, which in turn would at least partially and eventually address the problem of Indian hostility. Current Indian hostility required a new post in the region of the Black Hills, so the economic and military objectives were perfectly compatible. Politics, of course, played a role in the decision. The West versus East debate, always fractious, was heightened by the combination of Indian attacks and economics and was always underpinned by the westerners' hatred of the peace policies and the fundamental disagreement about giving fertile and productive land to Indians who did nothing with it but pass through now and then, hunting. Disenchantment with radical Republican policies for Reconstruction meant that more units of the much-reduced army could be redeployed to the frontier. All of these factors were at least reasonable explanations for Custer's expedition.

But it was also the climate of the time, a time of robber barons and political bribery that led to projects such as the Union Pacific and the Northern Pacific Railroads along with legitimate national interest. These projects infuriated the Indians and led to attacks against the construction crews. Those attacks—and Custer's (and others') reports about them—contributed significantly to the collapse of the NPRR's bond values and the subsequent collapse of Jay Cooke & Company. And that in turn triggered the depression in this country. Contributing to Indian hostility was the rampant corruption of the Indian agents, which was made possible by the casual ethics and greed of politicians, bureaucrats, and their cronies. But the Sioux were not simply innocent victims of a climate of corruption. Their inbred warlike culture was as much a driving force behind their hostility as their understandable rancor at seeing their traditional hunting grounds and territory gradually diminishing. Had there been no Indian hostility and attacks, there would have been no need for a new fort in the Black Hills, and there would have been no defensible rationale for Custer's mission. Perhaps the politicians would have found another. That sort of thing is their métier, after all. But perhaps they would not have.

The United States was not alone in enjoying a culture of greed and exuberant financial irresponsibility. The collapse of the Russian and Austrian banking systems, as the credit bubble burst, sparked the rise in Bank of England interest rates, which led to a spike in US rates that further contributed to Jay Cooke's demise and to the falling of the financial dominos that led to massive unemployment and business failures. And overarching all of this was the growth of international trade and the effect of the US exports on the European economies. To repeat the quote from Professor

Scott Nelson: "In the nineteenth century, most financial crises came after an omnipresent commodity suddenly became cheap."

How many degrees of separation are there between a suddenly penniless and debt-ridden Russian aristocrat and George Armstrong Custer at the head of the Seventh Cavalry as he went into the Black Hills? And assuming, as is undeniable, that Custer's expedition radicalized the Sioux fence-sitters and infuriated the non-treaty Sioux, is it possible to draw a line between the failure of the Russian wheat market and the disaster at the Little Bighorn? The line may be thin and not very straight, and it's not the only line, but it's there.

The worldwide financial crisis sparked the equally widespread depression, and the depression ratcheted up the pressure on the government to do *something*—something about the economy and inflation, something about the hostile Indians, something about opening up reservation land. Something.

And through most of these various forces, problems, and complexities, there was a common thread: gold.

CHAPTER ELEVEN

BUILD-UP

We are the marauders in this case.
—Bishop William Hare, 1874

*The only security these Indians can have in the possession of
their country would be in its utter worthlessness to the whites.*
—Lt. Gouverneur K. Warren

As the army senior officers and the government pondered the proposed Black Hills Expedition, they encountered two primary
obstacles—one was financial, the other legal. And along with the legal
obstacles came a problem of public relations.

The army was, as usual, on a short financial leash. Absurdly enough,
the first barrier to the expedition was getting authorization to pay for it.
By now well acquainted with the politics and finances of the army, Custer
would provide an answer. He was aided, ironically, by the searing heat and
drought around Fort Lincoln. Libbie described conditions that summer:

> We knew that we could not expect in that climate that the freshness of
> summer would last for more than a short time after the sun had come to
> its supremest in the way of heat. The drouth was unbroken; the dews were
> hardly perceptible. That year even our brief enjoyment of the verdure
> was cut short. A sirocco came up suddenly. The sky became copper-col-
> ored and the air murky and stifling. The slightest touch of metal, or even
> the door handles, almost blistered the fingers. The strong wind that blew
> seemed to shrivel the skin as it touched us. The grass was burned down
> to the roots [by the heat and sun]. . . . After that, during the summer, as

we walked over the little space allowed us, our shoes were cut by the crisp brown stubble, and the sod was dry and unyielding under out feet.[1]

Worse, that year there had been another invasion of grasshoppers that destroyed not only Libbie's garden but, more importantly, the crops of many farmers throughout much of the Midwest. This was the fourth year in a row that farmers suffered a disastrous, biblical infestation by these pests. (Wheat farmers who escaped the attacks were the source of the exports that undermined the European markets, but many western wheat growers were ruined.) Historian Watson Parker writes: "The damage they did was so severe that bills were introduced to Congress for the relief of settlers who had been forced to abandon their claims on public land [i.e., homesteaders]. Clouds of grasshoppers hung over Fort Sully, [South] Dakota 'like coal smoke from a steamer.' In some places insects covered the ground three or four inches deep."[2] This infestation had several effects. Coming in the context of the depression, the ruin of so many farms—and ranch grazing—exacerbated the already dreadful economic conditions. There were increased calls for the federal government to take some action, both for the relief of the farmers and for the economy as a whole. Further, the plague scattered many immigrant settlers who were thought to be part of the solution to the development of the west as well as to Indian hostilities. Discouraged with farming, many began to think that life in the old country was not so bad after all. There were no plagues of insects, no hostile natives; one could at least starve in peace. "The distress of the farmers caused by the destruction of their crops was augmented by the financial panic. Farm prices dropped. Railways, whose branch line building had offered employment, laid off construction crews. In Nebraska, as early as 1874, seven thousand destitute persons were threatened with starvation before the end of winter. Crime rates went up all over the nation as jobs became scarce. Bankruptcies from coast to coast were a daily news item."[3] (As an aside, when farm prices dropped and farmers defaulted because their crops were ruined, the banks holding mortgages on the land were left with titles to worthless land. Much like their Russian and Austrian counterparts, and much like their European counterparts, they collapsed.)

The awful Dakota weather conditions created what Libbie described as a "dreary waste."[4] And with the farmers' crops devastated, there was precious little available forage for the horses and mules, either nearby the fort or available from local farmers, whose grain fields had been destroyed. That meant that both grain and hay for the animals had to be purchased and shipped in by steamboat or the NPRR (which was still operating despite bankruptcy). Even had the local farmers' crops survived, the army would still have had to purchase the forage. There was no available (that is, free) grazing around the fort because the weather had destroyed the grass. And even if there had been, six hundred horses and six hundred mules would have made short work of it. The herds of animals would have had to travel each day farther and farther from the fort to find grass, so, too, the cattle herds, and all would have been exposed to Indian raids. This was no theoretical risk. In April of that year a band of Indians attacked some civilian herders not far from the fort and ran off eighty mules; Custer assembled six companies of cavalry and chased the raiders twenty miles and recovered all the stock. The raiders got away by abandoning the mules.[5]

Contemplating all this, Custer realized there was an opportunity to strengthen the argument for the Black Hills Expedition—it would be less expensive to take the regiment south than to keep them in garrison. He put his rationale in a letter to General Philip Sheridan, dated April 27, 1874:

> My dear General,
>
> Since your departure I have been calculating the comparative cost to the government of keeping the ten companies of the 7th Cavalry in garrison or sending them on the proposed reconnaissance. I have estimated the grain and hay allowance to each animal exactly in accordance with that fixed by regulations, the price being that which we pay for oats, corn and hay at this post. We feed one-half oats and one half corn; my calculations cover a train of 100 six-mule wagons, making 600 mules. I also estimate the cavalry horses at 600; from the subjoined figures which are correct it will be seen that my statement made to you last fall that the proposed reconnaissance can be made and result in an actual saving to the government was absolutely correct.[6]

It's significant that Custer wrote this proposal in April when green grass was beginning to poke through the last of the snow. At that time, if the weather cooperated, Custer could anticipate successful grazing all the way to the Hills and back—as long as the expedition could leave while spring still held back the wind, heat, and potential drought of summer.

Custer calculated that having the twelve hundred animals supplement their usual grain allowance with grazing along the trail south would result in a saving of $19,437.60, principally derived from the savings in hay— "principally," because in his proposal he figured four pounds of grain per animal per day, which was much less than usual; Custer was therefore being slightly devious in his calculation of savings. Elsewhere he mentioned that the usual amount of grain per animal was fourteen pounds,[7] but if he used that figure, the costs would obviously have been significantly higher, and the expedition would have needed many additional wagons to carry the extra forage—wagons that had to be hired along with civilian teamsters to drive them. Custer was betting that four pounds per animal would be sufficient, if only barely, and that grazing en route could make up for the shortfall. He also understood that there would be additional expenses, mostly the salaries of $30.00 a month for two months for one hundred civilian teamsters. Deducting that expense, Custer figured the savings would still be $13,437.60.

Custer went on to say that he had been questioning reasonably friendly Indians, some of whom he hired as guides, who knew the route southwest to the Hills and who reported that the grazing and the water along the entire trail were perfectly adequate, and more so. Then, once into the Hills, the grazing would be lush. Accepting this information at face value would seem to be something of a risk, since the wretched weather that destroyed the grass around Fort Lincoln might have done the same thing on the trail to the Hills, and maybe in the Hills themselves. Moreover, the Hills had long been the subject of fanciful stories, not only about gold but also about the potential for agriculture and ranching. What if all those stories were gross exaggerations? There was not enough grain to support the column from Fort Lincoln to the Hills and back again. Custer was risking his command, to say nothing of the twelve hundred or so horses and mules for which he was responsible.[8] But Custer was apparently untroubled. In a letter to General Alfred Terry, Custer wrote: "I have enlisted within the past few days scouts who are entirely familiar with every foot of the route from here and beyond to the Black Hills, giving every water course on the route. To verify this information I sent to the Standing Rock Agency and induced some Sioux to visit me who have hunted between here and the Black Hills every year. These Sioux confirm the accounts I previously obtained from the scouts enlisted by me; I feel entirely satisfied with the information thus obtained and deem it trustworthy in the fullest degree."[9] Custer's informants also told him that the country could easily be traversed by wagons, even heavily loaded. The rivers and streams were not major obstacles, although now and then the high banks would have to be cut down to allow wagons to cross and some temporary bridges would be required. Another informant said "that he had passed through the Black Hills by a pass practicable or capable of being made so for wagons, somewhere between Bear Butte and Bear Lodge . . . and once through this pass the interior country is of fine quality somewhat like a park."[10] There were known passes into the Hills, cut by streams, but these were heavily choked with trees, some lying tangled as a result of the beavers' unceasing labors. Other passes were too narrow for wagons. Custer's pioneer companies would have their work cut out for them building roads where necessary, reducing the banks of streams and ravines, felling trees, and clearing boulders and brush. But unlike previous attempts by whites to penetrate the Hills, Custer had the manpower and the engineering know-how to overcome the barriers en route to the Hills and to the ultimate penetration of this mysterious natural citadel.

In short, as far as Custer was concerned, there were no financial obstacles. The expedition would pay for itself. And despite his ineptitude in most business matters, Custer made a good case for the cost-saving nature of the expedition—as long as the grazing en route was as advertised and could in fact compensate for the reduced allowance of grain.

But there remained a legal question. Opponents of the expedition, both Sioux and white humanitarians and missionaries, such as Bishop William H. Hare, said the expedition was illegal according to the terms of the 1868 Treaty of Fort Laramie. The worthy bishop complained in person to President Ulysses S. Grant and also telegraphed his objections to the Secretary of the Interior. The key to the bishop's complaint was the treaty provision that said no white person was allowed on the reservation except "officers, agents and employees of the government."[11] Surely, the Bishop reasoned, that could not possibly mean an army of one thousand troops; a flotilla of wagons and teamsters; and a gang of civilian scientists, reporters, and, worst of all, miners; surely the phrase meant just those government employees attached to the agencies who lived there permanently, as well as the contractors who supplied the agencies. And the missionaries, of course. What's more, the expedition that the Sioux regarded as illegal would inevitably stir up the warlike elements, radicalize the fence-sitters, and risk conflagration.

Sioux chiefs living near Bismarck who were familiar with and even friendly with Custer agreed with Hare and called on Custer frequently to argue against the expedition. Libbie Custer observed some of these meetings: "They urged that white men must not go into the Hills—that it was dangerous and would bring on war."[12] Custer himself understood their point of view: "Love of country is almost a religion with them. It is not the value [i.e., usefulness] of the land that they consider, but their strong local attachment that the white man does not feel and consequently does not respect. He [the Indian] keenly feels the injustice that has been done him, and being of a proud and haughty nature, resents it."[13] Given the interconnection between the natural and the supernatural world, it would be fair to say that love of the country *was* a religious feeling. In fact, it would be more accurate to say that the Sioux made no distinction between the natural and supernatural. It was all one. And of all the land in the reservation, the Black Hills were among the most sacred. It was there that the Sioux hunted for eagle feathers to signify their coups, there that they found reliable hunting when the buffalo were scarce, there where the young men went to seek a vision that would guide their lives, there that they could escape the often wretched weather of the Plains. And it was there, some said, that the first man emerged from the underworld, guided by a wolf. As for the white argument that the Indians and the Sioux in particular never did anything with the land, the Sioux believed the whites were missing the point. They believed that "the Earth Mother *gives* us all she has."[14] In other words, the whites *took* from the land with plows and mines and saws and buffalo guns, but the Earth *gave* to the Lakota everything they needed and in return expected that the Indians would not violate the land and, in fact, would venerate it—both the land and its creatures (excepting enemies, of course). They would not use more than they needed. Not only did they not want to develop the land; they believed it was wrong to do so. The whites saw this as indolence; the Indians saw it as respect. The two attitudes toward natural resources could hardly have been more different. The Black Hills, along with the buffalo, were twin symbols of this dichotomy. And this dichotomy gives added meaning to the remark by Lakota chief Fast Bear when he referred to Custer's expedition and route as "that thieves' road," for a thief is obviously one who takes something that is not his to begin with and does so usually out of greed and only rarely out of need. The skinned carcasses of the buffalo, the sluice boxes of the gold mines were dramatic evidence of the white attitude toward natural resources. Further, the fact that the Lakota did not spend their lives in the Black Hills did not diminish the Hills' importance to them during their wanderings. The Hills existed powerfully in their imaginations, along with other culturally important places. Anthropologist Keith H. Basso writes:

> As Vine Deloria, Jr. (Standing Rock Sioux) has observed, most American Indian tribes embrace "spatial conceptions of history" in which places and their names—and all that these may symbolize—are accorded central importance. For Indian men and women , the past lies imbedded in features of the earth—in canyons and lakes, mountains and arroyos, rocks and vacant fields—which together endow their lands with multiple forms of significance that reach into their lives and shape the way they think. Knowledge of places is therefore closely linked to knowledge of the self, to grasping one's position in the larger scheme of things, including one's own community, and to securing a confident sense of who one is as a person.[15]

At the risk of descending into melodramatic sensitivity and generalization, one might say that certain territories functioned for the tribes as both temples and libraries. Basso addresses this risk: "Much has been made inside and outside of academic anthropology of the 'sacredness' of American Indian lands, the 'spiritual nature' of human relationships with them. At some vague and general level, I suppose this may be true. I also believe . . . that matters are much more complex and that outsiders seldom do justice to the subtlety and sophistication of native systems of thought."[16] In short, our language is not really equipped to express the Indian attitude with anything other than "vague" two-dimensional generalities, of which "sacred" is probably the most obvious and unsatisfactory example.

Custer glimpsed some of this feeling, but it was entirely foreign to the utilitarian westerners who dismissed it as rank sentimentality, the product of dewy-eyed philanthropists and apologists for Indian savagery cum indolence.

Opponents of the expedition were not limited to the Lakota and people like Bishop Hare. The always critical Private Theodore Ewert begins his journal of the expedition by accusing Custer of originating the idea in yet another effort to acquire glory and, further, of selling the idea to Sheridan, not knowing of course of Sheridan's long-held idea to place a fort in the "heart of the Indian country." Ewert goes on to say that by authorizing the expedition the government "forgot its honor, forgot the sacred treaty in force between itself and the Dakota Sioux, forgot its integrity."[17] Ewert was a trooper in Company H, which was commanded by Captain Frederick Benteen, who, as mentioned before, hated Custer. (Benteen even hated Libbie and called her "about as avaricious and parsimonious a woman as you can find in a day's walk." Few, if any, who knew Libbie, shared this opinion.[18]) It seems likely that Benteen's attitude rubbed off on receptive soldiers like Ewert—not that Benteen discussed such matters with a lowly private, but his body language, facial expressions, and off-the-cuff grumbling would have tipped off his observant troops on his opinion of Custer. Benteen did not make many attempts to disguise his feelings, and the regiment was a small community, subject to the gossip, rumors, and petty feuds that plague any village, especially one composed of ambitious career soldiers.

Despite the reasonable objections of the Sioux and their white advocates, the senior officers of the army were convinced that the expedition was perfectly legal according to the terms of the 1868 treaty. On June 16, General Sheridan wrote to Terry and Gen. William T. Sherman requesting their views on the expedition's legality. General Terry was one of the crafters of that treaty, and in his report to General Sheridan, Terry's elaborate explanation of the legality of the expedition reflected his pre–Civil War training as a lawyer.

I am unable to see that any just offence is given to the Indians by the expedition to the Black Hills. I cannot see that any of their rights which they have possessed from the beginning or those which are secured to them by treaty, are invaded. From the earliest times the Government has exercised the right of sending exploring parties into the unceded Indian Territory—exploring parties of a military character, and this expedition is nothing more. It is a large party, it is true, but that it should be large is made necessary by the fact that certain bands of Sioux are always ready to attack *small* parties either of civilians or troops. It was made large for the purpose of *preventing* hostilities.[19]

Characteristically, Sherman added a laconic endorsement to Terry's analysis. Terry's report is dated July 27, 1874, rather a long time after Sheridan's request. By this time Custer's expedition was already under way, and they were only a week or so away from the discovery that most of the west was hoping for.

Of course, the Black Hills were not part of the "unceded territories" but rather a part of the reservation. But the army obviously had other posts on reservations throughout the country, placed there to protect the agencies and keep the peace. There were already three such posts on the reservation created under the 1868 treaty. No one had objected to those, so the army reasoned, what possible objection could there be to a reconnaissance? Terry went on to say that there were two exceptions to the prohibition of white trespass: "Persons who are designated in and authorized by the treaty itself to reside [on the reservation]" and "Such officers, agents and employees of the Government as may be authorized to enter upon the Indian reservations in discharge of duties enjoined by law."[20] Since the treaty specifically identified the permanent employees and residents (agent, doctor, blacksmith, teacher, engineer, miller, and farmer) as the first exception, the second exception could only refer to the army—and to civilian contractors delivering supplies or working for the army. "That this provision was intended to exclude from the reservation the military forces of the Government, I cannot believe. As one of the Commissioners who made the treaty, I feel sure that the language of the section supports this construction."[21]

Perhaps if the language had been less ambiguous, there would have been less room for dispute. Cynics might say that the ambiguity was intentional and designed to achieve a treaty that left some maneuvering room later. More likely, the legal language was the product of a set of legal minds whose dedication to proper form outweighed any commitment to clarity. In either case, the dispute is yet another example of the yawning gap between two cultures, one which crafted elaborate legalisms and the other that neither understood the nuances of legal English nor cared about carefully worded sentences or indeed about the very idea of codified law. The Black Hills belonged to the Sioux, initially because they had conquered them and currently because of their agreement with the white man, an agreement that had the force of the white man's law. No soldiers should go there; that was the Indians' position. The Sioux perfectly understood what would happen if the troops should happen to discover gold. And even if the troopers failed at that, they would still discover the richness of the land. And if the Hills were not invaded by a horde of miners, they might well be invaded by a horde of farmers, lumber merchants, and ranchers. If the army had wanted to explore the barren wastes of the Badlands, the Sioux and their advocates would probably not have complained very much. But they knew what the Black Hills contained and what the soldiers would see when they got there.

Terry's report went on to say, in response to Bishop Hare's statement about marauders: "A marauder is one who roves in quest of booty or plunder. Plunder is not the object of the expedition. Neither is it sent out for the purpose of ascertaining the mineral or agricultural resources of the Black Hills. It seeks neither gold, timber nor arable land."[22]

Perhaps Terry believed that. But, in the end, even if the army officially did not intend to seek those resources, they found them, anyway.

In fairness to the army, it should be noted that they did go through this exercise of asking themselves whether what they wanted to do was consistent with their treaty obligations. There was a great deal of communication back and forth between the commanding general, the division commander, and the department commander on the subject of the Black Hills and the army's legal obligations. This self-analysis is a rebuttal to the idea that the government in general and the army in particular *always* rode roughshod over the Indians whenever they chose. Of course, there was an element of self-interest involved; the army did not particularly want war with the Sioux. War would be a last resort. But they did want a post in the

Nebraska borderland. Still, it's instructive to remember that they tried to follow the letter of the law and spent time debating what that letter was. The spirit of the law was something else, again. But in the army's eyes the Black Hills Expedition was not a violation of any treaty provisions. And their understanding of the law had its origins in Chief Justice John Marshall's 1831 Supreme Court decision (*Cherokee Nation v. Georgia*) that emphasized the federal government's overarching sovereignty: "They [the Indian tribes] and their country are considered by foreign nations, as well as by ourselves, as being so completely under the sovereignty and dominion of the United States, that any attempt to acquire their lands, or to form a political connexion with them, would be considered by all as an invasion of our territory, and an act of hostility." The reservation was within US territory, and the army believed it could legally go wherever it wanted to go. What's more, no soldier in his right mind would have agreed to a treaty in which raiders could leave the reservation, make an attack, and then return to a sanctuary to prepare for the next raid safe from reprisal, because the army was barred from the reservation. It was bad enough that the young warriors used the reservations as a winter sanctuary, but it was inconceivable that the army could be legally prevented from entering the reservation to find and chastise raiders.

The army also had a political and public relations problem with its critics, such as Bishop Hare and the eastern humanitarians. The army had to be seen to be doing the right and legal thing in order to mute the annoying criticism from this sector. So perhaps the discussion over legalities was not entirely disinterested. This public relations battle also played out in the editorials of the western and eastern press, and, not surprisingly, the positions of the two sectors were different. The *Minneapolis Tribune* said:

> There can be no doubt but that the government has a right to send an exploring expedition into the Black Hills of Dakota, regardless of the fact that most of that region is an Indian reservation. . . . There is good reason to believe that the Black Hills country is rich in minerals. If so, the white people want them, and the Indians do not [no fig leaves here]. Any other land is quite as useful to them, and as they only hold their reservation by permission of the Government, they have no right to attempt to shut out its representatives.[23]

In other words, since the Indians did not use, that is, develop, the land they lived on, they could live virtually anywhere, especially since they were supported by government handouts. Mineral-rich mountains and lush forests were essentially no different from dreary wastelands. A tepee could be pitched in either locale; aesthetics were irrelevant. The *New York Times*, on the other hand, took a slightly different view and attempted a bit of objectivity in presenting the two sides of the argument:

> These Indians have heretofore carefully guarded this country from white men, knowing that if once seen by them it would be coveted and eventually occupied, to their own exclusion . . . this beautiful land which they love as we do the home of our childhood. The philanthropist may view the encroachment of the whites with apprehension and sorrow, but in this stirring Western country no such feeling exists. The universal impression here is that a handful of Indians have no right to retard the progress of civilization, and that now, as in the past history of the world, the weaker nation must go to the wall.[24]

It was a clash of economies, a clash of theologies, a clash of radically different cultures—and a clash that the tribesmen must lose. Some might think it sad, perhaps, but in the end, the law of conquest was immutable, the advance of civilization, inexorable, the demands of economics, irresistible. That was the view of the westerners.

It's likely that some senior officers found the public relations aspect of the debate a little tiresome. After all, the Sioux had agreed in 1868 to stop raiding the railroads and the settlements, but Sioux attacks in '72 and '73 had brought the Northern Pacific construction program to a halt. That, in turn, contributed significantly to the current economic problems throughout the country. And it did little good to point out that those raids were committed by non-treaty Sioux under Sitting Bull, because all the world knew that young warriors from the reservation left in the summer. Some no doubt joined the northern raiders. Others attacked the settlements and ranches to the south. So in terms of treaty violations, the Sioux were in fact the primary offenders. If they had not been, there would have been no need for Sheridan's post on the Nebraska border and therefore no need for the expedition, which was, in the army's view, perfectly legal. As

General Sheridan wrote: "The expedition will examine a country hereto-fore unknown, and for the ultimate object of establishing a military post in the Black Hills, on or about the western line of the Sioux reservation, which seemed to meet the approval of the Secretary of the Interior at a consultation last fall in Washington, when the President, General Sherman and the Secretary of War were present."[25] The phrase "seemed to meet" suggests that the Secretary of the Interior (which oversaw the Indian Bureau) was less than enthusiastic about the project, but clearly the expedition was debated and approved at the highest level of government and the army.

Custer, of course, believed that the reconnaissance in force was after more than just a location of a proposed fort. As he wrote to his friend, actor Lawrence Barrett: "The expedition [is] entirely peaceful in its object, it being the intention to explore the country known as the Black Hills and gain some knowledge as to the nature of the latter. For many years it has been believed from statements made by the Indians that the Black Hills are rich in minerals."[26] Private Ewert wrote: "As we sat on our horses looking towards the supposed New Eldorado, the conversation naturally turned to 'filthy lucre'—Gold. If all accounts would prove true we would find plenty of it, surely. How would we carry it? We would empty our saddle pockets and fill them; this would be as much as a horse could carry. Then how could we smuggle several large nuggets into the wagons? Our claim (for every man intended taking one) should be staked and recorded according to law."[27] Ewert was destined for disappointment, but his comment surely proves that the troops felt the expedition was intended to find something more than a place to build a fort. How did he and the others expect to "stake" a claim in a reservation where white men were excluded? The comment suggests there was widespread expectation that the Sioux title to the Hills would soon be "extinguished" and that claims now staked could later be registered and made legal. In that, he was in line with popular western opinion and assumption, that is, that the expedition was the first step in acquiring the Hills from the Lakota, one way or the other. And it also suggests that Ewert's earlier indignation about the treaty violation was probably more the result of his dislike for Custer than legitimate concern about the nation's obligations.

And so the expedition was authorized. Custer planned to leave in June. Custer's preparations for the expedition were interrupted in May when reports reached him that one hundred Sioux warriors had left their Cheyenne River Agency, which was roughly due east of the Black Hills and along the Missouri River. The object was to attack their ancient enemies, the Arikara and Mandan at their agency at Fort Berthold, which was on the Upper Missouri, several hundred miles to the north. General Terry wrote to Custer that he should intercept these raiders and that "the Rees [Arikara] and Mandans should be protected [the] same as white settlers."[28] Custer sent scouting parties to the west and north. He led the northern scout personally. But he could find no trace of the raiders and soon abandoned the search, feeling that there was no real danger to the friendly tribes, since Fort Berthold had been warned about the possible attack. By mid-June the Sioux had arrived, and, using their traditional decoy tactics, they lured a handful of Arikara and Mandan from their camp and fired on them. They killed and mutilated five Arikara and one Mandan and then started the long journey south, apparently satisfied with their rather slender—given the numbers engaged—results.[29] The son of Bloody Knife, Custer's favorite Arikara scout, was one of those killed.[30]

Back at work on his preparations, Custer spent a good deal of time training his men at target practice "with the few serviceable arms at hand, and I find that they need this practice very much."[31] Custer's "finding" is curious on the surface. After all, he had led the Seventh Cavalry into the Yellowstone Valley the summer before and had fought two engagements with the Sioux. He should, therefore, have had some idea about the quality of his troops' marksmanship, or lack thereof. On the other hand, the army's woeful turnover rate through disease, discharge, and desertion meant that many of the troops were raw recruits. Moreover, Custer's adjutant, James Calhoun, reported that two-thirds of the troops were foreigners, most of whom had no prior military experience or experience with firearms. Then there was the chronic problem of funding for training. Custer was anticipating the arrival of the new Springfield .45-caliber carbines and so most likely felt he could use up the ammunition on hand for the various models of carbines that were in working order.

Given the fact that "four fifths of our carbines are unserviceable,"[32] that the new Springfield carbines and Colt .45 pistols and ammunition had not yet arrived, and that his troopers apparently were not very good shots to begin with, it may be another example of "Custer's luck" that he never found the Sioux raiders.

CHAPTER TWELVE

SOLDIERS, SCOUTS, AND SCIENTISTS

As I pen these lines I am in the midst of scenes of bustle and busy preparation attendant upon the organization of a large party for an important exploring expedition, on which I shall start before these pages reach the publishers' hands. During my absence I expect to visit a region of country as yet unseen by human eyes except those of the Indian—a country described by the latter as abounding in game of all varieties, rich in scientific interest, and of surpassing beauty in natural scenery. Bidding adieu to civilization for the next few months, I also now take leave of my readers, who, I trust, in accompanying me through my retrospect, have been able to gain a true insight into a cavalryman's "Life on the Plains."

—George Armstrong Custer,
My Life on the Plains, final paragraph

The Black Hills Expedition will move tomorrow morning. The new arms give great satisfaction. The Expedition considering its number is the most thoroughly equipped, armed and best organized force I have seen on the Plains.

—George Armstrong Custer to
Seventh Cavalry Headquarters.[1]

As Custer was finishing his memoirs, his men were in camp a few miles from the fort. They had already "bid adieu to civilization." Custer thought it would be good to get them reacquainted with life under canvas, although he intended to remain in the comforts of his home at Fort Lincoln. And his home was indeed comfortable. In February his original house had burned to the ground, and he had it rebuilt with additions and improvements. It was good to be the commanding officer. His troops left Fort Lincoln on June 20 and marched probably no more than two miles away, where they bivouacked and spent the next twelve days making sure that their preparations for the expedition were complete. No doubt the troops would have preferred to stay in garrison until the last minute, too, for their camp was regularly attacked by swarms of mosquitoes. William Curtis, the *Chicago Inter Ocean* correspondent, described the men as "groaning through the dark and gloomy night because of the pestiferous mosquitoes which make the valley of the Missouri the vilest place in the world. One lives with gloves and a head shield during the day and sleeps with his shield and gloves under blankets and bars [to secure the blanket flaps, presumably] during the night. Lift up your shield to speak to your neighbor and in fifteen minutes your lips and chin feel as mammoth as the Andes Mountains. Take off your gloves to button your collar closer, and your hand is a swollen and unseemly thing."[2] Nor were the mosquitos the only unwelcome visitors. Chief Engineer Bvt. Lt. Colonel William Ludlow, wrote: "While still in camp near Fort Lincoln during the last days of June, the grasshoppers were very numerous. I counted twenty five on one morning on what I judged to be an average square foot of ground; a brief calculation gives at that rate over a million to the acre; and as they are often much more numerous than observed, and are exceedingly rapacious, their capacity for destruction to living vegetation may be imagined."[3] If Custer worried over the possibility of having the grazing destroyed by these pests, he did not mention it. By this time he was in no mood to think about canceling or postponing the expedition. There had been too many delays as it was.

One of those delays was due to the later than expected arrival of the promised carbines, pistols, and ammunition. They did not arrive until the end of June and were issued to the men on July 1. Even so the officers and men were glad to get their hands on these recently designed weapons. The carbine fired a .45-caliber lead bullet weighing 405 grains and propelled either by 70 grains or 55 grains of black powder.[4] The smaller (55 grain) powder charge was introduced to reduce recoil; the shorter (22-inch barrel) carbine weighed less than the 45.70 trapdoor infantry rifle and so was more susceptible to uncomfortable recoil. The carbine (and the longer infantry-version rifle) were called "trapdoor" because the trooper loaded the weapon by pulling back the hammer to half cock, flipping a lever and opening the trapdoor just forward of the hammer, inserting a metallic cartridge, closing the trapdoor, pulling the hammer back to full cock and firing. To reload, he opened the trap, which activated an ejector that spit the empty shell out, and inserted another cartridge. A well-trained trooper (of whom there were precious few) could get off ten to thirteen rounds a minute. The practical range of the carbine, depending on the skill of the shooter, was anywhere from three hundred to six hundred yards, although beyond three hundred the comparatively slow-moving bullet tended to drop significantly. At longer ranges the shooter had to adjust his elevation and factor in wind conditions. But it was a rare trooper who could hit anything at extreme ranges—or who could be bothered to try. In the army it was generally accepted that three hundred yards was about the first time a human target could be hit with a bullet from a trapdoor carbine. Of course, the actual bullet could travel much farther—perhaps up to twelve hundred yards— but in combat the object was accuracy, not maximum distance. Nor did the Indian fighting require long-range shooting, as a rule; for that there was artillery.[5] Civilian guides and officers often carried longer-range hunting rifles, but the enlisted troops were generally limited to government-issued weapons. There is clearly a great advantage to a command if all the troops are using the same weapons and ammunition. In a combat situation when ammunition runs low or some weapons are damaged or jammed, to be able to use those of wounded or killed comrades can be vital.

The cartridge case for the carbine was initially made of copper. After the Little Bighorn there were complaints that the soft copper case jammed, either because it expanded from heat caused by firing, or because the ejectors cut through the heat-softened metal of the copper rims; the troopers had to pry the expended cartridge out with their knives. (Carbines were not initially equipped with ramrods, so there was no alternative to the knife.) Since the Sioux and Cheyenne made off with most, if not all, of Custer's weapons, it's difficult to determine how significant this factor was in Custer's sector of the battle. There were similar criticisms from troops fighting on Reno Hill, however, and ultimately the army switched from copper to brass casings, which were harder and less susceptible to jamming.

The other new weapon was the Colt revolver. It fired six rounds of a .45-caliber bullet weighing 250 grains and propelled by 30 grains of black powder. The Colt was a single-action weapon, which means the hammer had to be cocked before each shot. (Double action means the weapon can be fired by pulling the trigger repeatedly, an action that automatically cocks the hammer with each trigger pull. Double-action army-issue handguns were introduced much later.) The army-issue Colt .45 had a seven-and-a-half-inch barrel and, along with its shorter-barreled cousins, was known as the Peacemaker: "the gun that won the west." The Colt was popular with the troops, even though it took longer to load than other handguns because loading meant opening a "gate" on the side behind the barrel and inserting one bullet at a time. Ejecting the spent cartridges required the same action. This was not easy to do on horseback, especially.[6] But the pistol was popular because it was accurate. Accuracy in a handgun, though, is a relative term. It was and is strictly a close-range weapon. A good shot with the Colt .45 pistol could hit a man-sized target with every shot at twenty-five yards. Beyond that, accuracy tended to drop off—especially in the chaos of battle with dust swirling and multiple enemies returning fire, and fear and excitement unsteadying the hand. And, of course, close-range enemy fighters were rarely standing upright and still. Imagine the situation of a new recruit, most likely a recent immigrant, dismounted, in the middle of his first battle with weirdly painted warriors dashing everywhere, some mounted, some charging toward him on foot, shouting war cries. In that terrifying situation a soldier would be happy to have a straight-shooting pistol, but he'd be lucky to hit anything beyond ten yards. Even worse, most likely he wouldn't need to.

As Custer said, the officers and men were pleased with their new weapons, and they were more than ready to leave the swarms of insects along the Missouri banks and head south. As the dyspeptic Private Ewert wrote: "The latest pattern of improved carbines were issued, two hundred rounds of ammunition per man, and all to assure the Indians that we really mean peace and nothing but peace. It is true that the Indians had broken the existing treaty themselves, time and time again and they could, with right, be considered as enemies—in fact should have been treated as such long since—but it can only be treated as strange that a Government as powerful as the United States should offer a willful lie in opposition to a few hundred Indians."[7] No matter where Ewert looked, apparently, he found something to grumble about. It was, and is, the eternal prerogative—almost the obligation—of the American enlisted man, immigrant or not.

One of the key officers of the expedition was Brevet Lt. Colonel William Ludlow. Ludlow was the Chief Engineer of the Dakota Territory and the chief engineer of the expedition. Historian Donald Jackson wrote about Ludlow: "Although he was not considered a fighting soldier, and was classed with the bug hunters by the troops, Ludlow had the respect of the line officers."[8] In this, Jackson overlooked the fact that the engineers and topographical engineers from West Point were the Point's most prestigious graduates. The "scientific corps" was open only to those who had the highest academic record, and being accepted to the engineers was the goal of nearly every cadet. As Lt. John Tidball wrote, "We were taught with every breath we drew at West Point the utmost reverence for this [hierarchy]; consequently it [became] a kind of fixture in our minds that the engineers were a species of god, next to which came the 'topogs' [topographical engineers] only a grade below—they were but demi-gods. The line was simply the line, whether of horse or infantry."[9] Nor were engineers excused from combat. Ludlow, Class of '64, received three brevets for gallantry during the Civil War. Engineers fought, and indeed the venerable professors at the Point, who determined the curriculum, valued engineering, including combat engineering, above all other skills, since the ability to understand (and prepare) the terrain, to build defensive positions and artillery emplacements, and to spot weaknesses in enemy positions was vital in wars against nation-states. (Engineering officer Captain Robert E. Lee distinguished himself in the Mexican War by making hazardous reconnaissances of enemy positions and emplacements. And, as mentioned, Gouverneur Warren, who by the Civil War had risen to brigadier general of engineers, was a hero at Gettysburg.) Further, during peacetime the engineering graduates of the Point were assigned to major public works projects, the construction of coastal defenses, and surveys of unmapped territories, while the cadets who did poorly were likely to be assigned to the infantry or cavalry. If they were lucky, they were sent to well-appointed forts like Lincoln, where they could swat insects alongside their troopers but at least live in congenial quarters along with their families and comrades. Others who were not so lucky were sent to shabby one- or two-company posts on the frontier—ramshackle places like Fort Buchanan in Arizona. Ludlow, who would be responsible for navigating and plotting the expedition, came with the automatic prestige of his West Point training and was popular with his brother officers perhaps in part because he did not patronize the cavalry and infantry officers who would have understood the West Point—and army—hierarchies as well as Ludlow. Besides, Ludlow had a solid war record and had the brevets to prove it. The enlisted men did not understand these not-so-subtle social and professional gradations, but the officers certainly did. Ludlow had accompanied Custer on the 1873 Yellowstone expedition, but Custer had some even earlier history with Ludlow. When Custer was an upperclassman at West Point and acting as officer of the guard, he failed to break up a fight between Ludlow and another cadet. The officer of the day was the even-then prickly William Hazen, then a lieutenant, and he arrested Custer and had him court-martialed.[10] The court reprimanded Custer, but that was all. No doubt Custer admired Ludlow's spunk, and no doubt he always remembered Hazen's treatment. This was the same Hazen who preferred infantry to cavalry in fighting Indians, the same Hazen who would attack the Northern Pacific Railroad's real estate claims, and the same Hazen whom Custer would rebut on behalf of the NPRR. Sincerely annoyed, Hazen went on to criticize Custer's book *My Life on the Plains*, joining Captain Frederick Benteen in attacking Custer's version of the facts surrounding the Battle of Washita.[11] These are the kinds of things an author does not forgive or forget. And if the entire army was undermanned, small and scattered, the officer corps was smaller still, a petri dish of rumor, jealousy, professional hatred, and cliques. Custer versus Hazen was a microcosm of the whole.

For the upcoming Black Hills Expedition, Custer intended to travel fast. The speed of the expedition would frustrate some of the civilian scientific gentlemen. Most complained at some point that Custer's urge to get to the Hills and then return quickly meant that careful geological, botanical, and zoological analysis was impossible. Like many, if not most, scientists, they would have been content to potter around peering at insects, rock formations, and plants, oblivious to passing time. They had little sensitivity to the problems of supply for both men and animals; they did not seem to understand that as travel days accumulated, supplies dwindled— supplies that were fuel for animals that were, in turn, their only means of returning home. There was no time to waste; Custer figured he had two months to make the round trip. There was a beef herd to supplement supplies for the troops, but the soldiers would hunt antelope, deer, and elk so successfully that most of the beef herd would return to Fort Lincoln—and in better condition than when they left. But it was forage for the horses and mules that concerned Custer and his quartermaster, 1st Lt. Algernon "Fresh" Smith, another member of Custer's favored circle. (Like most of the "royal family," Smith would die at the Little Bighorn.) The horses and mules were on short commons to begin with, and to run out while still far from Fort Lincoln would be disastrous.

The most junior scientist would become the most renowned—George Bird Grinnell. Grinnell was only four years out of Yale, but he was already an assistant in paleontology at Yale's Peabody Museum. Grinnell worked for Yale professor Othniel Marsh. Marsh was a personal friend of General Sheridan who had invited Marsh to join the expedition. Marsh could not go but sent Grinnell as his surrogate (Yale apparently paid Grinnell's expenses). Grinnell was eager to go, for the lure of the West had already seduced him. As an undergraduate he had joined a Yale expedition to hunt fossils in Nebraska, and the following year he had come west to hunt buffalo. Grinnell would go on to the most varied and distinguished career of all the scientists on the expedition, and indeed a career that would compare favorably to any scientist of the period in terms of service to the country and service to a variety of academic fields, including ethnology. From the first, he was fascinated by the Plains Indians and ultimately wrote a number of books about the Pawnee and the Cheyenne, doing his own fieldwork and spending long periods of time with the people, learning their stories and their histories and recounting them for the white readers with respect and care. (It was Grinnell who retold the story of the coyote and the grebes in his book *By Cheyenne Campfires*.) Grinnell would also become editor of *Forest and Stream* magazine, a publication devoted to outdoor sport. He was an avid hunter and a founder of the Boone and Crockett Club as well as an ardent bird fancier and founder of the Audubon Society. He was an important activist in preserving both Yellowstone and Glacier National Parks. (Perhaps predictably, the opening of Yellowstone National Park in 1872 aroused the interest of Jay Cooke, who saw it as a potential tourist attraction to be serviced by his railroad.) Not surprisingly, Grinnell was a friend of Teddy Roosevelt, for the two men shared almost identical passions and convictions about the environment, conservation (of both wilderness and animals), and the outdoors.

Grinnell's role in the expedition was zoologist, and he would spend most of the trip collecting specimens of birds and animals and making lists of what he saw. He hoped to find buffalo, but the only traces he found were skulls and skeletons, along with an arrangement obviously made by Indians of five rows of buffalo skulls, each row containing twelve heads painted red and blue and facing east. It would have been an unsettling and at the same time fascinating spectacle for a budding anthropologist. He also poked around fossil beds and found a few prehistoric turtle shells and the femur of a dinosaur, but in general the fossil hunting was disappointing.

As though straight from the pages of a novel in which the young hero always seems to have a sidekick, Grinnell was assisted by a rough-and-ready frontiersman named Luther North. North had guided Grinnell on his first buffalo hunt and was a veteran of the Pawnee Battalion that had battled the Sioux and Cheyenne during the Civil War and had later patrolled the Union Pacific as it crept inexorably across the Plains. (Like the Crow and Arikara, the Pawnee were inveterate enemies of the Sioux.) Grinnell would later write a book about Luther and his brother, Frank. And, not to be outdone by the growing number of writers who were smitten by the romance of the West, Grinnell also wrote novels: *Jack, the Young Trapper* and *Jack, the Young Ranchman*. Designed for boys, these were a kind of combination of Owen Wister (another friend of Teddy Roosevelt) and Zane Grey. Grinnell wrote them around the turn of the century when the West was not so wild anymore but still a place of adventure that would stimulate the imaginations of countless adolescent boys back east. Undoubtedly, more than a few succumbed to the call of the wild, just as Grinnell had done thirty years before. Indeed, as a model of the outdoorsman, conservationist cum gentleman scholar and author, Grinnell could hardly be surpassed and was perhaps only equaled by his friend T. R.

Naturally, Custer took to Grinnell, for they had many interests in common. Custer would later invite Grinnell to go along on the 1876 Bighorn campaign. Grinnell had to decline; he was too busy with his academic work and so missed Custer's "appointment in Samarra." Of Custer and his subsequent Little Bighorn defeat, Grinnell would write: "He was a good soldier and a good fighter, but like most white men he did not understand Indians and underrated them."[12]

Custer also wanted to hire a geologist to accompany the Black Hills Expedition. He wrote to General Alfred Terry: "Is there no way by which the services of a geologist can be had with the expedition? The country to be visited is so new and believed to be so interesting that it will be a pity not to improve to the fullest extent the opportunity to determine all that is possible of its character, scientific and otherwise."[13] To some this may seem that Custer was giving the game away, in other words, that his primary object was really to look for gold. Perhaps. But a geologist is not necessarily a miner, and it's useful to keep in mind that the army often combined scientific exploration with military objectives. As mentioned, the very curriculum of West Point emphasized the natural sciences as part of its overall emphasis on engineering. Even an indifferent student like Custer would have been imbued with this ethic. Besides, the two ideas are not incompatible. If a geologist who was examining and analyzing the land happened to see formations that might harbor gold, so much the better. If not, there would still be a treasure trove of new scientific information about a hitherto unknown territory. What's more, there was a commonly perceived difference between a "practical miner" and an academic geologist, for, as the *Bismarck Tribune* sniffed, "When did a geologist ever discover a single gold mine in all recorded history?"[14]

Colonel Ludlow also wrote to his superiors in Washington suggesting that the expedition could profit from the services of a geologist and asked permission to hire one at a salary of $150 a month. Washington wrote back saying the army had no objection to a geologist but had no money to pay for one. Ultimately, though, the army unbelted for $450 to pay the salary of Professor Newton Winchell of the University of Minnesota. Winchell would produce a credible geological map of the Black Hills, although again the speed of the expedition meant that he had to leave many areas of the Hills unexplored and therefore unmapped. Winchell would also have a major role in the controversy over the extent, even the legitimacy, of the gold strike. At that point Custer probably wished he had done without that particular professor. But that controversy was in the future.

The fourth member of the civilian scientists was A. B. Donaldson, who was also associated with the University of Minnesota as a botanist. Apparently Donaldson funded himself by writing articles for the *St. Paul Daily Pioneer*, and although he poked around collecting botanical samples here and there, he seemed more interested in his journalism. Probably, it paid better.

Another civilian—perhaps an auxiliary member of the "bug hunters"—was photographer William H. Illingworth. His spring wagon was equipped as a nineteenth-century version of a traveling darkroom, complete with chemicals for developing the glass plates that would then be turned into stereoscopic images of the expedition and would record for history how massive the expedition truly was and in so doing give a fair and visual commentary on the skills of the soldiers and their civilian employees who were managing this complicated undertaking. Illingworth planned to sell his photographs to a public eager to gain a glimpse of life in the West.

Then, last but not least, were the two practical miners—Horatio Nelson Ross and William McKay. It's not certain who paid their expenses. Some say Custer contributed; others that the two men paid their own way. In either case, their objective was the clearest and most single-minded of all. Their participation and purpose were hardly a secret. As the *Bismarck Tribune* wrote on the eve of the expedition's departure: "Ross and McKay, the practical miners and explorers who are to accompany Custer's expe-dition, have packed their 'keisters,' sharpened their picks, primed their pieces, and are now ready to go at a moment's notice. Take care of your scalps, boys. Bismarck can't afford to [lose] you"[15] ("keister" was slang for "satchel").

To the thoroughly appropriate tune of "The Girl I Left Behind Me," as well as the inevitable "Garryowen," the expedition got under way on

July 2, 1874. The sixteen band members were mounted on white horses and made a noble sight, regardless of their musical talents, one way or the other. Custer was at the head of the column, of course. He was dressed in buckskins and riding his bay, "Dandy." His stag hounds gamboled ahead. His staff and headquarters elements followed. Then came the band followed by a contingent of Indian scouts. A small squad of them was sent ahead each day to scout the country and act as an early warning. There are differing reports of the exact number of scouts, although several estimates, including Private Ewert's, claim there were about seventy-five in total— thirty-nine Arikara, twenty-nine Santee, and a handful of Sioux, of undetermined bands. The Santee came from their agency in the northeast corner of Nebraska. The Arikara arrived from their agency at Fort Berthold, and many were still furious about the recent Lakota raid and were out for blood. The Santee (aka Dakota) were a branch of the greater Sioux nation and language family and had settled on the reservation after the disastrous US-Dakota War in Minnesota in 1862—a war in which hundreds of white settlers were attacked and killed or captured all along the Minnesota River. In the end one hundred and fifty Santee warriors were killed in a series of sharp engagements with the army, which lost nearly eighty troops killed in action. When the Santee surrendered, thirty-eight were hanged in a public execution; the rest were moved to reservations outside Minnesota. Originally three hundred and three were condemned to the gallows, but after reviewing the evidence, President Abraham Lincoln commuted the sentences of all but thirty-eight. Some had obviously decided it was the better part of valor to work as scouts, and according to Custer they knew the Black Hills territory very well. (Not all were reconciled, however, for the famous Lakota holy man Black Elk reported that there were Santee and Yanktonai camped with the Lakota and Cheyenne at the Battle of the Little Bighorn.)[16] The handful of Sioux scouts, by which commentators no doubt meant Lakota, probably came from the area around Fort Lincoln, perhaps as a result of Custer's personal recruiting. One named Goose was said to be a Hunkpapa, the same band led by Sitting Bull. His presence along with the other Lakota is further evidence of the wide differences of opinion and policy among the various tribesmen, even those of the same band. Black Elk, who as a boy traveled with his second cousin, Crazy Horse, referred with some contempt to the reservation Indians as "hang-around-the-fort people."[17] These were led primarily by Red Cloud and Spotted Tail, whereas the non-treaty tribesmen were led by Sitting Bull, Gall, and Crazy Horse, among others.

The scouts were under the command of 2nd Lt. George Wallace, with the able assistance of Custer's favorite, Bloody Knife, who ranked as a corporal. Bloody Knife was still grieving over the death of his son and was out to live up to his name.

Next came the "pioneer wagon," which was filled with tools for bridging, cutting, and digging. Assignment to the "pioneer company" would be rotated among the line companies, since the pioneers would have the heavy work of cutting riverbanks, chopping trees, and bridging the streams.

Following the pioneer wagon was the artillery detachment—the three Gatling guns and the three-inch caliber cannon. These were followed by the four ambulances. This order of march was useful because Custer knew he would have a number of creeks and rivers to cross. Many would require temporary bridging, and he needed the lightest wagons to start the crossing to test its sturdiness before the heavy mule wagons could attempt to cross.

The civilian scientists and reporters marched or rode in their wagons near the head of the column.

After the advance units came the 110 wagons, each drawn by six mules and heavily laden with forage, food for the troops, and ammunition. As mentioned, the forage for the horses and mules was reduced to around four pounds, but even so four pounds of grain for twelve hundred horses and mules for sixty days added up to something like 144 tons of grain. And that is using Custer's original proposal figures for the animals: twelve hundred horses and mules for sixty days. In fact, he had nearly a thousand troops and civilians under his command, and only two companies of them were infantry, so he had more than twelve hundred government animals to worry about, so his total freightage for them almost certainly exceeded 144 tons. Either that, or he was planning on even smaller grain supplements and relying almost entirely on grazing, or he was planning to make the trip in less than sixty days.

The food for the troops consisted mainly of hardtack, coffee, bacon, and beans. The wagons also carried some flour so the cooks could bake bread when the column stopped early enough or (rarely) lingered at a campsite. While out on the treeless Plains the wagons would travel in four columns, but once inside the Black Hills where many of the canyons and passes were narrow, the wagons would go in single file, and the column would be approximately two miles long. The cavalry were divided into two battalions under the commands of Majors George Forsyth and Joseph Tilford. Each battalion was assigned to march alongside the wagon train. The infantry would march behind the train, and a rearguard of cavalry came last. Traveling at his own discretion was the expedition's sutler, the primary source of alcohol for the troops—"primary" because it is impossible to believe that some of the men did not carry their own, regardless of regulations. Needless to say, this near monopoly on a valued commodity meant good profits for the sutler, but unlike the campaign of the prior year no accusations of financial shenanigans have surfaced. Accompanying the sutler was his cook, Sarah Campbell, also known as Aunt Sally.

CHAPTER THIRTEEN

ALKALI AND COMETS, GRASS AND STARS

When beggars die there are no comets seen.
—William Shakespeare,
Julius Caesar, act 2, scene 2

Chief Engineer Brevet Lt. Colonel William Ludlow wrote: "Prairie travel resembles that by sea which indeed the landscape not unfrequently [*sic*] suggests. . . . The direct course is not always the best, and the probabilities of finding wood, water and grass, and a good road, compare with those of obtaining favorable and moderate winds and a smooth sea."[1]

Prairie travel also resembled a sea voyage because the prairie, while rarely flat, was also empty. You could look in any direction, through all three hundred and sixty degrees of the compass, and see virtually nothing but your own wake, nothing other than empty prairie. In the case of the Black Hills Expedition, the wake consisted of wagon ruts and the prints and leavings of walking men, horses, and mules.

But the comparison to sea travel only goes so far, for unlike ships that as much as possible carried the necessities of life with them, travelers on the Plains depended on the Plains for the basic elements of survival. As Major George "Sandy" Forsyth wrote in his memoirs, "A day's march is commonly from water to water, and that may be anywhere from eight to 28 miles."[2] In fact, during Custer's expedition there were at least four marches that stretched to over thirty miles, as the expedition tacked back and forth "from water to water." And there was more to the problem than finding just any kind of water. Many of the streams on the Plains were alkaline and undrinkable; others were muddy. Still others dried up in the summer, although their dry riverbeds could turn into raging flash floods during and after the astonishing rainstorms that regularly swept the Plains. Still other creeks were little more than rivulets that could hardly support the needs of men and animals. An Indian scout who was used to relying on tiny streams he could step over soon learned that the army and its animals needed more substantial flows. As Private Theodore Ewert wrote: "It is remarkable what a tendency towards high sounding and exaggerated names the first explorers of this territory had. Every brook or creek, be it ever so small and insignificant, is christened a river, every mud puddle is dubbed a creek."[3] Going from water to water" was easier said than done.

It was water and grazing that mattered most; the men could get by without wood for cook fires, though they did not like it. But the animals obviously could not survive long without water. And, given their heavy workload under the scorching summer sun, they needed more water than they would require in garrison. The expedition was therefore entirely dependent on finding streams. They did carry some kegs but could not begin to carry enough water to meet the needs of the animals. Now and then a rainstorm would leave a pool of standing water, a miniature lake, but such a large expedition could not rely on these occasional and unpredictable gifts. What's more, those same rainstorms also turned the spongy prairie soil into a sticky gumbo that could and did suck heavily laden wagons down to their axles. With typical Western irony, these violent storms were called "Dakota zephyrs." Capable of blowing down the men's tents and scattering their equipment, the west wind gusted at gale force. But at least it was a change from the blistering heat of the sun.

Then there was the problem of grazing. Horses typically need to consume forage equal to 1 to 2 percent of their body weight per day. The average cavalry horse weighed nearly eleven hundred pounds, which meant a horse would need at least seven pounds of grass to supplement its allowance of four pounds of grain. And that was the bare minimum. It's reasonable to assume that at that rate a horse would gradually lose condition, especially after the fatigues of a long day on the march.[4] And when the expedition was forced to camp where there was poor grazing or no grazing at all, the gradual deterioration of fitness accelerated. As Lt. James Calhoun wrote in his July 9 entry: "I pity the poor horses that have to carry such heavy burdens. I know many in the command weighing nearly two hundred pounds and add to this the weight of saddle equipments, arms, accoutrements, etc., etc., I think the horses have a pretty heavy load."[5] Apparently, many of the men, and not a few officers, evaded the regulation weight limitations of one hundred and sixty-five pounds. (The four-foot-eight-inch Private Ewert, on the other hand, did not overburden his horse, "Monkey.")

The constraints imposed by the horse's needs and capabilities naturally affected army operations. As mentioned, each company of cavalry generally required three supply wagons to carry food, ammunition, and forage. That meant that the horsemen could only leave their wagons for short periods. They could only enter terrain unsuited for wagons or follow the trail of fleeing enemies and be away from the base of supplies for as long as they could carry food for themselves and their animals. (Pack mules greatly extended a patrol's range.) But traveling with supply wagons also meant that some men had to be detailed to stay with the wagons to protect them against attack. Further, as Colonel William Hazen was quick to point out, cavalry horses often broke down after only a few days of rigorous campaigning, and they were not the equal of the smaller Indian ponies that could live on grass and needed no grain supplement. (It also meant that Indian ponies endured very hungry winters, which, in turn, meant that winter warfare was essentially impossible.) Consequently the cavalry was constantly entering races they could rarely, if ever, win. Hazen's carping, though, is contradicted by Custer's scout that led to the Little Bighorn. Still, the point remains: the needs of the cavalry horses placed significant restrictions on the army's operations and tactics—a patrol running short on supplies might well be tempted into a precipitate attack.

The Plains were for most of the route a series of rolling hills, inevitably compared to ocean swells, as Ludlow observed. Ludlow along with his sergeants would use celestial navigation to mark the latitude and longitude of each campsite and each important landmark. Using the traditional navigational tools of the seafarer—the sextant and celestial tables—Ludlow and his assistants would measure angles of the sun and certain stars and thereby generate "fixes," that is, positions of the sun and stars as measured by the sextant and, after consultation of the tables, drawn on the map to mark a man's place on the earth. Given the fact that the horizon was irregular, unlike the horizon at sea, the measurements were not always precise, but they were as close as humanly possible in that country. (To measure the angle of the sun or star, the navigator uses the sextant to pull the image of the star down to the flat horizon; an irregular horizon broken by hills and mountain ranges made exact measurements impossible.) Undoubtedly the navigators were frustrated more than once when their "fix" looked like three lines surrounding an empty triangular space instead of the desired three lines crossing precisely at the same spot. But for their purposes, an approximation would have to be good enough. The latest fix gave Custer and Ludlow a starting point for the next day's march, a starting point from which they could draw a new compass course toward the Hills. Inevitably the demands of water, grazing, and wood and the broken terrain meant that the initial compass course would undergo frequent changes on the march. But at least Custer and Ludlow knew where they were each morning when they started, and the initial compass course served as a general guideline as the expedition frequently changed direction to find the easiest wagon route and the next camping place. Ludlow and his men plotted these changes and would ultimately translate them into a course map of the expedition. Following a set course was far less important than following the guides' and scouts' information about water and grazing. Fortunately the expedition's goal—the Black Hills—was so prominent and extensive that making the ultimate "landfall" would hardly be much of a navigational achievement, especially since there were scouts and guides available to ride ahead—a luxury unavailable to a ship at sea. But finding and improving a good road there was something else again.

Ludlow used a barometer to measure the elevation of various mountains they encountered. This device was even less accurate than his other equipment and techniques. Barometric calculations to ascertain elevation were complicated and imprecise. (Ludlow estimated Harney Peak at 9,700 feet. Harney Peak was the highest in the Black Hills but was 2,500 feet lower than Ludlow's calculation.)[6] Ludlow's work would therefore yield only a preliminary survey and map. More accurate topographical information would have to wait for later expeditions in which a survey was the primary object. Custer's expedition was moving too quickly for topographical precision.

Still, despite the need to move expeditiously, Ludlow's calculations would result in a useful map of the expedition's route and topography. And the quality of the map Ludlow and his staff ultimately produced shows that his calculations were extremely good, despite the difficulties he faced.

Each day Ludlow's team measured distances traveled to the tenth of a mile by means of two odometers that were attached to the wheels of two vehicles: an ambulance and a two-wheeled cart. At the end of the day the readings from the two were compared and reconciled, although as the expedition wound its way south regularly changing directions in order to find the easiest trail, the odometers registered miles over the ground but did not measure the crow's-flight distance to the Hills. The expedition might march fifteen miles only to advance half of that distance toward the objective. Further, the trail south was covered with rolling hills, which added odometer miles as the wagons rolled up one side and down the other.

The first day, July 2, was representative in some ways of the difficulties the expedition would encounter. Lt. Calhoun writes:

About five miles from our starting point we found a good supply of wholesome water, refreshing to man and beast.[7] [It's worth noting that the men and animals needed "refreshing" after only five miles, because of the brutal heat. Temperatures routinely exceeded 100 degrees.] The wagon train had several bad [river] crossings which caused a delay of several hours. Four wagons sunk into the mire and had to be unloaded. The contents of one wagon had to be left on the prairie [to be retrieved later]. Several NCO and privates belonging to the Infantry Battalion fell down from the effects of oppressive heat and had to ride in the ambulances. Saw a bright comet this evening.[8]

And this was just the first day. But after unloading the wagons and pulling them out of the mud, the expedition carried on and camped that night 15.1 miles from their starting point.[9]

What of the comet? Comets had long been a signal that something momentous was in the works. Whether the coming event was a good thing or the reverse was never clear, even to the soothsayers. It's said that a comet appeared as William the Conqueror was leaving to invade England. It seemed a good omen to him. Apparently he was an optimist; he is supposed to have called it a wonderful sign from heaven. And for him, that's how it turned out. His adversary, however, the Saxon, King Harold, may have seen things differently had he survived the battle. It's at least reasonable to assume that Custer was aware of this story. He was an indifferent student at West Point, and West Point, oddly, paid almost no attention to world or national history. But a famous anecdote from a famous military leader was most likely known to many cadets and officers alike. And although Custer finished last in his class, it was not from lack of intelligence or curiosity. Rather, like more than a few high-spirited young men, he only did enough academically to get by. And when he fell behind, he applied himself to catch up. Also, those same high spirits led him into a series of pranks and violations of the Academy's maze of punishable offenses, including frequent visits to Benny Havens's tavern—an off-limits spot popular with the boys after hours. (Clearly, this was before Custer "took the pledge.") These adventures led to a string of demerits that affected his class standing. Also, it's worth pointing out that simply graduating from West Point was considered more than a routine achievement. Cadet George Derby (Class of '46) wrote to his mother: "It is not thought a disgrace to be dismissed from here, for the studies and discipline are very hard, and a man who succeeds should be thought uncommonly talented, and one found deficient should not be blamed, for I verily believe that not one half of those appointed can possibly graduate."[10] Derby had his numbers exactly right; West Point's attrition rate averaged 50 percent.

If Custer actually had heard of William the Conqueror and the comet, and if he assigned any significance to it this first night of the expedition, he most likely saw it as a good omen for him and his men—and probably for the future as well. Probably he saw it as an astrological affirmation of Custer's luck. And since this is all speculation, it's interesting to wonder how long a comet's predictive powers, whether for tragic or happy results, can last. Two months? Two years? Or is it a fickle and therefore unpredictable omen? Perhaps Shakespeare had the answer: "When beggars die there are no comets seen; the heavens themselves blaze forth the death of princes" (*Julius Caesar*, act 2, scene 2). In two years, America's version of a warrior prince would, like King Harold, meet his end. There is, however, a slight difference between the two, for in Custer's case, he was the attacker.

What the Indians thought of the comet is another question. But certainly they thought something. And given Custer's presence—of which they were well aware—they probably regarded it as ominous. Black Elk, who was eleven at the time and camping somewhere in the Black Hills as the troops marched south, said: "Afterward I learned that it was Pahuska ["long hair"] who had led his soldiers into the Black Hills that summer to see what he could find. He had no right to go there because all that country was ours. . . . Later I learned that Pahuska had found much of the yellow metal that makes the Wasichus [whites] crazy, and that is what made bad trouble, just as it did before when the hundred [Fetterman et al.] were wiped out."[11]

One of the subjects taught at West Point was castrametation—the art of setting up a military camp. Of the courses taught there, it was probably among the most useful to the professional soldier. Compared to outdated tactics, which explained how to line regiments up and march into the teeth of enemy fire, the techniques of setting up a camp not only dealt with the security of the camp but also considered the health and to whatever extent possible the comfort of the troops, the safety of their animals, and the security of the supply wagons. (In contrast to the regular army troops, who camped apart from the volunteer soldiers during the Mexican War, the volunteers suffered disproportionally from disease, in part because their officers were essentially civilian politicians who knew nothing about setting up and maintaining a healthy camp. For every one US soldier killed in action, another seven died from diseases that were mostly preventable.)[12]

Custer routinely selected the next camping place several hours ahead of the main body. Once there, he established a perimeter of pickets, or vedettes, all around the proposed site. These spread out several hundred yards around the site. He sent Indian scouts out beyond the pickets. When the wagons rumbled in, the men set about caring for their animals and erecting their tents. The tents would form a massive square, with the wagons parked in the middle. The animals would be allowed to graze, assuming the grazing was adequate, but at sundown the mules were tied to their wagons and the horses were tied outside the tents of the men. Guards were of course stationed outside the perimeter, and on at least one occasion a nervous vedette fired at what he thought were lurking Indians. The whole camp was aroused, and rumors flew that they were under attack by thousands of Indians. Nervous soldiers were understandably liable to mistake a clump of brush or an enterprising coyote for a crawling enemy. The disgusted Private Ewert was one of those rudely awakened: "I can assure you that alarms of this kind occur frequently in a hostile country, and that the men are always mad when told that no Indians are around waiting to attack the camp and that they can return to their blankets and finish the broken 'nap.'"[13] For days there had been rumors that the Sioux would attack the column. There were smoke signals in the distance, and armed parties had been spotted. There was no doubt that the Sioux were watching and perhaps awaiting their chance. When the expedition left Fort Lincoln, more than a few of the troopers foresaw disaster. As Private Ewert wrote, "We all believed that scarce half our number would return."[14] Rumors are the currency of an army, and the rumors spread by some of the Indian scouts suggested that Sioux in their thousands were waiting to attack. That gave the rolling prairie all the more sinister aspect, for it was easy to imagine mounted hordes of warriors hidden in the arroyos or behind one of those strange-looking buttes that unaccountably dotted the landscape. Others thought the Sioux would wait until the command reached the Black Hills, where they would use the landscape to their advantage, fighting a guerilla war behind the trees and boulders. According to Ewert some of the troops would have welcomed an attack as an alternative to the numbing monotony of the march across the endless prairie. This is easy to say, and for some small minority, it may even have been true. But the majority of men, like most soldiers, would have been well satisfied if the Sioux ignored them.

The days were long for the troopers. Few if any of them had Custer's energy and sense of purpose. Some nights they would straggle into camp, and after looking after their horses, it might be midnight before they could roll into their blankets. Since reveille came at three in the morning, the men sometimes didn't bother with their shelter tents, which, when it rained, provided no shelter and which, when hit with a Dakota zephyr, blew away.

Custer's tent was somewhat more elaborate. It was a wall tent that was supplied by the Northern Pacific Railroad—another indication of the close relationship between the army in general and Custer in particular and the NPRR. Speaking of tents, Private Ewert said:

> The men raised no tents as it was near midnight 'ere the horses were fed and groomed, and the men got their supper, but the officers, Oh! These gentlemen. They could not sleep these few hours without having their large wall tents pitched. They did not have to put them up and the poor men—well what does an officer care how tired or worn out or even ill a man is. Their imperial will would at all times have to be obeyed; humanity is something that is foreign to their feelings and a little kindness is but seldom or never shown to one of the rank and file.[15]

Ewert had a point. As mentioned, the army's discipline was harsh, in part because of the character of many of the men—hardcases, to say the least. But there was also a clear sense of class differences between officers and men. Of course, there were obvious differences in education, family, and social status. But for an officer, effective leadership involves ignoring those differences, not in the sense of becoming "one of the boys," but in the sense of diligently looking after the welfare of the men—and being seen to do so. At the very least, Custer's officers could have done without their tents on those late nights. His officers could have done better; Custer should have seen to it. That is the point of command.

It's worth remembering that Custer did not really know where he was going as he set off across the Plains. He knew, of course, that the Black Hills were some three hundred zigzagging miles to the southwest, but he did not know the country between Fort Lincoln and the Hills. The army's earlier attempts to map the territory were incomplete. Lt. Gouverneur K. Warren had been turned back by the Lakota as he approached the western side of the Hills in 1857, and Captain W. F. Raynolds had done a little mapping on the northern edges of the Hills in 1859 as he traveled west to the Yellowstone and Powder River country.[16] But there were no maps of the route to the Hills from Fort Lincoln, and of course no one but the Lakota knew anything about the vast interior of the Hills themselves. In truth, the expedition would have to transit one terra incognita in order to reach and explore another.

Custer was relying on information provided by more or less friendly

Indians and on the experience of scouts and guides, both white and native, who did not really know as much as Custer might have wished. The Indians knew where the rivers were, but they had no experience managing wagon trains, nor did they understand fully the quality of roadways the wagons required. While the scouts might be content to slide their ponies down a steep arroyo wall to reach a useful river and drinking water, the wagon train might have to detour for miles to find a place where the pioneer company could carve a wagon-wide ramp down to the water—and then another back up the other side. It's also useful to remember that there was a difference between a scout and a guide. The Indian scouts' primary duty was to ride ahead and be on the lookout for enemies (and in some cases to carry dispatches back to Fort Lincoln). Secondarily, they might find a decent trail for the train, but that was not really their area of expertise. If they spoke English at all it was only at the most primitive level—hardly the basis for understanding the army's civil engineering and road-building needs. The guides were supposed to know where they were going, but there were only three men listed as such: "Lonesome" Charley Reynolds, Louis Agard (a French Canadian who doubled as interpreter), and Boston Custer. As a guide Boston was useless—and an example to Custer critics of the General's lining his family's pockets. But Custer liked having his youngest brother around, and he wrote to Libbie that "Bos takes to life on the plains as naturally as if he was bred to it."[17] But Boston was as ignorant of the country as the rawest recruit. Lonesome Charley was more useful, but he would be with the command for only part of the expedition. Custer would send him with historically important dispatches halfway through the mission.

In the end, finding the route was mainly Custer's job. He would lead the column, and he would relish the task. As usual, Custer was tireless and led a small detachment of trailblazers and the pioneer company to seek out the best roadways and campsites, and he got so far ahead some days that he arrived at that evening's campground hours before the wagon train. He was apparently unconcerned about the risks. It was the not first time he exposed himself and a small detachment to possible attack in hostile territory.

As reporter William Curtis gushed in the *Chicago Inter Ocean*: "General Custer is a famous road maker, and to him, as to the great Napoleon, nothing is impossible."[18] (While perhaps a little over the top, this comment had some merit; on more than one occasion once inside the Black Hills Custer personally found a way out of what seemed to be an impassable canyon.) As much as possible, this work might be reasonably permanent, an actual road, for it was understood that Custer's expedition would not be the last, military or civilian, to head for the Black Hills. After all, the object was to find a place to build a fort and therefore in the future there would be communication from Fort Lincoln in the north and another road from Fort Laramie in the south. The Lakota saw it that way, too, and they could remember that the evils of a previous road, the Bozeman Trail, had on their hunting grounds and on their relations with the whites, both civilian and government. This new road was even worse, for it would run through the prairie and into the mountains, both of which were guaranteed to them by treaty. There was no ambiguity in their minds about who owned this country and about this new pernicious road.

As far as Custer was concerned, however, the problem was not finding the Hills but rather getting to them and back with minimal loss and damage to the expedition, its men, animals, and equipment—and, if possible, avoiding a scrap, or worse, with the Indians. While this attitude seems to contradict the conventional characterization of Custer—an egomaniacal war lover—it is perfectly consistent with his understanding of the mission and its possible results. There's no doubt he reveled in publicity and fame, but he was astute enough to understand that the expedition alone would be more than enough to burnish his credentials, especially if he found what he expected to find. On his return, a reporter asked him if he was disappointed in "not having a brush with the Sioux." In response, Custer said: "Yes, I was somewhat disappointed for, though I had sent pacific messages and had taken every precaution to avoid hostilities, I had reason to anticipate trouble. I was disappointed and am heartily glad of it. Some thought I courted an engagement—such was not the case, and I congratulate myself and the country on the return of the expedition without bloodshed."[19] He was not out for a fight. He was, as usual, out to make a mark in history.

The environment could well be a greater hazard to the expedition than the Sioux. Hostile Sioux may or may not be there, but the rugged countryside, the brutal summer heat, and the occasional, violent rain and wind storms most certainly were there, and they awaited Custer and the Seventh

Cavalry. Grazing, water, and wood for cooking were not always where Custer wanted or needed to find them. Indeed, the most impressive feature of the Plains, then and now, is the relative lack of trees and water. The rolling prairie seems to go on forever with only an occasional thin line of cottonwoods lining a creek or small river. As Curtis wrote: "A Wisconsin lumberman would laugh at the use of the word 'wood' as applied to a cluster of timber that would not turn out 10,000 feet of planking, but let him live in this country a while and he would value even the stunted shrubbery that occasionally makes a feeble attempt at existence on the banks of some sluggish stream."[20] And of all trees, cottonwoods least deserve the title "timber," for their wood is soft and pulpy, as the infantry at Fort Lincoln learned when they tried using it to build palisades. It did not take long for the walls to deteriorate. But cottonwood would burn and would usually be the only choice for campfire fuel along with the "shrubs" that Curtis mentioned. (On the Plains buffalo chips were a common substitute, but as George Bird Grinnell noted, there were no buffalo around to produce the fuel.) Cottonwoods are the fastest-growing trees on the Plains, and they can grow to well over a hundred feet and live over a hundred years, which in tree ages seems unimpressive. But despite their utilitarian shortcomings, they are welcome sights from a distance—welcome to thirsty travelers who know that cottonwoods are almost invariably a sign of water, either flowing or subterranean. Whether the water is drinkable or not is a different matter, since cottonwoods are "alkaline tolerant" and can live on water that will lay a soldier low with dysentery. But after miles in a saddle, the sight of a grove of cottonwoods in the distance meant that the troops would at least have fuel for their campfires and, with luck, drinkable water.

The Plains were more like a checkerboard of vegetation. Now and then the troops would come to an outcropping of stone; now and then a weird-looking pyramid-shaped butte would appear, incongruously; now and then there would be a dry arroyo that would have to be gone around or reduced by the pioneers. But those were the exceptions. Beyond these anomalies, there was the grass and rolling hills and above it all a relentless sun that raised the temperatures above one hundred degrees on a landscape that offered nothing in the way of shade. Patches of green grass, patches of brown grass, here and there gray stone, here and there slag-colored remnants of some prehistoric eruption—after a while both the monotony and the unrelenting sun began to wear on the men. As the reporter for the *St. Paul Daily Pioneer* wrote: "Only two days out and the sun has set its mark upon us. Lips unprotected by a moustache awning, blistered skins, noses red as lobsters boiled, ears that shame the glowing color of the turkey gobblers gills, and the cuticle peeling of the whole face, make us even more hideous in appearance than our red brethren."[21] William Curtis added:

> People who sit in cool, dark parlors and shaded offices may envy us, but if they consider seven and eight and ten and fourteen hours in the saddle, under a sun that raises the mercury a hundred degrees on a parched dusty plain, an experience to be envied, four days such as we have spent would convince them to the contrary. No one, so far, very fortunately has felt fatally the terrible suffering, but the ambulances are full of poor soldiers who have fallen out by the way. The animals feel the heat and the want of sufficient water even more than the men, and whenever the train stops the air is hideous with the braying of the poor, thirsty, tired mules. Most of the bottom lands in this region are covered with a sediment of alkali, which is as fine as the finest powder, and sifts through veil or any other protections a person can wear, and sifted through is very painful, getting into the pores of the skin, and burning and smarting till one imagines himself in the process of cremation. The heat and wind parches and cracks our lips and faces, and this dust settling on the blistered flesh is about as serious a torture as the strictest disciplinarian can desire.[22]

Immigrant soldiers and their eastern native-born comrades could be excused for finding the Plains a trifle otherworldly. To a man used to forests of mixed-growth timber, pine and oak and birch, and only rare glimpses of a far horizon, the emptiness of the Plains was at first strange and then, to some, gradually unsettling. The land rose and fell in some places like ocean waves, and in other places, where the hillocks were more pronounced, like waves at sea during a storm, the kind of storm no mariner wants to be in. Wherever the troops looked there was usually nothing for miles, nothing but grass, and much of that burned brown. The Irish soldiers might have initially seen something that reminded them of home, especially in places where the grass was green, for in these places the prairie resembled the sheep meadows of home. But after a while the memory of the old country would seem like a dream, while the reality of this place began to unsettle them, for there were no ancient gray stone walls separating one farm from another, no whitewashed cottages with thatched roofs, no sheep grazing peacefully, no signs of humanity. It was as though humankind had abandoned this part of the world or, more realistically, had never come here at all, as though the troopers were the first people there. Of course they weren't, and the occasional smoke on the horizon made the point that there were other people around, somewhere. But those other people were the Sioux, a strange race of people so different that they hardly seemed human at all. They were a race who could communicate with smoke, and their otherness blended perfectly with the strange, unnatural prairie that was unlike anything most of the troops had ever seen. On realizing that no matter where they looked there was mostly nothingness, more than one trooper was glad not to be alone out there and to see the wagons, the cavalry, the infantry, and to hear the constant cursing of the teamsters. It was reassuring; they had brought a portion of their world to an empty wilderness. Even so, the maudlin old song "Bury Me Not on the Lone Prairie" acquired some new meaning, for no one knew what lay ahead, and no one wanted to remain in that place for eternity. But some would.

And as they trudged along day after day they worried about practical and mundane questions, too—would Custer and the advanced units find a decent place to camp that night? Would there be enough grass for the animals? Would there be water and firewood? Would they arrive in time for the cooks to bake bread, or would it be hardtack and coffee, or worse, a dry camp again?

And it was not always rolling grasslands and alkali bottomlands. Now and then they encountered rougher terrain. The report written for the *St. Paul Daily Pioneer* on July 9 pictures a typical day in some of the roughest country the troops would encounter:

> After crossing Hidden Timber Creek, we wended our way out of the valley and over the hills. Rocky pinnacles and ledges were all around us. Passing the creek bluffs we descend to a rolling plain. Every elevation is covered with siliceous limestone, petrified wood or sandrock, literally paved and wedged in so that between the separate pieces a blade of grass

can scarcely grow. The country becomes more sterile. Bare clay and sand and alkali and prickly cactus are all abounding. It is hard to trail over a surface so broken into gullies. Our trail is indirect and serpentine.[23]

Without grass the horses and mules would have to get by on their four pounds of grain, for there was no budget for extra rations. And on that, everyone knew, the animals could not last for long. Custer's own report for that same day states: "When we struck the tributaries of the Grand River we entered into a less desirable portion of the country, nearly all the streams flowing into Grand River being more or less impregnated with alkali."[24]

William Curtis described the travails of the trail:

Traveling with our wagon train in this sort of country is next to impossible. The ground is hard enough, except when we strike an alkali bottom as we frequently do, but the canyons and gulches are so frequent it keeps us digging and bridging all the time. When we reach a gulch that cannot be spanned, a grade is made to its bottom and up again; when we meet a stream that we cannot ford or a sluice that is bottomless, to bridge it is the work of a moment. . . . Reaching a place that has to be bridged, the General selects the most available point and with a shovel in his hand directs and assists at the work himself. If cobblestones and sod or willow branches and rushes will not make a roadbed, the train master cried "poles." And every teamster brings the extra wagon tongue he always carries with him and lays it devotedly down at the General's feet. These poles are then placed crosswise—two or three layers of them . . . and the crevices are filled with brush, sod, mown rushes and every available substance three or four hundred bridge builders can lay their hands on. The bridge done, the artillery and ambulances are sent across, being of the lightest tonnage, and when they cut through repairs are made; then the mule teams are sent across."[25]

The poles, of course, were recovered after the last wagon crossed. This picture puts Custer in a more favorable light, under the leadership principle of not asking your men to do anything you would not do yourself. It goes some way to balancing his account against when he stayed at Fort Lincoln while the men were tormented by mosquitos. And, in fairness, there was a great amount of paperwork to do for the expedition, not least writing the extensive orders for the line of march and the conduct of the expedition while on the trail. Plus he wanted to finish his memoir.

Lt. Calhoun's diary for that same day reports: "Goose, an Indian [Lakota] scout informed the commanding officer that no timber would be seen for many miles, and that wood would have to be carried in the wagons for purposes of fuel. The company commanders were informed accordingly." As an afterthought, Calhoun wrote: "Lt. McIntosh kicked by a horse."[26] From the perspective of a century and a half this may seem comical, but it illustrates a fundamental fact of military life then—accidents were as likely to injure, and worse, a soldier, as enemy action. Indeed, historian Robert Utley suggests that a soldier on the frontier could expect a fight with the Indians about once every five years.[27] He was far more likely to meet his maker from an accident or malady. Fractious animals; ever-present firearms that could and did go off accidentally; unwieldy equipment such as wagons; uneven trails; bad weather; poor food (and the wrong kind); contaminated drinking water; to say nothing of too much alcohol, also of the wrong kind; sudden storms that drenched soldiers who had, at best, one change of underwear—all were accidents or diseases waiting to snare the unlucky or inattentive soldier. In one of the many crossings Curtis described a teamster who was thrown under the wheels of his wagon; his leg was broken in two places.[28] Then, too, the Plains had more than its share of troublesome critters: "One horse, Company K, 7th Cavalry, bitten by a rattlesnake. Ammonia administered."[29] There is not much mention of these creatures in the soldiers' diaries, but they do mention that the troopers were careful to beat the ground around their proposed tent site before setting up. It was hardly the most reassuring way to begin the night's much-needed rest. (The horse survived.) One of the teamsters, a man known as Antelope Fred, said the prairie was alive with rattlers. Antelope Fred drove the General's private ambulance, which housed Custer's growing collection of animals and creatures, including several rattlesnakes. Custer was an inveterate collector of animals, alive and dead, and ultimately donated his Black Hills collection to an eastern zoo. Ewert, with some justification, criticizes this: "The best ambulance was taken to transport Negro servants [Aunt Sally, the cook], rattlesnakes, porcupines, owls, etc., while the enlisted man, for whose use all the ambulances were taken, had to crawl into an old broken-springed one, there to have the remaining spark of life jolted out of him."[30] Implicit in this statement is the fact that the ambulances had better springs than other army wagons.

Happily the prairie was well supplied with game. Pronghorn antelope abounded and seemed to have little fear of the strange procession crossing their territory. Indeed, the hunting was so good that most of the beef herd made it back to Fort Lincoln in good condition. Game took their place. As Grinnell says of the hunting in general and Custer in particular: "General Custer was friendly, sociable and agreeable. He was very fond of hunting and a great believer in his skill as a rifle shot. He had with him a pack of greyhounds and scotch deer hounds that he thought very highly of and which he told everyone had overtaken and killed many antelope. They did nothing of this kind on the Black Hills Expedition and, though they chased antelope frequently, they never caught any. They did kill plenty of jack rabbits."[31] With tongue placed gently in cheek, Grinnell is suggesting that Custer's opinion of his own marksmanship was something short of accurate. Grinnell's sidekick, Luther North, once "wiped Custer's eye" by shooting the heads off three swimming ducks after Custer had missed all three. And since the pronghorn is the fastest mammal in the Western Hemisphere, it seems that Custer's claims about his hounds might not bear too much scrutiny. (Interestingly, pronghorns can run like the wind, but they cannot jump.)

The appearance of antelope caused great excitement among the troops. In one case the troops assigned to a Gatling gun abandoned their team to chase pronghorns, whereupon the startled horses broke and ran and over-turned the Gatling. Other troops began firing in all directions, once again demonstrating that they could be as dangerous to each other as the hostile Sioux. The incident resulted in orders there would be no firing within five hundred yards of the outermost troopers. But organized hunting did continue, to the delight of the men assigned and to the delight of the men provided with fresh meat.

Beyond whether there would be hot coffee that night, other questions nagged the troopers—where were the Sioux, and when would they attack? People interested in history look back on an event like this expedition and conclude that it was pretty tame. Nothing much really happened—though the subsequent events turned out to be significant. But for a soldier or an officer, there was the here and now, and there was a future that was only something to be imagined. And many of these imaginings were disturbing, if not frightful. A fighting man cannot know what lies ahead. The mere fact of his willingness to go is, in many ways, his most important badge of courage, because he goes into the unknown and confronts sometimes dreadful images in his imagination. Some troopers, of course, had no choice. But that didn't matter—they still had to look into the face of what they feared. Ernest Hemingway, much maligned by some for his hairy-chested posture on combat, was in fact correct when he said that cowardice is essentially the inability to control the imagination.[32]

Some of the places along the trail were truly appalling. As Ewert wrote: "The country around the caves is poor, rocky and literally one vast cactus bed. Our horses were in constant misery; their fetlocks were pierced by thousands of their sharp needles causing our trail to be spotted with quite an amount of blood."[33]

The "caves" Ewert refers to was Ludlow's Cave, named in honor of Chief Engineer William Ludlow. Scouts Goose and Bloody Knife both extolled the wonders of this place and its mysterious functions, and so Custer took time out to explore it. The sandstone walls of the cave were covered with petroglyphs of animals and people. Outside they found a human skull with a bullet hole above the eye. The surgeons examined it and decided it was the skull of a white man. Goose and Bloody Knife explained that the cave was the home of the Great Spirit, to which a waggish reporter responded: "My opinion is that the God or Gods of the Indian could find a more agreeable place to spend his leisure time were they to try very hard."[34] Ewert was similarly unimpressed with the cave, although the officers and men did find a variety of utensils scattered on the floor of the cave. Custer found a flintlock pistol.

As the expedition wound its way southwest and then turned south, the general opinion about the value of the country was pretty strongly negative. July 17 was a representative day. As they approached the Black Hills they traversed country along the border of Wyoming and South Dakota and suffered through some rough going. The reporter for the *St. Paul*

Daily Pioneer Press wrote: "To add to the nothingness of the vegetation, a scraggly brush plant called by the Indians 'Grease weed,' puts in an appearance and helps suck up the little moisture from the heated earth and air. The better parts of this miserable region are settled by prairie dogs and rattlesnakes."[35] Lieutenant Col. Fred Grant added to this: "Went into camp on a bluff on the edge of some of the worst country I have ever seen. Grass very good, water poor and no wood in camp."[36] If it was not one thing, it was another. Some camps had drinkable water but poor grazing; others had the grazing but poor water. And wood was a continuing problem. After a long day traveling through rugged country, they went into camp only to be greeted by a Dakota zephyr that arrived without its usual partner in mischief, the rain. Captain Ludlow wrote: "During the night heavy clouds and lightning appeared, and toward morning, a severe windstorm routed us from our sleep and covered us with sand."[37] Correspondent Curtis added: "Near midnight everyone awakened by the swaying and flapping of his tent, and terrible clouds of dust drifted under the curtains with every gust. The whole heavens were covered with heavy, black-hooded, rifting clouds, broken momentarily by vivid flashes of lightning. The air was hot, dry and heavy, and the wind came in sudden gusts with a force that tore the tent pins from the earth as if they were leaves."[38] The only advantage gained from the storm was that it blew away the clouds of mosquitos that had descended prior to the awakening of the wind.

The terrible weather was the sort of thing that discouraged civilian observers of the expedition. They had come thinking they might be introduced to an Eden, rich in natural beauty and natural resources, and were disgusted at the reality of what they saw. A few eruptions of lignite here and there offered nothing in the way of potential wealth. (Lignite is a soft, brown, combustible fuel, midway between peat and bituminous coal.) The nearly unanimous opinion of the reporters and the "bug hunters" to this point was to let the Indians have the place and good luck to them. As Curtis wrote: "A few such nights will leave life little worth living for."[39]

But Custer's luck seemed to be holding, if only just. He had found enough grazing and enough water and enough wood—although not always together—to get the column to the Hills, or close enough to them. On July 18 the expedition finally arrived at the Belle Fourche River, and from there the troops could glimpse the dark massif that was their goal. The darkness alone was encouraging, because it came from the pines that seemed to be endless. There would finally be sufficient wood. And although the darkness and the escarpments of the Hills were in some ways ominous, at least the troops could look forward to hot food, and there would be good mountain springwater and meadows of grass for the overworked and underfed animals. The basics of life would be provided and not in the improvised fashion of the expedition so far. Everything suddenly seemed hopeful. And, maybe . . . maybe there was gold in that looming darkness. People said that it was there. Many believed it. Now the troops would find out for themselves, and now their often miserable journey to this point seemed, perhaps, worthwhile.

CHAPTER FOURTEEN

IN THE MOON OF
BLACK CHERRIES

*We cut plenty of tepee poles up along the creeks that came
down the east side of the Black Hills, and there was all we
wanted to eat, for the Hills were like a big food pack for our
people.*

—Black Elk[1]

The health of my command continues excellent.

—Custer Dispatch to Headquarters[2]

The rain came as the troops were camped along the Belle Fourche, and since the earth was slippery clay, the wagons could not move. Custer used the day to give the men some much-needed rest and to scout the trail for the next day. As it turned out, that trail would lead south along the western edges of the Hills.

In general, for such a large expedition, Custer was right about the health of this command. There was no fighting and would be none, so there would be no combat casualties. But there was disease and dispute. One trooper named Roller shot another soldier for no apparent reason other than bad blood. The two had fought before with fists, but this time there were guns involved. The wounded man died that night with a bullet in his spine. The shooter was, of course, arrested.[3]

And there were other casualties. Before the expedition returned home, three men would die of dysentery from drinking alkali water and from the neglect of the surgeons who pronounced the men fit for service, although they could not stay upright in their saddles. The two doctors thereafter became the pariahs of Pvt. Theodore Ewert's Company H, in particular. It is touching to read Ewert's descriptions of his own and his comrades' reactions. The men were not killed in action against the enemy. But they had given their lives, reluctantly, of course, and they were legitimate casualties of war. The first dysentery casualty and the man shot by a comrade were buried with appropriate honors (the other two would die later in the expedition). Three shots were fired over their graves and a bugler sounded "Taps." But then a fire was built over their graves to obscure their resting places so that the Indians would not dig up the bodies to collect what they wanted to collect. That, in itself, was disturbing to the troops. They were saddened by the deaths—to be shot by a comrade or to be neglected by someone in authority on whom you had no recourse but to rely was profoundly depressing to the troops. It was a sad fate to be buried in the wilderness in a grave obscured by fires, and the soldiers felt it keenly. They knew these men, and it was not hard to imagine themselves suffering a similar fate. They were left behind forever, for who of their families would ever come to tend these graves? How could they even find them?[4]

But soon everything changed. The troops had arrived in a country that was the polar opposite of the inhospitable prairie they had just traversed. They had reached the Black Hills. What had been a miserably inconsistent country, hardly a modern Eden, now changed into what the troops had hoped for. As Lt. James Calhoun described the route through the valley leading to the Hills he said: "Passed through a magnificent country. The finest quality of grass I ever saw."[5] He went on to say: "As I gaze upon this particular spot, I think that it is a great pity that this rich country should remain in a wild state, uncultivated and uninhabited by civilized men. Here the wheel of industry could move to advantage. The propelling power of life in the shape of human labor is only wanting to make this a region of prosperity."[6] From the Lakota point of view, of course, it already was a region of prosperity and needed no assistance from the wheel of industry. If a circular image was appropriate, it would be the "sacred hoop of the people." But Calhoun of course saw things differently: "Man is the noblest work of God. In this wild region man will ultimately be seen in the full enjoyment of happiness obtained by honest labor. For the hives of industry will take the place of dirty wigwams. Civilization will ere long reign supreme and throw heathen barbarism into oblivion."[7] You could scarcely get a more succinct example of conventional white thought—labor, industry, civilization, and religion all combining to create true happiness. Wealth also was a welcome by-product—or the result of a properly organized way of life and living. The Black Hills therefore became a metaphor with two radically different meanings. For the whites the Hills were the next step in the advance of civilization and its agreed-upon virtues of labor, development, and wealth production. For the Lakota they represented nature's bounty and were therefore perfect as they were and needed no help from humans. They were living benefactors of the people, not an economic project. They dispensed the good things of life without being asked and required only appreciation and reverence. The Hills were an active natural force, not a passive resource to be exploited. As for honest labor, well, that was for women.

Suddenly the opinions of even the most skeptical civilians in the expedition made a dramatic turn. Calhoun goes on: "I asked several citizens accompanying the Expedition their opinion regarding the country travelled over today, and they told me freely that up to yesterday they had formed a very unfavorable impression concerning this region, but this morning their unfavorable opinion vanished like the 'morning cloud and early dew,' and they were astonished to behold such a sudden change. That it eclipsed anything they ever saw before, and that the valleys passed through could not be surpassed for agricultural purposes and natural beauty."[8]

Implicit in these observations is the assumption that the government would ultimately, and probably sooner rather than later, decide to acquire the Black Hills. The agricultural potential alone would be irresistible, especially since all the world knew that the current owners did not farm, and would not farm, which meant that all this potential was simply wasted on them. And that acquisition, that transfer from one culture to another, would in fact happen within just a few years. But by then Calhoun would have been killed along with his brother-in-law in a battle that hardened the government's determination to extinguish the Lakota title to the Hills. And so it's at least reasonable to say that although Custer and his men lost the battle of the Little Bighorn, they won or at least contributed to winning or, perhaps more accurately, to *acquiring* the Black Hills.

The expedition passed Inyan Kara Mountain in Wyoming and camped near its base. This was where the troops buried the two men, one the victim of dysentery, the other of a gunshot. The next day the command did not move, while Custer and some of the scientists and two companies left to explore Inyan Kara partially in the hope of spotting an entry into the Hills to the east, but the hazy atmosphere frustrated them. The next day, July 24, the expedition moved out and entered the Hills proper. Calhoun writes: "We travelled through the Hills and encountered many bad roads. I never thought it possible that a wagon train could move in such a country."[9] The Indian scouts agreed. Not so Custer. The pioneers were kept busy clearing rocks and cutting trees, and the wagons struggled up one side of the mountain and then down again as the troops and teamsters had to rope the heavy wagons down the side of rocky and tree-choked "road." It was hard work, to say the least, but the men were in better spirits because there were clear streams of pure water, plenty of wood, and grazing for the animals. Custer deserves credit for his determination and his engineering know-how, although of course in the latter case he had help. But no one could replace his will to proceed against very stiff environmental odds. After all, the difficulty of access had been one of the reasons no one had really penetrated the Hills before, certainly not a large expedition with wagons. Crossing and recrossing streams, the expedition wagons rumbled along slowly in single file, the teamsters swearing and sweating, the pioneer company chopping and levering obstacles, building bridges, and in general defeating terrain with muscle and know-how. The train gradually became strung out for miles, a situation that occurred frequently as Custer willed a line of heavy vehicles through country that could hardly accommodate a man on horseback. Had there been hostile Lakota in the vicinity, they would have had a cornucopia of easy targets and an escape route back into the Hills that could not have been followed. But there were no Lakota there now.

Finally the troops entered a valley that was covered with uncountable wildflowers of bewildering varieties and colors. The men were stunned by the beauty of the place, and they picked bouquets and wove strands of flowers and decorated their hats and their horses' manes. They camped there that night, and Samuel Barrows, the correspondent for the *Chicago Inter Ocean*, wrote that the band serenaded the men with "strains of music for the first time heard in paradise."[10] His use of the word "paradise" underscores the dramatic, almost unbelievable contrast between the dreary Plains and the sublime Black Hills. Perhaps some of the men also began to understand Lakota devotion to this place. And others, perhaps former farmers or stockmen, imagined coming back to this place as a civilian and building a ranch or farm here. And of course the chief fantasy on the minds of most was the possibility of gold. And was it a fantasy? They would soon know or at least have strong indications. All along the expedition trail the practical miners had been at work, but whenever they found a likely-looking location, they dug or panned and found nothing. But now they were in the Hills, and these pure streams must surely yield some "color." After all, the Hills had so far provided not only aesthetics but also abundant grazing, pure water, and endless timber. It only stood to reason that they would yield up the fourth natural resource the white men sought.

On July 26 scouts reported the presence of a small Lakota village. Apparently, these Lakota were entirely ignorant of the army's presence. There were five lodges and twenty-seven individuals, and so offered no threat, unless of course they were merely an outpost of a larger village. Custer led two companies of cavalry to the site and after surrounding and reconnoitering the still-unsuspecting village, he sent an interpreter and three scouts with a flag of truce into the suddenly astonished village. Guide Louis Agard explained that the army meant them no harm, and Custer came down to parlay. The village chief was out hunting, but the Lakota sent some children to fetch him. Also in the village was Slow Bull and his wife, who was said to be the daughter of Red Cloud. While waiting for the chief to arrive Slow Bull's wife, vastly relieved that the soldiers meant no harm, invited Custer and Barrows into her tepee. "A not uncomely squaw she was," wrote Barrows, "and was so glad that her husband and little ones were not going to be killed that she became very agreeable, and entertained us in a most lively manner. Her tepee was the cleanest and neatest of the five, in fact one of the few Indian tepees that invite an entrance."[11] As an aside, it's worth mentioning that Custer critics, who in some quarters caricature him as a homicidal Indian hater, might be abashed to recognize that, if Custer simply wanted to kill Indians, especially Sioux, here was a perfect opportunity.[12] His two companies of troops could have obliterated this tiny encampment with one or two volleys. There was no one around, no one to complain, no one to dispute the reason for an attack, and the after-action report could easily portray the village as hostile. Barrows was a witness, but he was friendly to Custer and could probably be relied upon to substantiate any claim Custer made. Besides, it would have been easy to precipitate a battle by merely charging into the camp. It would be the easiest of victories. The Arikara scouts, who hated the Sioux and were bent on revenge anyway, were all for it. But Custer had no intention of inflicting harm.

The chief arrived in due time—an ancient, rather ragged man in a battered felt hat with shirt and breechclout of a quality to match. His name was One Stab. He and Custer smoked a peace pipe, and Custer questioned him about the geography of the Hills. Not completely satisfied with the information, Custer invited One Stab and the others to come to Custer's camp, so that they could exchange sugar and coffee and bacon for more information. Four of the Lakota joined One Stab in camp later that afternoon, but angry looks were exchanged between them and the Arikara, especially Bloody Knife, who was looking for vengeance for the death of his son. Any Lakota would do. To emphasize his point, Bloody Knife and the other Arikara had put on their war paint, and the Lakota visitors were understandably alarmed. Accordingly, two of the four slipped away, only to be followed by the other two, who jumped on their horses and galloped away toward their village, leaving One Stab with Custer. Custer sent the scouts after the four, and there was tussle between one of the scouts and a Lakota who tried to grab the scout's rifle and, not succeeding, jumped back on his horse and rode away as fast as possible. But not fast enough, for the scout fired at him and, from the traces of blood found afterward, obviously hit something, whether horse or rider no one could tell. Custer said: "I hope that neither [horse nor rider] was seriously hurt, although the Indians had thus their bad faith as the sole ground for the collision."[13] This "bad faith" in part consisted of a typical Indian ruse, not unlike the decoy, for while the four and One Stab were visiting camp, the rest of the village was packing up and escaping. When the scouts went to the site of One Stab's village the inhabitants were gone. Custer decided to keep One Stab as a hostage cum guide, but toward the end of the expedition he released One Stab with his horse, rifle, and sufficient rations to sustain him on his trip back to the Red Cloud Agency—much to the disgust of Bloody Knife, who wanted to kill and scalp the elderly chief. And while Custer did not learn very much from One Stab, he did determine that the Black Hills were not alive with enemies. He and his men were the only warriors for miles. Well, almost. The band, including a young Black Elk, had been camping in the Black Hills, too, but when they learned that the soldiers were coming, they packed up and fled into the night. So Custer and his men had the Black Hills to themselves.

> *THE MOST BEAUTIFUL VALLEYS THE EYE HAS EVER RESTED UPON. GOLD AND SILVER IN IMMENSE QUANTITIES. NO FIGHTING WITH THE SIOUX.*
> —*Bismarck Tribune*, headline,
> August 12, 1874

Having visited and camped in lovely places like the Floral Valley, the expedition's labors were not over. Camping in lush valleys meant climbing steep ridges and mountain trails or thrashing through ravines clogged by rocks, trees, and underbrush to find the next valley, the next creek. Sometimes they struggled into blind canyons and had to reverse course. As Calhoun wrote in his July 29 diary entry:

> This is a hard day's march for the wagon train—Very bad roads. Hard work for the pioneer party. Travelled through narrow ravines, timbered hills, steep and stony places. Arriving in the valley encountered four bad crossings. The Hills had a beautiful silver appearance, caused by the shining surface of mica. One artillery carriage broken. Lt. Chance, 17th Infantry, Officer in Charge of the Artillery Det. received a kick from a horse ridden by Captain French and was badly hurt. A private in Company C, 7th Cavalry, accidently wounded in the right arm from a carbine shot. The wagon train did not reach our camp tonight.[14]

On the thirtieth day of July the troops went into camp near French Creek, a small rivulet that runs through a valley south of Harney Peak. A reasonably fit person could jump over it. The following day would be a day of rest. While Custer, Brevet Lt. Col. William Ludlow, and Major "Sandy" Forsyth led a small detachment about ten miles north to explore Harney Peak, the men played baseball; the "Athletes" versus the "Actives," with the Actives winning 11 to 6. Later, while the cat was still away, Major Joseph Tilford hosted a champagne supper for a number of the officers. The Company H "glee club" serenaded the party and received a couple of bottles of whiskey from correspondent Barrows in return for the music. Brevet Lt. Col. Fred Grant participated in the champagne festivities enthusiastically, and although he apparently had what the Irish call "a strong weakness" for alcohol, he was by no means unique among the officers, and he did not seem to be a troublesome drinker. Photographer William Illingworth recorded the festivities. Glowering in the rear of the photograph is Captain Frederick Benteen; he and Tilford shared not only a bottle or two but also their enduring distaste for their commander.

While the officers and men were enjoying their rest, the two miners were panning French Creek. They found promising "color."

July gave way to August, the month the Lakota called The Moon of Black Cherries, and the command moved downstream a few miles and set up what they intended to be a more permanent camp. Calhoun writes:

> Made a short march of 3 ½ miles. The change of camp was desirable on account of grazing. Before our view spreads forth a lovely sight. In our front extends one of the most beautiful parks the human eye ever beheld. I have travelled extensively both in Europe and America, and I have never seen a more elegant park. Here Nature in all her glory has performed a system of created things perfect and wonderful. The ornamental parks and graceful enclosures which I have seen in London, Liverpool, Paris, New York and Philadelphia cannot present such a natural appearance for beauty as this park. . . . Excellent grazing. A large stream of water running through camp.[15]

What could be better? Even if there was no gold in the Black Hills, the quality of the countryside and environment would draw farmers and ranchmen and timber companies, once the news of the new Eden reached civilization. But there was still more good news to come. The next day,

August 2, Calhoun's laconic diary entry read: "The prospectors accompanying the Expedition discovered gold this morning."[16]

Having found hopeful indications when panning the creek, the miners began digging. They dug a grave-sized hole next to French Creek and extracted about fifty pinhead-sized grains of gold. It could hardly qualify as a bonanza, but it was enough, for this was the start of the Black Hills gold rush and the beginning of the end for the Lakota title to the Hills.

The miners estimated that when properly worked the diggings could result in ten cents a pan. In *Custer's Gold* historian Donald Jackson suggests that an average team of miners with even marginal experience could shovel fifteen hundred pans a day; at that rate the find seemed to justify enthusiasm. One hundred and fifty dollars a day is roughly $3,100 in 2015 currency. One of the miners, Ross, was sure that there were richer diggings nearby, but he doubted that the finds along this section would yield more than seventy-five dollars a day. Even so, to a thirteen-dollar-a-month trooper, that was big money. And it was big money to unemployed laborers in eastern slums and western frontier towns, big money to farmers suffering from drought and grasshopper infestations, big money to immigrants bewildered by the lack of opportunity in what they had thought was the land of opportunity. Small wonder then that excitement about the find spread—and would spread quickly throughout the country. Custer would see to it, helped by the journalists whose excitement about the find was enhanced and redoubled by the glittering prospect of a scoop.

The troops gathered along the creek and started digging with whatever tools they could find or borrow from the pioneer wagon. Twenty-one of the more entrepreneurial and forward-looking formed the Custer Park Mining Company and staked claims along the creek, both above and below the initial dig. Aunt Sally, the sutler's cook, was one of the members of the company. Of course, these claims were not legal, since they were on Sioux land. But few if any of the troops worried about that, for they operated as if they were quite certain that the Sioux title was soon to be a matter of history, after which the company's claims could be registered and made legal.

It's significant that the very next day after the discovery Custer took five companies of cavalry on a scout to the south. The stated objective was to explore the lower half of the Hills and to examine the South Fork of the Cheyenne River. But also to the south lay Fort Laramie, the nearest telegraph station, and when they got to the southern edges of the Hills, "Lonesome" Charley Reynolds set off on a ninety-mile solo ride to Fort Laramie. He carried Custer's report to headquarters, and he carried the journalists' stories. In her book *Boots and Saddles* Libbie Custer describes Reynolds's ride: "He had only his compass to guide him, for there was not even a trail. The country was infested with Indians, and he could only travel at night. During the day he hid his horse as well as he could in the underbrush, and lay down in the long grass. In spite of these precautions he was sometimes so exposed that he could hear the voices of the Indians passing near." Water was either scarce or nonexistent. By the end of the ride "his lips were so parched and his throat so swollen that he could not close his mouth."[17] His horse was so exhausted that Reynolds had to lead him. But after four nights of travel, he delivered the news.

Custer's report recounts the expedition's adventures to this point, and when he gets to the subject of the Hills' natural resources, he writes:

> The main portion of that passed over since entering the unexplored portion of the Black Hills consists of beautiful parks and valleys, through which flows a stream of clear, cold water, perfectly free from alkali, while bounding these parks or valley is invariably found unlimited supplies of timber, much of it capable of being made into good lumber. In no portion of the United States, not excepting the famous blue-grass region of Kentucky [which Custer knew well], have I ever seen grazing superior to that found growing wild in this hitherto unknown region. I know of no portion of our country where nature has done so much to prepare homes for husbandmen, and left so little for the latter to do, than here. . . . I could contrast the bright green verdure of these lovely parks with the sunburned and dried yellow herbage to be seen on the outer plains.[18]

As he wrote this, Custer must have breathed an inward sigh of relief that he had successfully crossed the dried-out prairie and reached these Hills with his stock still intact. Of course, there was still the return trip to contemplate, but there would be time to let the men and animals rest, regain weight and fitness, and prepare for the arduous journey home.

Custer also no doubt recognized that the superior quality of grazing in the Hills would have been just as important to the Lakota, since their ponies approached starvation on the Plains in the winter but could actually do well if grazed in the Hills. As Calhoun writes: "From reliable sources. . . . I am informed that Indian ponies wintered in the Black Hills all come out fat in the spring."[19] Whether that was true or not, Custer and the other officers believed it. Custer writes: "Cattle could winter in these valleys without other food or shelter than that to be obtained from running at large."[20] And since Indians intent on depredations were dependent upon their ponies, which, in turn, were entirely dependent on grass, Custer and his officers would have regarded the Hills as the equivalent of an enemy fuel and supply dump and, for that reason alone, as a valuable capture and an additional justification for placing a fort in the vicinity. So whether or not the Hills eventually became a hive of white industry and agriculture, they had significant military value that had only been theorized before; now the theory had been proved.

But Custer was saving the best for last. He goes on for seven pages before dropping his bombshell:

> As there are scientists accompanying the expedition who are examining into the mineral resources of this region, the result of whose researches will accompany my detailed report, I omit all present reference to that portion of our explorations until the return of the expedition except to state, *what will appear in any event in the public prints* that gold has been found at several places, and it is the belief of those who are giving their attention to this subject that it will be found in paying quantities. I have on my table forty or fifty small particles of pure gold, in size averaging that of a small pinhead, and most of it obtained today from one panful of earth.[21](italics added)

Custer's nose for publicity was keenly developed. It's reasonable to assume he knew exactly what he was doing as he wrote the report. First he extolled the aesthetic and the agricultural potential of the Hills—and by those criteria alone implied that the Hills were a paradise for sturdy yeomen farmers, stockmen, and loggers. And by placing the discovery of gold toward the end of the report he suggested that it was unwise to get too excited, that so far they had only collected fifty or so grains of *pure gold* and that most of it had come from *one panful of earth*. And he went on to say that "veins of lead and strong indications of silver have been found." *But . . . let's not get carried away quite yet*: "Until further examination is made regarding the richness of the gold, no opinion should be formed."[22]

Custer's report is a classic example of diplomacy and self-promotion by modesty and indirection. And it's even fair to think that he may have been entirely sincere, that he did favor the obvious agricultural resources and was hesitant about the mineral finds, which, after all, were not obvious and had to be investigated further. But even if he was sincere in his caution, he knew that he had achieved a coup. If there turned out to be rich gold, he would have the credit for discovering it. If it turned out that, in either quantity or quality, the gold was not worth digging for, he would not have made any unjustifiable or exaggerated claims. He was simply reporting the facts. Further, his position on the matter would be made clear to all concerned, because he could be confident his entire report would be reprinted in the national press, just as his earlier reports on the Yellowstone expedition had been. And if, as it turned out, the journalists' stories that Lonesome Charley was also carrying were less retrained and measured, well, there was nothing Custer could do about that. They were an excitable lot, these journalists—some of them, anyway. Custer could not control what they might say. But in his private letter to Libbie, written that same day, August 2, he said: "I wish I could go into more detail in describing the expedition, which has exceeded all previous ones, and in success has surpassed my most sanguine expectations. . . . *We have discovered gold without a doubt*, and probably other valuable metals."[23] His public position was cautious for reasons of diplomacy and public image, but his letter to Libbie contained no hedging. Despite his officially conservative stance, he must have known he had just pulled the army's and the government's institutional finger from the dike. When the news got out, the miners would come flooding in.

"Confirmed!!" blared the headlines of the August 12 *Bismarck Tribune*. "Custer's Official Report! The Black Hills Country. Gold Bearing Quartz Crops Out in Every Hill. Fifty Pieces of Gold as Large as Pin Heads from One Pan." The accompanying story said: "Here in Custer's Valley, rich gold and silver mines have been discovered, both placer and quartz diggings; and this immense section bids fair to become the El Dorado of America."[24] (A placer mine is one that the rankest amateur can manage; it involves digging shovelfuls of dirt and then washing it with a pan or in a sluice box to separate the heavier grains of gold from the dirt. Of course, the miner has to be able to distinguish gold from other materials, but that education was relatively quick and painless, although none other than Mark Twain as a neophyte miner had several hours of euphoria when he mistook fool's gold for the real thing. Quartz mining requires heavier equipment to crush gold-bearing rock.)

Headlines in the *Chicago Inter Ocean* competed in sensationalizing the story: "The Glittering Treasure Found At Last," "A Belt of Gold Territory Thirty Miles Wide."[25] William Curtis's story for the *Chicago Inter Ocean* was equally effusive: "All the camp is aglow with gold fever. . . . This is the first opportunity our miners have had to make a really fair test of the 'color,' and it has yielded them abundantly. . . . *From the grass roots down it was 'pay dirt,'* and after a dozen pans or more had been washed out, the two persevering men who will be the pioneers of a new golden state came into camp with a little yellow dust wrapped carefully up in the leaf of an old account book."[26]

"From the grass roots down, it was paydirt." It was the siren song to desperate and ambitious men everywhere. "If the whole army of the United States stood in the way, the wave of emigration would pass over it to seek the valley where gold was to be found." This from US Senator John Sherman, the general's brother. And he made this statement to the Senate in 1867, well before the depression had arrived and with it the hordes of unemployed native-born Americans and the corresponding influx of impoverished immigrants. In the year of the Black Hills expedition the depression was crushing the economy, and the *Bismarck Tribune* said: "As the Christian looks forward with hope and faith to that land of pure delight, so the miner looks forward to the Black Hills, a region of fabulous wealth, where the rills repose on beds of gold and the rocks are studded with precious metals."[27] It's not hard to imagine the effect this sort of prose had on an unemployed artisan living in an eastern slum or on a farmer surveying dusty fields laid waste by drought and grasshoppers. Their first thought would be to grab a shovel, their second to wonder how they could get to the Hills—and how quickly. Many would take the Northern Pacific Railroad, still operating under bankruptcy and no doubt grateful for the sudden swell of new passenger business. (Returning to Bismarck the following winter, Libbie Custer describes an NPRR train equipped with snow plows and "the Black Hills miners who filled the passenger coaches."[28] And this in the dead of the dreadful Dakota winter.)

Never mind that there were cautionary voices, such as William Barrows. In his report to the *New York Tribune* he reminded his readers that the Hills were owned by the Sioux, who were committed to blocking any white incursion into tribal lands. They had objected strenuously to the army's expedition even though that could be viewed as technically legal—and was viewed that way by the government. But an invasion of white miners was strictly illegal and undeniably so, and the Sioux would consider it within their rights to attack and massacre shovel-wielding white men. Barrows wrote: "Those who seek the Hills only for gold must be prepared to take their chances. . . . The Black Hills . . . are not without ready-made monuments for the martyrs who might perish in their parks."[29] But Barrows didn't say there was no gold there, only that it would be dangerous to seek it. To a rough-and-ready frontiersman, to an unemployed laborer, to a recent immigrant with no understanding of the West and its fearsome natives, that warning would be filed under the "noted" category. Disregarding any and all pessimistic or cautionary voices, the would-be miners would pack their gear, say good-bye to loved ones, and head for the Hills to search for what Black Elk called "the yellow metal that makes the Wasichus crazy."[30]

CHAPTER FIFTEEN

HOMEWARD BOUND

I have achieved the hunter's highest round of fame. I have killed my grizzly.

> —George Armstrong Custer,
> letter to his wife, Libbie

I knew it was no grizzly, but a genuine cinnamon. . . . General Custer, of course, wishes to magnify his discoveries to the fullest extent.

> —Private Theodore Ewert,
> *Private Theodore Ewert's Diary of the*
> *Black Hills Expedition of 1874*, 1976

On his scout to the south, Custer had reached the South Fork of the Cheyenne River on the southern edge of the Black Hills. That part of the Hills was less appealing than the northern half. As Lt. James Calhoun wrote on August 4, "The greater part of the country travelled over today is uninviting and not worthy of notice."[1] And by the time the troops reached the river they could see the dreary Plains stretching southward. From there Custer sent "Lonesome" Charley Reynolds on his dangerous mission to Fort Laramie and turned around and headed back toward French Creek. There he reorganized the expedition and prepared to start for home the following day, August 6.

Custer and the expedition headed north, back to Fort Lincoln from the "permanent camp" along French Creek. He had completed most of his mission. He had explored the Black Hills and found them rich in natural resources of the kind to gladden the hearts of farmers, ranchers, and timber merchants. And he had discovered gold. Gold! What's more, the broad valleys in the Hills offered various locations for a fort, and assuming, as he no doubt did, that the Sioux title would be extinguished, and soon, a fort in the interior would be useful to protect the influx of miners and settlers, an influx that was as inevitable as the resulting Sioux enmity. True, supplying such a fort might prove difficult given the rugged access into the Hills, but it could be done. Certainly he believed that the army could build and maintain sufficient access roads to make a fort in the interior a viable proposition. Given enough manpower and proper leadership, the army could do almost anything involving engineering. The Black Hills escarpments and narrow canyons that had daunted civilian explorers would be widened and smoothed by army engineers and pioneer companies. If he could now get his command back to Lincoln with a minimum of loss to his troops and his animals, he could justifiably regard the expedition as a smashing success. And he had no difficulty imagining the laurels he would receive.

But while still on the expedition Custer intended to examine another possible site for a fort on the Plains. For that reason he intended to move the column northeast to explore the region around Bear Butte, which was on the Plains just a handful of miles from the Black Hills. In other words, he would not go home exactly the way he came. This makes perfect sense in retrospect, for, after all, there was every possibility that new and important discoveries lay to the northeast, and nothing more could be learned by retracing his route to the Hills. There was of course the thorny question of grazing and water, but the trip down to the Hills had been sketchy in those departments, so there was an even chance that a different route north would be better. As it turned out, though, it wasn't.

On August 7 Custer and a small entourage arrived at that evening's campsite far ahead of the train, as usual, and, thinking to use the rest of the day scouting the trail for the next day, he rode ahead with Bloody Knife, Colonel William Ludlow, and his orderly, Private John Noonan. Bloody Knife was the first to spot a bear lolling on the hillside "about seventy five yards away."[2] Whether it was a grizzly or a "cinnamon" was a question that only the skeptical Ewert seemed to ask. A "cinnamon" bear is a black bear with a lighter-colored coat. And, as many people know, there's a significant difference between a black bear and a grizzly. Black bears are generally shy and usually not dangerous unless startled or aggressively confronted. Most often, when they see a human, they will scamper away at a surprisingly high rate of speed. Grizzly bears are much larger, bad-tempered, and dangerous all the time, and if they are running in any direction it's probably toward, rather than away from, you. Not for nothing is the grizzly designated "Ursus arctos horribilis."

Custer took the first and second shots and hit the old stager, first in the thigh and then in some undetermined place. Seventy-five yards is a very short rifle shot, especially with the Remington hunting rifle Custer was using, and although he didn't miss, Custer might have done better. Had George Bird Grinnell been there he would have remembered his sly comment that Custer was "a great believer in his skill as a rifle shot."[3] The other three men opened fire, too, and the bear went down. Bloody Knife finally had a chance to live up to his name and finished the bear by cutting his jugular. Photographer William Illingworth arrived on the scene later and took a picture of the four men and the bear, which was well past its prime; its broken teeth and scars showed the effects of many ancient battles. Still, everyone except the dismissive Private Ewert agreed it was a grizzly, and even though all four men fired, and all four hit the bear, the honors were awarded to the general, as might be expected. The meat was distributed to the troops, but it was tough and rank, and, although some of the men may have appreciated the gesture, they did not care much for the meat.[4]

The trip to Bear Butte was difficult. Simply finding a way out of the Hills was a problem. As Custer reported: "In every instance we were led into deep, broken canyons, impassable even to horsemen."[5] His use of the passive voice here is interesting, since he generally was the pathfinder—he and the scouts. More than once the command had to turn around and retrace their steps. Calhoun wrote: "Dead and fallen trees lie across our path. Nothing but huge rocks and concretion of earth welcome our onward march."[6] But there was pure water and plenty of wood and grazing. And it rained. The rain was not unwelcome. Memories of the treeless, water-less prairie made a few showers at the very least tolerable. As Calhoun wrote: "We had a copious shower today. [August 10] I have omitted to mention that rains are copious and frequent, rendering irrigation unnecessary. There is constant moisture in the ground, caused by heavy dews, and everything tends to make this a most desirable farming country."[7]

The welcome combination of water, grazing, and wood would disappear when they finally found an exit from the Black Hills bastion—which they did on August 14, after burying another trooper who died from an unspecified disease and, according to Ewert, from the criminal neglect of the "inhuman brutes with us called doctors."[8] The soldier, a man called King, was popular with his company, and there were mutterings about an eye for an eye, for it would have been easy enough to inflict a similar fate on one or both of the doctors. It was, after all, a big country—an easy place to disappear in. But nothing happened, and the doctors continued their bibulous travels homeward, while the troopers mourned their "dear, good, honored and respected comrade."[9] It's worth mentioning that during the expedition two of the three deaths from disease were suffered by men in Company H, which was commanded by Frederick Benteen. It's fair to say that a commander who had the welfare of his troops uppermost in his mind would have been more alert to the severity of the men's condition and more active in ensuring proper medical treatment. The doctors were not the only ones who could be charged with neglect. Benteen proved that he was a good and courageous combat leader on Reno Hill during the Battle of the Little Bighorn. But whether he was a good officer is another question.

Finally the expedition was back on the Plains again. Calhoun wrote:

We are bidding adieu to a country which has been to us a source of real pleasure. Farewell ye lofty hills of western beauty. Farewell ye meadows of verdant pasture. Farewell ye rich valleys and timbered hills. We know that this is the best country that can be found in any of the Northwestern states, and when we move for days upon an open prairie beneath a burning sun, with nothing but warm alkali water to quench our thirst, we will be reminded of the many cold springs of pure water which flowed sweetly from the mountain side, and often will we turn round and cast a wistful desire toward these prominent hills which for many a day afforded us so much enjoyment.[10]

Custer agreed. In his second report to Headquarters, written on August 15, he said, in part: "Behind us the grass and foliage was [*sic*] clothed in green of the freshness of May. In front of us as we cast our eyes over the Plains below, we saw nothing but a comparatively parched, dried surface, the sunburnt pasturage of which offered a most uninviting prospect both to horse and rider."[10] No doubt the prospect was a little daunting; he still had a couple of hundred miles to go, and the sight of that parched grass was surely worrisome. But he went on in his report to extoll the many virtues of the Black Hills, this time with slightly less restraint than in his first report:

> From the fact that in all our principal marches through the Black Hills we have taken, without serious obstacle, a heavily laden train of over one hundred wagons, it may be inferred that the Black Hills do not constitute the impenetrable region heretofore represented. In entering the Black Hills from any direction, the most serious, if not the only obstacles, were encountered at once, near the outer base. This probably accounts for the mystery which has long existed regarding the character of the interior. . . . No portion of the United States can boast of a richer soil, better pasturage, purer water . . . and of greater advantages generally to the farmer or stock raiser than can be found in the Black Hills. . . . Building stone of the best quality is to be found in inexhaustible quantities; wood for fuel and lumber sufficient for all time to come. Rains are frequent with no evidence in the country of either drouths or freshets. The season, perhaps, is too short and the nights too cool for corn, but I believe all other grain could be produced in wonderful abundance. Wheat would particularly yield largely.[11]

It's worth remembering that Custer was raised on a farm and so could be expected to know at least something about agricultural potential. Then, too, certainly many of his officers and noncommissioned officers would have agricultural experience worth listening to. It's also significant that he mentions wheat in particular, since, as mentioned earlier, wheat was the nation's principal export in the early 1870s—obviously transported from those farms, mostly midwestern, that had escaped the grasshopper infestations. Further, the news that wheat might be grown in high altitudes that avoided the infestations would have been welcome to struggling farmers on the Plains. Custer was certainly aware of the plight of the prairie farmers when he wrote this report.

Then there was the heart of the matter: gold: "I referred in a former dispatch of the discovery of gold. Subsequent examinations at numerous points confirm and strengthen the fact of the existence of gold in the Black Hills. On some of the water courses almost every panful of earth produced gold in small, yet paying quantities. . . . It has not required an expert to find gold in the Black Hills, as men without former experience in mining have discovered it at an expense of little time or labor."[12] Here he must have been referring to the troops who had joined the practical miners alongside French Creek.

In conclusion, Custer said that his beef herd, after traveling hundreds of miles to date, was in better condition than when he left; hunting had provided the expedition with most of its fresh meat: "I have never seen so many deer as in the Black Hills."[13] With his knowledge of the Plains Indians, Custer certainly understood that the Sioux and the tribes before them cherished the Black Hills *primarily because* it was a paradise for the hunter. It would not be difficult for a Sioux leader or ordinary warrior on the reservation to realize that, if they were deprived of this cornucopia of game, they would become almost entirely dependent on government handouts—handouts that were managed by often corrupt agents, and handouts that could be withheld if the tribes did not conform to the government's latest whims and demands. Even the non-treaty Indians who were still roaming and hunting would understand that a vast and vital hunting resource—forty-five hundred square miles of it—would have disappeared, leaving them to pursue the dwindling buffalo herds. Both actually and symbolically, the Black Hills stood between the Sioux and potential starvation, as well as the virtual end of their nomadic hunting culture.

Wrapping up his second report, Custer wrote: "We had no collision with hostile Indians."[14] Interestingly, Custer does not make any mention of a potential location for a fort; all his attention is on the richness of the Black Hills' natural resources. Perhaps he was waiting to discuss the issue with his superiors in person, but a skeptic might draw different conclusions. To wit: "I have seen and documented the richness of the Black Hills; now it's time to do something about their ownership."

An unemployed worker anywhere in the country would interpret Custer's message with no difficulty at all—gold was there in quantity and quality. Mining experience and capital were not necessary; a shovel, a pan, and a strong back were the only requirements. While you were gathering your wealth, you could live quite happily on game; you could cook it over a generous fire, for firewood was inexhaustible. And if you should wish to build a cabin, there was plenty of timber available and stone for walls and chimneys. You wouldn't go thirsty; water was abundant and pure. Your animals would thrive on the grasses. Once you got your wagons into the Hills, it was pretty easy going. Even better, the stories about dangerous Indians were exaggerated. After all, Custer didn't find many, and he was probably looking for them. The ragged handful he did find ran away. Of course, there may be a risk or two, but the risk/reward ratio was much more favorable than people had been led to believe.

The *Chicago Inter Ocean* agreed. An August 27 editorial said: "It would be a sin against the country and against the world to permit this region, so rich in treasure to remain unimproved and unoccupied, merely to furnish hunting grounds to savages."[15] This was more of the same sort of thing that was bruited before the expedition, but it had renewed and, ultimately, irresistible force, because of Custer's discoveries. Whereas the Black Hills' various riches had been before a matter of rumor and conjecture, now they were a matter of fact. The editorial was the result of William Curtis's reporting, for on the August 27 the expedition had not yet reached Fort Lincoln. Curtis's story had gone with the scouts who couriered Custer's second report back to Fort Lincoln.

Custer wrote his report beside Bear Butte, another of those startling ancient eruptions that dotted the Plains. The army would ultimately build a fort nearby—Fort Meade, which, as mentioned much earlier, was built to protect the growing number of mining towns and miners that had sprouted in the Black Hills because of the Custer expedition. But that fort was not built until 1878, well after Custer and his men had paid the price for their discovery—and for Custer's impetuosity. (No fort was ever built in the Black Hills proper. No doubt the army regarded cutting roads into and through the difficult access points to be unnecessary work and expense. Building on the Plains was easier; so was supply.)

But despite the optimism of Custer's second report and the euphoria of the journalist's stories, there was still a long stretch of barren prairie to cover before the expedition was successfully completed. And there was the ever-present danger of Indian attack.

Describing the homeward route, the reporter for the *St. Paul Daily Pioneer* wrote: "As a rule the grass becomes thinner and poorer and more dried up as we recede from the Hills. Cactus and small sage plant grows almost everywhere. Down some of the dry and dusty creek channels great torrents sometimes thirty feet high have at times washed down. Not a single spring has been found."[16]

Worse, as the column moved north they discovered huge swaths of prairie (fifty to seventy-five square miles[17]) where the grass had been burned, leaving only blackened and inedible stubble for as far as they could see. There was no way to know whether the fires had been caused by lightning or by the Indians (who often used prairie fires against their enemies or as a means of stampeding and concentrating game), or even possibly spread by careless campfires of the troops on the first leg of the expedition (a stiff west wind could spread grass fires with frightening speed). Whatever the cause, it was worrying; Custer had the same problem returning home as he did on the initial leg—there was not enough grain to go around if the grazing was inadequate. He responded by driving the men and animals harder and farther, and marches of thirty-plus miles per day were the occasional result. As usual, Custer was the pathfinder, and he managed to find enough unburned grass to keep the command moving. But it was the "nearest run thing." And gradually the animals began breaking down.

Rumors of imminent Indian attacks further enlivened the early stages of the march north. Some of the scouts had run across four Sioux on their way home to the Cheyenne River Agency. The four told the scouts that thousands of hostiles were waiting to attack the column somewhere near the Little Missouri River. They also said the hostiles had burned the grass for miles and miles; what's more, they had poisoned the streams. The rumors spread quickly and somehow and mysteriously even reached the eastern newspapers, which hysterically reported an actual battle. (Mail-carrying scouts were most likely the source of the stories.) None of that happened. The four Sioux were apparently exercising their talent for humor and no doubt rode away smiling. According to George Bird Grinnell, the Indian placed honesty alongside courage as a cardinal virtue,[18] but that did not extend to enemies, against whom any ruse was fair play.

The column went on heightened alert but continued on its weary and thirsty journey. On August 19 Calhoun wrote: "Thirty Five (35) mules played out today. Several horses abandoned. Bad water. Very little green herbage to be found. Marched 35 ½ miles."[19] The animals that were abandoned were shot to prevent their falling into the hands of the Indians, who could revive them and put them to good use. The ones that might have been saved but were too weak to be serviceable were unsaddled or unhitched and gathered into a herd of sorts that trudged along with the column. Calhoun's entry for the following day read: "As far as the eye can see the prairie is black with burnt grass. Water obtained about every ten miles. Several men very sick with typhoid dysentery. Marched thirty miles. Camped on the bank of the Little Missouri River. Good grazing."[20]

The Indians were said to be waiting in the valley of the Little Missouri, the precise destination of the expedition. But there were no hostiles and there was water and good grass there, and the played-out mules and horses rejoiced. Antelope Fred recalled: "It was astonishing to see horses and mules that could scarcely move during the day trot and even run to the water. The stream was literally black with them. It was very shallow and many of them laid down and could not rise without assistance."[21]

It would be another week before these travails would end. "The prairie is black all over;" wrote Calhoun on August 23. "No grass (except in isolated spots) to be found for our animals. Our animals are falling away fast. Lt. Chance had some trouble to get his artillery carriages into camp because so many of his horses played out. The grain which is given to the public animals would be quite sufficient if the grazing was good. It is the belief of many that the Indians put of pure mischief have set fire to the surrounding grass."[22] It was a reasonable supposition.

The implication of entries like this one is that the column was strung out over quite a distance. After all, the artillery's assigned position in the march was near the front of the column, yet on this day the artillery horses and their guns and caissons were barely able to struggle into an already pitched camp. Had there been anything like the numbers of hostile Indians that rumors had placed in the area, the Indians would have been sorely tempted to attack the stragglers in the column, to say nothing of the herd of exhausted horses and mules.

But Custer's luck held, barely. There were no hostiles nearby. And on August 26 the column finally reached the place where it would turn due east toward Fort Lincoln. Calhoun writes: "Traveled over very good country. The grazing in this vicinity is noted down as excellent. We came to the grave of Dan Malloy, a teamster who was killed last year [i.e., during the Yellowstone survey] by a wagon running over him. Passed Heart River where wood and water were put in the wagons. Near a prominent butte I observed a stake of the NPRR Co. marked 4877; I made a calculation and find that we are 92 miles from Lincoln."[23] The only sad note on this day was the burial of a Sergeant Stempker, another victim of disease. Stempker was assigned to Company L, commanded by Tom Custer.

Calhoun's penultimate entry, August 27, signaled the beginning of the end of the expedition's ordeals: "We have at last reached good grazing. The country before us is clothed with good grass of excellent quality, and no more signs of burnt prairie. Water and grass in abundance to satisfy all demands."[24] They were due west of Fort Lincoln.

Calhoun's last entry began: "The General obtained two (2) porcupines." No doubt Private Ewert disapproved, but at least he had the satisfaction of knowing that he and the rest of the column, minus only four of their comrades, were just about home. Despite the troops' initial premonitions of disaster ("that scarce half our number would return"[25]), they had made it. The wagon trains had traveled 883 odometer miles, and the army's side trips and scouts had added another 322 miles for an expedition total of 1,205 miles.[26] Given the objectives, both explicit and implicit, the expedition was a resounding success, and that success can be laid at the feet of its commander, where he would be sure to reach down and pick it up. Most agreed with that assessment, except, of course, Private Ewert, whose final entry in his diary reads: "I had never been able to definitely ascertain the loss of horses and mules, but I should guess the number being near fifty. That is quite a 'gain' for the Government. As a whole the majority will vote the expedition a failure."[27] As it turned out, from the perspective of the army, in particular, and white civilization, in general, Ewert was dead wrong. From the perspective of the Sioux who owned the Black Hills, the expedition's very success was a catastrophe—and led to further catastrophes, and not just to themselves.

To the inevitable strains of "Garryowen," Custer led the expedition into Fort Lincoln. One by one the officers dropped out of the column to meet their wives, who were standing by the parade ground anxiously scanning the troops to make sure their husbands were among them. And in a cinematic moment, Libbie came rushing out to greet the general, who jumped off his horse and took her in his arms, whereupon she fainted, for a moment, which led Ewert to observe sourly that it was "a very pretty piece of by-play for the men of the command."[28] Apparently, Ewert had no sympathy for nineteenth-century melodrama or romantic tableaux. As a four-foot-eight-inch army private, he was hardly a figure of romance, and perhaps he regretted that, as well as the fact that no one was rushing out to welcome him. A soldier coming home to no one will inevitably have mixed feelings.[29]

> *Custer had made a landfall in paradise, given the economy*
> *a lift, brought a glint to the eye of the railroad financier,*
> *the merchant, the land speculator, the idle laborer, the*
> *languishing adventurer.*
>
> —Donald Jackson[30]

> *Let us weigh the gain and the loss in wagering that God is. Let*
> *us estimate these two chances. If you gain, you gain all; if you*
> *lose, you lose nothing.*
>
> —Blaise Pascal, *Pensées*, 1669

After the euphoria came the backlash. While the western press and inhabitants were going wild with excitement, cooler heads began to wonder whether fifty grains of gold really amounted to a bonanza, or even a potential bonanza. Chief among the skeptics was Professor Newton Winchell, the expedition geologist, who gave a speech before the Academy of Natural Sciences after he returned to the University of Minnesota. He not only said he doubted the existence of gold, since he had never been shown a sample, but he also impugned the character of the practical miners who, he said, at the very least were guilty of exaggerating their claims. Perhaps unstated but implied was the suggestion that the miners might even have "salted" the diggings for reasons of their own.

The *Bismarck Tribune* was outraged. "If Professor Winchell has made such reports . . . he has written himself an ass and deserves the appellation of a Dogberry of the first water."[31] Custer also responded, "Why Professor Winchell saw no gold was simply due to the fact that he neglected to look for it."[32] And who, the westerners asked, was a more reliable source of information: the nation's leading Indian fighter or some weedy professor who was, after all, merely a geologist? And as the *Bismarck Tribune* had already sniffed, geologists were not miners; they were dusty academics who spent their time poking among worthless rocks and theorizing about volcanic eruptions and dreaming about the earth's core, while practical men went about the business of discovering wealth.

There was another naysayer. The Reverend Samuel Hinman was an Episcopal missionary to the Sioux, primarily to the Dakota, or Santee, tribe. On August 5 he set off on an exploration of the southern edges of the Black Hills. Two companies of the Third Cavalry and some practical miners accompanied Hinman, whose object was to find a potentially new site for the Spotted Tail Agency. Not having either the manpower or perhaps the engineering skills of the Custer expedition, Hinman's wagon train was stalled near the southern entrance, and he was forced to divide his men into small groups. His miners prospected but found nothing, and Hinman returned to report that any tales of gold in the Black Hills were the stuff of dreams, and that further, as historian Watson Parker wrote, "the Hills were bleak . . . forbidding, sterile, useless for agriculture, and swept by fearful storms, both in winter and summer."[33]

Hinman was ignored. And with some justification. He had explored only the southern edges of the Hills, the same area that Custer visited on his southern scout—with much the same results and evaluation. Obviously Hinman's miners were looking in the wrong places. Moreover Hinman was thought to have a conflict of interest. Known as an "Indian lover," his assessment of the Hills' potential was thought to be skewed by his own desire to protect not only his flock but also his influence and opportunities with them. Indeed, Hinman would later be dismissed by his boss, Bishop William Hare, under charges of financial and sexual misconduct. Hinman's negative report was easy to dismiss. Besides, the westerners and the eastern immigrants and unemployed hopefuls *wanted* to believe in the gold. There were all the old stories that rumored its existence, and now they had Custer's word for it. What was the opinion of a psalm-singing parson with a notorious eye for Indian women compared to the nation's most famous cavalry leader?

More troubling were the remarks of Lt. Col. Fred Grant, who returned to his staff job and when interviewed expressed his own misgivings. He gave interviews to that effect and wrote in his journal: "We had several Miners along who had nothing to lose and everything to gain; they all lived together and could concoct any plan they wished. After we got near Harney's Peak they said they found gold. . . . Also they came each day and showed specimens and would say 'I got this from one pan of earth today,' and I noticed that they showed the same pieces every day. . . . I saw about all the gold that was produced in the hands of different miners and I don't believe there was two dollars all put together."[34]

This was harder to swallow, and Custer no doubt felt more than a soupçon of irritation over what might have appeared to him to be a betrayal of sorts. And it's fair to wonder what possible motive the practical miners could have in essentially committing fraud. What was there to gain? Perhaps they believed they could go into the real estate business selling claims to gullible miners. Such things had happened at other gold strikes. (Mark Twain in *Roughing It* describes the lively speculation in gold claims—claims that had nothing to do with actual gold strikes.) But Grant did not elaborate or explain his suspicions; it was enough that he expressed them. It's also fair to wonder how Grant was able to identify pinhead grains of gold and determine that they were the same grains, day after day.

The eastern press picked up on these stories. The *New York Times* was quick to point out the self-interested motivations of the western towns that expected and hoped for an influx of eager miners who would need everything from supplies to life insurance, and that the Northern Pacific Railroad was also loud in its advertisements of inexpensive transportation to Bismarck. To them it didn't matter whether there was gold or not; they would profit from the deluge of optimistic miners, one way or the other. The railroad would even make money hauling disappointed miners back to their homes.

But the readers of the *New York Times* were generally not impoverished immigrants or unemployed laborers. And even if the miners did hear a discouraging word from some sectors, they heard the seductive calls from others, from the western press that was supported by the comments of none other than General Custer, who, after all, was actually there and saw the gold. Given the choice between the eastern naysayers and their predictable dismissiveness on the one hand, and the western "boomers" on the other, the eager miners and immigrants chose optimism. Besides, it was like Pascal's Wager: if they went to the Hills and got rich, they would achieve dreams that were otherwise well beyond them. If they went there and found nothing, what had they given up? Virtually nothing. A few months of travel and labor, that's all. At the very least they would have had an adventure and a period of hopefulness; that alone was better than the dreary life of unemployment or starvation wages. Of course, there was also the possibility of losing their scalps and their lives, but that risk seemed small enough and worth taking. Therefore, the East versus West controversy about whether there was gold or not was, to an unemployed adventurer or out-of-pocket miner, much ado about nothing. Gold was calling to them, and they would answer.

After his return to Fort Lincoln, Custer said: "The extinguishment of the Indian title to the Black Hills and the establishment of a military post in the vicinity of Harney's Peak and another at some point on the Little Missouri will settle the Indian question so far as the northwest is concerned."[35] Interestingly, Custer is linking the extinguishment of the Sioux title with the establishment of a fort in the Black Hills, even though he and his superiors had gone to great lengths before the expedition to prove that the two issues were not related, that the army had every right to place a fort on the reservation lands and to travel through them. There were three other posts already on the reservation. And since there was no apparent legal impediment to a fourth post, why could the Sioux not retain their title to the Hills? The obvious conclusion is that Custer perfectly understood that the gold discovery would unleash a horde of immigrants, miners, and settlers and that the Hills would then inevitably have to be acquired, either by negotiation or by other means. There was no stopping any of it. As far as the miners were concerned, there would be no distinction between de jure and de facto ownership. They'd be there, and that would be that. The estimable Captain John Gregory Bourke, who was one of General George Crook's top aides and a future Indian ethnologist wondered: "Why should not Indians be permitted to hold mining or any other kind of land? The whites could mine on shares or on a royalty."[36] This may have been a good idea in theory, but Custer's discoveries released a horde of prospectors well before any negotiation with the tribes could have occurred. It would have been difficult, if not impossible, to establish royalties retroactively once hundreds of miners had begun staking claims (illegal except among themselves) and finding gold. Far easier simply to acquire the Black Hills from the Indians and let the miners continue to develop them.

Once again, all this raises the question: was Custer's expedition designed simply to find a fort, or was it a cleverly subtle way of prying the Hills from the Sioux, once the anticipated gold was discovered? A cynic would of course answer the latter. But most likely the army was not being that subtle, although anyone who thought about the possibilities could easily predict the future if gold were discovered. Just as the Sioux knew all along, it would be gold, not the army, that would doom their ownership of "Paha Sapa" (Black Hills). But the army's object was a post, and, besides, before the expedition they had no proof that there was gold in the Hills. Stories of gold were mere rumors, while the army was dealing with the fact of Sioux depredations that the proposed fort was designed to interdict. Looking for gold was not the army's hidden agenda, although it was almost certainly Custer's. As we shall see, after the flood of miners began to stream into the Hills, the army tried to keep them out and only gave up later when the impossibility of the task became obvious.

Custer also recommended that the best route to the gold fields was through Bismarck, which was a nod to his old friends at the NPRR. In other words, the miners should come west by rail and from there follow what Chief Fast Bear later called that "Thieves' Road."

CHAPTER SIXTEEN

INVASION

Plate sin with gold and the strong lance of justice hurtless breaks.

—*King Lear*, act 4, scene 6

He that maketh haste to be rich shall not be innocent.

—Proverbs 28:20

Wildly excited citizens of the frontier towns prepared to head for the Black Hills. The *Bismarck Tribune* reported that half the men in town intended to go prospecting; the other half were poised to sell supplies and material to the eager pilgrims.[1] Companies were formed. Meanwhile all the frontier towns along the Missouri River and in Wyoming competed with each other to entice the eastern hopefuls to come their way, saying that the best route to the Hills lay through their precincts and that their merchants could provide the best equipment and supplies. As territorial politician and Yankton resident W. W. Brookings said to his supporters: "We must congratulate ourselves on the splendid prospect for all of southern Dakota. Every farmer or dealer must receive more for his articles sold; a score of hotels would be full; in short, Yankton's rapidly increasing business must be doubled in the next year to meet the demands of the new El Dorado. [The Black Hills] must be opened at once, doubling or quadrupling our already large immigration."[2] Brookings made this speech on August 29, while Custer's Expedition was still on the march home to Fort Lincoln, although the news of the gold find had already been published across the country. And his speech might very well stand as the synthesis of western attitudes toward not only gold but to the trickle-down economic benefits that the mere *possibility* of gold would provide. Men following dreams were in a hurry and not likely to worry over nickels and dimes; they'd pay the asking prices. In truth, they would have no choice. The merchants of Yankton were rubbing their hands in anticipation, but they did not lack for competition. Bismarck boosters pointed out that the route to the Hills from Yankton involved traversing dangerous reservation land; and Fort Laramie offered the same drawbacks as a jumping-off point. Bismarck on the other hand was the terminus of the Northern Pacific Railroad and the starting point of the road well blazed by none other than General Custer—who, significantly, encountered no hostile Indians along the way to the Hills or back. Yankton responded in the August 27 issue of the *Yankton Press & Dakotaian* by saying: "From Yankton westward, the fast and elegant steamers run up the Missouri River through a country of the most picturesque, varied and romantic scenery."[3] The paper did not explain why "romantic scenery" was a good reason to travel via Yankton; they must have known that very few prospectors were poets or artists carrying sketch books. But no possible allurement should go unmentioned. Captain John Gregory Bourke wrote from Wyoming Territory: "Cheyenne was then wild with excitement concerning . . . the settlement of the Black Hills in which gold in unheard of sums was alleged to lay hidden. No story was too wild, too absurd, to be swallowed with eagerness and published as a fact in the papers of the town. Along the streets were camped long trains of wagons loading for the Black Hills; every store advertised a supply of goods suited to the Black Hills trade; the hotels were crowded with men on their way to the new El Dorado; even the stage drivers, boot blacks, and bell boys could talk of nothing but Black Hills—Black Hills."[4] Even the local barber got into the act: "Before you start, go to Hardin's Barber shop, on Eddy Street, and get your hair cut."[5] Undoubtedly a miner on his way to Indian country hoped that a trim at Hardin's would be the only loss of hair forthcoming. A local pharmacy advertised Humphrey's Homeopathic Number 28, which was good for "nervous debility, viral weakness or depression, a weak exhausted feeling, no energy or courage, the result of mental overwork, indiscretion or excess."[6] Aside from "indiscretion or excess," which sounds very much like a hangover, these other ailments would seem to disqualify anyone from the prospecting business. But the belief in panaceas was apparently almost as strong as the belief in the new El Dorado. On a perhaps less optimistic note, another advertisement in the *Yankton Press & Dakotaian* pointed out that "no sensible man will think of going to the Black Hills without first insuring his life."[7] As it turned out, that was good advice for a number of unlucky prospectors. In short, all the frontier towns in the vicinity of the Black Hills were excited at the prospect of servicing and, in some cases, fleecing the miners. Prices certainly would go up; they always did in gold rush towns. (Brookings told local farmers to cut and store as much hay as possible, for miners arriving before the grass turned green would have no choice but to pay five dollars a ton to feed their animals.[8]) Some prospectors might get rich; most would not. Western merchants might not get rich, but they would certainly become more "comfortable." What's more, no one doubted that some of the immigrants, whether successful in the gold fields or not, would stay, once they saw the country. Farmers and ranchers would follow. Land values would increase; real estate development offered new avenues for making money. New town lots could be surveyed and sold. Entrepreneurs offering services would proliferate. Spearfish, for example, a new town on the northern end of the Hills, sprouted up not as a mining camp but as a service center offering lumber and farm produce to the miners.[9]

Of the eventual collection of miners in the Hills, 40 percent were from the eastern and midwestern states. Another 40 percent were foreigners, although that statistic probably referred to first-generation immigrants, happy for more than one reason to leave the eastern cities and their wretched slums behind. The number of foreign-born miners almost approached the percentage of foreigners in the army, and no doubt some of the miners had only recently left the army, some even legally. The remaining 20 percent were westerners, many of whom arrived from other gold fields. Having failed elsewhere, or perhaps succeeded only modestly, they were undaunted and eager to try their luck in the new El Dorado.[10]

Black Hills historian Watson Parker described the basic miner's equipment: "The well-equipped 'pilgrim,' as he was called had a rubber ground-sheet, rubber hip boots, two woolen blankets, and a rifle, pistol and ammunition. Two tin plates, a dipper, knife, fork, and large spoon, some towels, and matches completed his personal outfit. Two men together might carry a round pointed steel shovel, miner's pick, and other mining equipment. Messes of five or six shared a Dutch oven, frying pan, tin pail, handsaw, ax, and tent. Army-style provisions for three months cost less than $20 per man, and the entire personal outfit came to about $50."[11] Most would travel by wagons pulled by mules or oxen—hence the need for Yankton's expensive hay.

Despite the widespread euphoria, the anticipated invasion of miners, supported by eager merchants, was, unfortunately, illegal. The Acting Secretary of the Interior wrote to the governor of the Dakota Territory to inform him of something the governor already knew—that the Black Hills were part of the Sioux reservation and would remain so unless and until Congress saw fit to find a way to extinguish the Sioux title. No civilian expeditions would be permitted until then. The distasteful job of keeping fellow citizens away from glittering opportunity fell to the army. On September 3—mere days after Custer's return—General Philip Sheridan telegraphed his Dakota Department head, General Alfred Terry:

> Should the companies now organizing at Sioux City and Yankton trespass on the Sioux Indian Reservation, you are hereby directed to use the force at your command to burn the wagon trains, destroy the outfits and arrest the leaders, confining them at the nearest post in the Indian country. Should they succeed in reaching the interior, you are directed to send such force of cavalry in pursuit as will accomplish the purpose above named. Should Congress open up the country for settlement by extinguishing the treaty rights of the Indians, the undersigned will give cordial support to the settlement of the Black Hills.

But not until then. The telegram was reprinted in the *Yankton Press & Dakotaian* on September 10.[12] The locals viewed Sheridan's statement as an abuse of authority and made plans to ignore it. But at least the miners knew what they were up against; now they had two adversaries to avoid— the Sioux and the army. Although many hundreds and ultimately thousands passed through the army's rather flimsy net, not all did. One of the first freighters who tried to ship supplies into the mining district was Fred T. Evans. He started out from Sioux City with a wagon train bound for the diggings in April of 1875. He followed along Nebraska's Niobrara River planning to turn north to the Hills, but the army found him and burned his entire train. Though furious, Evans was undaunted and with other local investors formed the Black Hills Transportation Company. He and his partners knew that freighting goods *to* the diggings was apt to be more profitable than wielding a shovel *at* the diggings. And so it turned out. At the height of the gold rush Evans's company "employed 1000 to 1500 men, 1500 oxen, 250 mules and 400 wagons."[13] Like many of his fellow teamsters, Evans was well versed in profanity. Overhearing Evans in full flight one day, a Methodist minister suggested that Evans exercise a little moderation, whereupon Evans offered to bet the worthy divine one thousand dollars that he could not drive a yoke of oxen to Deadwood without cussing. The minister did not take the bet; perhaps he did not have a thousand dollars to lose.[14]

Few, if any, of the regular army officers welcomed the task of burning and destroying the investments of fellow citizens on behalf of the Sioux. The army really wanted no part of this business, but the senior generals had no choice. They were caught, not for the first time, between competing interests—the eastern politicians and philanthropists, the Department of Interior bureaucrats, the western editorialists and settlers, miners from all over the country, and the treaty Sioux who saw these developments quite correctly as a threat to their rights and, ultimately, to their way of life. And then there were the non-treaty Sioux who were belligerent and whose position would attract increasing numbers of disaffected reservation warriors, especially the young men, angry over the Black Hills invasion, eager to assert their rights and also to proclaim their manhood and gather the laurels of war. Overarching all of these interests were the interests of the nation's population that was suffering under the weight of economic depression and, in some regions, agricultural disaster. People were clamoring for the government to do something. Standing in the middle of these crosscurrents was the army, faced with a task they did not like and could not effectively perform. It seems fair to suggest that the harsh tone of Sheridan's telegram reflected, at least in part, his frustration over his orders to stop unstoppable forces, to put his institutional finger back in a dike that was already crumbling around him. As Senator John Sherman had said: "If the whole army of the United States stood in the way, the wave of emigration would pass over it to seek the valley where gold was to be found." Sheridan knew that, as did the senator's brother, the commanding general. So did President Ulysses S. Grant, and ultimately he would act.

As Bourke recounted: "In the winter of that year [1874–85] a large party of miners without waiting for the consent of the Indians to be obtained, settled on the waters of Frenchman, or French Creek, built a stockade, and began to work. . . . These miners were driven from point to point by detachments of troops, but succeeded in maintaining a foothold until the next year."[15] (There is some irony in that picture, because apparently the miners could scatter as efficiently as the Sioux, whenever the cavalry got near.) The winter of '74 was a particularly harsh one, as Bourke wrote: "One of the commands sent to look them [the miners] up and to drive them out was the company of the Third Cavalry commanded by Brevet Lt. Colonel Guy V. Henry, which was caught in a blizzard and nearly destroyed."[16] Winter campaigning in the west was a dangerous and chancy business, regardless of who the adversaries were. Henry found no miners. They were there, but Henry's failure to find them was not only a function of the brutal weather but also due to the size and scope of the Hills. Forty-five hundred square miles of mountains and valleys and forests can hide more than a few intrepid miners. One group, known as the Gordon party, left Sioux City in October and traveled across the reservation to the Hills and French Creek. There were twenty-eight people in the party, including one woman. They built a stockade and cabins at French Creek, but an army patrol discovered them and evicted them in the spring.

It seems more than possible that some in the administration and the army had a secret hope that gold in the Black Hills was really a mirage; that the few pinheads of pure gold Custer saw were about the extent of it; and that once that information was made clear to the public, the various political and Indian problems would go away. Discouraged miners would eventually give up and leave the Hills to the Sioux, once and for all. On the other hand, there were the thorny questions of the national debt and the sagging economy. If the Black Hills truly were a new El Dorado, they might be worth the difficulties of wresting them away from the Sioux, by hook or by crook. The problem was, no one knew how much gold was there. The government could not make or amend its policies regarding the Black Hills until it knew what the Hills were really worth. It made perfect sense, therefore, to send another expedition into the Hills, this time with increased scientific manpower. The only object of this expedition would be to evaluate the gold and silver opportunities. Custer himself had sensibly recommended a second expedition with that purpose. William Curtis of the *Chicago Inter Ocean* also endorsed the idea. Despite his enthusiasm for the initial discoveries, he understood that the fifty grains of gold were really just an indication of what *might be*, not what definitely *was*. Custer probably thought he would lead the second expedition, but the army had different ideas. Custer was too closely identified in the public mind with Indian fighting; the government wanted to position this expedition as merely scientific exploration. And in fact from this point on until the Battle of Little Bighorn, Custer would be more or less marginalized. He would follow events from Fort Lincoln or during extended periods of leave in Monroe, Michigan, or New York City.

The Department of the Interior took charge of the follow-up. If this was a cosmetic move to assure the Sioux that it was not a military mission, it could not possibly have worked, since the expedition was escorted by six companies of cavalry and two of infantry, all under the command of Colonel Richard Dodge. Early in May of 1875 the expedition got under way from Fort Laramie. The leading civilian scientist was Walter P. Jenney of the New York School of Mines. The object of the mission was not only to determine exactly how rich, if at all, the Black Hills were in gold, but also to decide—if there was gold there—how difficult (and therefore economically feasible) it would be to extract. Jenney and his party poked around French Creek and were not impressed by the placer potential. But they then moved north and dug holes anywhere that seemed promising. Jenney's overall findings might have dampened a little of the enthusiasm, but not much, because he said there definitely was gold there. Getting to it would take a little more work than simply washing panfuls of dirt, and more elaborate equipment would be needed. That in turn meant investment capital. But . . . properly worked, the mines of the Black Hills would pay. And as it turned out, there were productive placers even farther north, placers that the Jenney party did not locate but that would be found and exploited by the horde of miners soon to arrive, placers in the area that would come to be known as Deadwood.

The subject of investment capital complicated matters. Investors, whether individuals or institutions, were reluctant to put major money into heavy equipment and mining operations until the Indian question was solved—specifically until the ownership of the Hills was transferred to the government, which would then recognize claims by individual miners or mining companies, and which would authorize the army to establish posts nearby to prevent attacks by outraged Sioux. The need for capital as determined by Jenney's report, therefore, increased the pressure on Congress to do something about acquiring the title to the Hills. Without that, investors would hold back, and if investors held back, the richest deposits of Black Hills gold could not be developed. As with the railroads, here was once again a situation in which private capital and government policy needed to operate together in the national interest. Miners with pans were one thing; ore-stamping mills financed by stock or bond issues were something else.

By the time of Jenney's expedition, there were already an estimated eight hundred miners scattered throughout the Hills.[17] Many had been unsuccessful thus far, but they had staked claims. Their presence in the Hills, though, would become a problem for the government, once they opened talks with the (reservation) chiefs about the possible sale of the Hills. Annoyed by the unauthorized miners, the Sioux were not inclined to sell. In fact, even if the miners had not been there, the Sioux would have been reluctant to sell. Meanwhile miners continued to come into the forbidden territory. As Bourke wrote: "During the closing hours of 1875 the miners kept going into the Black Hills, and the Indians kept annoying all wagon trains and small parties found on the roads. There were some killed and others wounded and a number of wagons destroyed, but hostilities did not reach a dangerous state, and were confined almost entirely to the country claimed by the Indians as their own."[18] All things considered, the Sioux response to the invasion of miners seemed measured and restrained, although that was cold comfort to those miners who were attacked. Still, despite the government's embarrassment over the influx of miners, negotiations with the Sioux continued. It was at one of these meetings that Red Cloud and Spotted Tail and other important treaty chiefs made their demands. If they decided to sell, they would want a lot of money for the Hills. Their asking price was $70 million.[19] Spotted Tail said: "As long as we live on this earth we will expect pay. We want to leave the amount with the President at interest, forever. By doing that I think it will be so that I can live. I want to live on the interest of my money."[20] Red Cloud demanded guaranteed annuities for the next seven generations.

The commissioners, on the other hand, were authorized to offer $6 million for on an outright sale, or $400,000 a year for the mining rights. Black Elk was in the vicinity of the meetings: "They talked and talked for days, but it was just like wind blowing in the end. I asked my father what they were talking about in there, and he told me that the Grandfather at Washington wanted to lease the Black Hills so that the Wasichus could dig yellow metal, and that the chief of the soldiers said that if we did not do this, the Black Hills would be just like melting snow in our hands, because the Wasichus would take that country anyway."[21]

The Sioux rejected the government's offers, and there was an impasse. The meetings broke up. The frustrated commissioners reported their failure and said that the Sioux would not sell the Hills "until they are made to feel the power as well as the magnanimity of the Government . . . [and] if the Government will interpose its power and authority, they are not in a condition to resist."[22] They recommended that Congress simply set a price and insist that the Indians take it. Or else. The government had leverage, of course. The 1868 Treaty of Fort Laramie had only promised the Sioux rations for the next four years.[23] The rations had been continued either out of governmental philanthropy or as a way to keep the lid on a potentially boiling pot. Regardless of the government's prior motivations, those rations could now be curtailed or eliminated completely. There was very little subtlety about the new proposition, as Chief Standing Elk observed in one meeting: "Whenever we don't agree to anything that is said in council, they give us the same reply— 'You won't get any food.'"[24] Starkly put, the new offer was "sign or starve." Here indeed was the proverbial rock and hard place. The Black Hills were valuable to the Sioux in large part because they were a hedge against government whim and agency corruption regarding promised rations, as well as substandard rations. Now the Indians were threatened with loss of that "meat pack," and that would place them in even greater thrall to the vagaries of government budgets and the still-rife corruption of the agents—to say nothing of the loss of a way of life that in many crucially important ways defined the Sioux sense of identity. And yet, if they did not agree, the current rations might, and probably would, be withdrawn completely. And if they rejected it all and left the reservations to live and hunt with the non-treaty Sioux, they knew the army would order them to return or declare them hostile—which is essentially what happened in 1876, not only to Sitting Bull and the non-treaty Sioux but also to the summer roamers. Besides, with the buffalo herds dwindling, could the Lakota even survive as free roamers? In short, the government was offering an entirely legal (under the terms of the 1868 treaty) and yet sinful proposition. Aside from the "unceded territories" to the west, the Black Hills were the last shred of productive hunting ground and, therefore, economic—and cultural—independence, that the reservation Indians had. Without those lands, the reservation Indians would become utterly dependent on a government and a race of people whose trustworthiness was, at the very least, suspect. Small wonder that Spotted Tail wanted to be able to live on his interest. Government promises were one thing; invested capital was another. As Black Elk said about the white man's promises: "They made a treaty with Red Cloud that said our country would be ours as long as the grass should grow and water flow. You can see that it is not the grass and the water that have forgotten."[25]

In the summer of 1875 the army sent General George Crook to the Hills, where he called a meeting of the miners and explained the ticklish nature of the negotiations with the Indians. As Bourke wrote: "Instructions of a positive character were sent to General Crook, directing the expulsion from the Black Hills of all unauthorized persons there assembled. General Crook went across country to the stockade erected on French Creek, Dakota, and there had an interview with the miners, who promised to leave the country, first having properly recorded their claims, and await the action of Congress in regard to the opening of the region to settlement."[26] Whether Crook also offered a wink and a nudge, the result was the same. The miners agreed to go away, and all understood that action by Congress was under way and that the Sioux title would soon be extinguished, at which point the miners could return to their claims. A committee of miners was established to maintain the records of the claims.

The impasse with the Sioux continued, and by the winter of 1875 President Grant was growing frustrated, both with the lack of progress in negotiations with the Sioux and with the need to use the army to police the vast territory of the Hills—caused, he understood, by the lawless prospectors who ignored all strictures in their headlong dash toward gold, the "yellow metal that makes the Wasichus crazy."[27] Grant regarded the mission as fruitless and inappropriate for the army, one best calculated to aggravate the already thorny problem of desertion. Moreover, winter patrols and campaigns in the Hills were a hardship and danger to men and animals alike. And they were expensive. If prospectors wanted to go there in the dead of winter and risk not only Sioux enmity but also the ravages of winter, well, that was their worry. Grant had had enough. Accordingly, he called a meeting with Generals William T. Sherman and Philip Sheridan as well as the Secretaries of War and the Interior. The meeting ended with a decision to remove the army from the Hills and to halt all attempts to prevent miners from entering the Black Hills. Going there would still be technically against the law, but with no one to enforce it, the law had no teeth. It had very few teeth to begin with, when the army was trying, but now even the most timid of prospectors could ignore it. No announcement was made; to proclaim such a major policy shift would bring howls of protest from the eastern philanthropists, Quakers, and assorted Indian advocates—as well as Grant's political opponents who were always on the lookout for partisan political openings. The army would instead be quietly withdrawn from the Black Hills and surrounding areas. Grant and the other senior officials understood, of course, what this change would mean. Was the decision simply a matter of bowing to reality and necessity . . . an acknowledgment of the impossibility of policing the vast Hills with limited troops? Or was it a cynical ploy designed to put pressure on the Sioux leaders by presenting them with a fait accompli, meaning thousands of miners squatting in the Hills, miners who were dug in and impossible to evict? Most likely this is not an either/or question. But the fact that Grant did not announce this change of policy certainly suggests that there was a whiff of Machiavellian thinking involved. Perhaps more than a whiff. Some historians postulate that the move was really designed to precipitate a war that could lead to the final solution to the Sioux problem.[28] But given the fact that the Black Hills dispute was a reservation issue and that the only Sioux the government was negotiating with were already on the reservation and therefore largely peaceful (excepting of course the young warriors who were summer roamers), removal of the troops from the Hills was more likely designed to apply negotiating pressure on the reservation chiefs— assuming it was *designed* to do anything other than remove an arduous and virtually impossible task from the army and its limited resources.

At that same meeting, however, it was also agreed that the non-treaty Sioux and Cheyenne who were roaming the unceded territories to the north and west of the reservation should be removed and settled on reservations.[29] The unceded territory would no longer be open to the Lakota wanderers. Exactly how that would be accomplished was a separate question, since these unceded territories were also Sioux by right of the 1868 treaty. War against these bands might and probably would be necessary. So it proved. The action that precipitated the summer of '76 war was a government proclamation requiring all Sioux who were not on the reservations to come in by a certain date or be regarded as hostile. While this may well have been designed to start a war with the non-treaty hostiles, it seems reasonable to regard it as mostly separate from the negotiations over the Black Hills, which had more or less boiled down to, and stalled over, the question of money—although intertribal politics as well as objections from the non-treaty Sioux contributed to the impasse. There was a significant gulf between the free roamers and the "hang around the fort people," and between the two were the young men who operated in both camps, depending on mood and season.

The westerners didn't have to be told that the army was being withdrawn from the Hills; they noticed, and word spread. As the army turned its back on the Black Hills, the miners arrived in ever greater numbers. By January of 1876 an estimated four thousand miners were in the Hills.[30] The area of initial discovery, next to French Creek, had become almost overnight a town of one thousand people, mostly miners, along with the usual handful of bartenders, gamblers, and "soiled doves."

The name of the town was "Custer."

EPILOGUE

By the end of June 1876, Custer and 262 of his men were dead. The Sioux and Cheyenne had won a great battle that would lose them the Black Hills and the unceded territories. The reservation chiefs continued to resist the sale of the Hills, while their young men, radicalized by the "illegal" invasion of the Hills and lured by the old way of life and by the glory of war, left the reservation in larger numbers than usual and joined Sitting Bull and Crazy Horse. And they had joined in destroying the very man and many of the same troops who had traveled down the Thieves' Road just two years before. While the army made plans for campaigns designed to whip the hostiles militarily and then send the remnants to the reservations, the impasse over the Black Hills remained. The nation mourned Custer's loss through its centennial, and certainly the shock of the battle intensified white hatred of the Plains tribes and intensified the calls for vengeance. No doubt, too, those calls and the subsequent military campaigns made the peacefully inclined reservation chiefs a little nervous—as well they might have been, for in August a riled-up Congress passed a bill requiring the Lakota to relinquish title to all their lands that were west of 103 degrees longitude, a line that runs ten miles or so east of the Black Hills. They were to give up not only the Black Hills but also the unceded territories granted in the 1868 Treaty of Fort Laramie, which meant that Sitting Bull and his followers would have to come into the reservations. The estimable historian Robert Utley suggests that there was linkage between the two propositions, saying that the second proposal was designed to "curb the power of the Sitting Bull Indians and thus their power to obstruct the sale of the Hills."[1] Should the Sioux refuse this latest offer, Congress would no longer authorize appropriations for rations. With the buffalo nearly gone, with the miners swarming through the Black

Hills, with the army campaigning against the non-treaty belligerents in and around the unceded territories, the peacefully inclined chiefs had no real option; this latest proposal from Congress was more an ultimatum than a proposal.

A commission was appointed to travel to the Lakota agencies and sell the government's plan, since even though government policy had been to cease making treaties with the Indians, there was still the problem of the Peace Policy advocates and humanitarian concern for the tribes— a problem that was essentially political. Accordingly, the government appointed a seven-man commission headed by a well-known spokesman for the humanitarians, George Manypenny, to sell the changes to the reservation chiefs and thereby paste a fig leaf over what essentially was annexation and removal. One of the commissioners, the Reverend Henry Whipple, explained: "In return for giving up the Black Hills and the unceded territory . . . the president would provide rations, clothing, farm equipment and schools 'until such time as you are able to support and take care of yourselves.'"[2] It was the same old story. The Lakota would become self-sufficient farmers, and their children would be taught from the white man's syllabus. It was a formula for cultural despair. But there was no choice. Red Cloud and Spotted Tail and other prominent chiefs "touched the pen." None of the militants under Sitting Bull or Crazy Horse came in and signed, however. Their capitulation would come later. Congress ratified the agreement in October of 1876, at which point the Lakota titles to the Black Hills and the unceded territories were extinguished, even though only about 10 percent of the Lakota agreed to the proposal.[3]

As Black Elk later said: "Every good thing seemed to be going away."[4]

The Black Hills now belonged to the United States, which in turn allowed miners and mining companies—and their assorted and predictable camp followers—to go legally into the Hills. Unfortunately, the Custer expedition's discovery of gold in the Black Hills and the subsequent gold rush did not do what much of the white culture hoped it would do. In fact the Black Hills only provided the mildest kind of stimulus to the national economy, if any. It did not reduce the national debt, much less eliminate it as the *Yankton Press and Dakotaian* predicted it would. The national debt was gradually reduced over the next several decades, up until the First World War. But the new availability of gold from the Black Hills did little or nothing to advance the process of repayment. Nor did the gold rush significantly reduce unemployment. Since unemployment figures were not kept with any precision, there's no way to determine just how important, if at all, the gold rush was to national unemployment statistics. At the height of the gold rush the Black Hills census showed a total of roughly 18,500 people, although "a fair guess would be that from 1874 to 1880 more than thirty thousand [people] passed through the Hills."[5] Most were miners; most went away disappointed. Of course, the gold rush did provide some temporary employment, especially once the problems with the Sioux were resolved and the "monied interests" felt comfortable investing in heavy equipment and major mining operations. Disappointed miners whose own claims turned out to be worthless found jobs working for the mining companies like the Homestake Mine in Lead. Lead (pronounced "leed") was the mountainside town a couple of miles from Deadwood. But jobs like that were a drop in the bucket in the context of national unemployment. The gold rush did give a boost to local economies and to the regional economy as well. Hardware stores and freight companies did good business; so did farmers and ranchers who supplied the miners' food. Then there were the barbers, patent-medicine salesmen, insurance agents, bartenders, prostitutes, and gamblers—all of whom did pretty well during the boom. Newspapers did a lively business both in increased advertising and circulation as they went about the business of promoting their towns—a process called "booming." And the gold rush did increase traffic on the suffering railroads, such as the Northern Pacific. A miner paid $49.25 for a first-class ticket from Chicago to Bismarck, and included in that fare was the cost of a stagecoach ride to Deadwood. But that increase in business was not nearly enough to lift the NPRR out of bankruptcy. That would not happen until 1879, when the national economy finally emerged from five years of frightful depression, so that the NPRR could at last return to the credit markets and resume its slow and expensive construction westward, this time without much fear of hostile Indians. Steamboats, too, did good business transporting miners up the Missouri to Fort Pierre from where the miners could go to the Hills by stagecoach or wagon. The steamboat *Big Horn* "made the Yankton-Fort Pierre trip every week carrying one hundred tons of freight, eight staterooms full of women, and as many miners as could crowd aboard. Another boat, the *Black Hills*, also made a weekly trip, and in 1877 it carried over four million pounds of goods and passengers from Yankton up the river to Fort Pierre."[6] It's not known what the women who were cramming the staterooms had in mind by going to the diggings. Perhaps some were wives of the miners.

As for the actual production of gold, however, there was a vast gulf between hopes and subsequent reality. As usual. But not everyone was disappointed. The estimates of gold finds during the five years of the height of the gold rush, from '76 to '80 are wildly inaccurate, because the gold "dust" and nuggets were used as local currency—as they were in other gold rush towns—instead of being immediately entered into the financial systems, that is, sold to the banks, which in turn sold to the Treasury. One miner's "poke" might be passed around many times before the ultimate beneficiary sent it into the banking system. But the closest estimates are that roughly 17.5 million dollars' worth of Black Hills gold was mined in the five years of the height of the gold rush. Much of this was from placer mines, but after the question of Sioux title had been answered, capital began to flow into the Hills. The aforementioned Homestake Mine was a hard-rock operation involving massive pit mines and heavy equipment, and it was productive over many decades, only closing in 2002. During that time it produced forty-four million ounces of gold. The dollar value of that production is, of course, difficult, if not impossible to determine, given the fluctuating price of gold over the years. (As of this writing the market price of gold is roughly $1,300 an ounce.) But by any standard forty-four million ounces of gold is a great deal of money. But it came gradually, over many years.

By 1880, there were at least twenty-two towns and villages scattered around the Black Hills, the largest and most notorious being Deadwood, with a population of almost four thousand. Wild Bill Hickok lived there for a while in 1876. Just over a month after Custer's defeat, Hickok, while playing cards in a saloon, was shot in the back of the head by Jack McCall, who was subsequently acquitted for acting in self-defense—a verdict so outrageous that he was later retried in Yankton because the court ruled the earlier miner's court trial had no "legal standing."[7] McCall was found guilty and hanged. And while Hickok's national fame increased the intensity of the news coverage, the murder was symptomatic of the degraded culture that spread like a fungus throughout the Hills in the mining camps scattered around the diggings. The aesthetic and cultural catastrophe that the Lakota feared and anticipated is symbolized in muddy streets and saloons of Deadwood and, perhaps, in Wild Bill himself, a gambler, gunman, and sometime vagrant, suffering from an unnamed venereal disease.

Despite the gold rush and the transformation of the Black Hills from a pristine wilderness into a beehive of energy and activity, it's fair to say that Custer's discovery did not come close to achieving the ecstatic dreams of the white culture. But it did do everything the Sioux feared it would do. Swarming over the Hills, grubbing in the dirt and mud, doing work that was to the Lakota degrading by definition, the miners stripped away the surface of the earth using shovels and sluice boxes in the same way the buffalo hunters stripped away the hides and left the meat to rot. If that seems melodramatic, it is very much in line with how the Lakota saw it. As far as they were concerned, the Black Hills were a living benefactor to the "People," just as the disappearing buffalo were. Or, rather, had been.

Now both were gone. And with them, much of what it meant to be Lakota. Looking back on that time, when he was still a young boy, Black Elk said: "I did not know then how much was ended."[8]

In history we must look for multiple causality.
—Patrick O'Brian, *Treason's Harbour*, 1983

The Lakota owned the Black Hills, first by right of conquest over the Kiowa and later by treaty as a result of their victory during the Red Cloud War. How then did they lose them? It's always tempting in looking at major historical events to try to find a logical series of events, moving from cause to effect to the next cause again with inexorable logic or at least a recognizable structure, some sort of reconstructible line. And accordingly the simplest explanation of how the Sioux lost the Black Hills is to say Custer's discovery of gold unleashed the inherent greed of the white civilization, and that overwhelmed the resistance, both political and military, of the Sioux. And, of course, there is more than a little truth in that. But, as usual, the story is more complicated. A variety of historical factors came together and *in their combination* resulted in the loss of the Hills. Had any one of these factors been different, things might have worked out in other ways.

When it comes to the Sioux ownership of their "Paha Sapa," it's hard to escape the fact that the beginning of the end came with the raids of warriors leaving from the reservation and traveling to the settlements and travel routes south of the Dakota border. It was those raids that motivated General Sheridan to authorize a new army post somewhere along the border. That required a reconnaissance in force to find a site. The force had to be large, because of the perceived, and probably real, danger that the Lakota would attack a smaller unit. Had there been no raids, it's unlikely that Sheridan would have sent Custer on a scout through the Hills. The senior generals were dealing with an army of limited size, budget, and capability, and the idea of building and manning yet another fort had no appeal. True, there had been reports and rumors of gold in the Hills, but those rumors had been circulating for decades. And verifying those rumors was not the army's business. Those rumors, however, piqued the interest of George Custer, who quite intentionally brought civilian miners along to substantiate or refute the stories of gold. He saw no inconsistency in combining military and civilian objectives; after all, there was nothing to be lost as far as Custer was concerned and much to be gained, potentially. Custer's interest was certainly a product of his own ambition and desire for further national acclaim. As he wrote: "In years long numbered with the past, when I was merging upon manhood, my every thought was ambitious—not to be wealthy, not to be learned, but to be great. I desired to link my name with acts and men, and in such manner as to be a mark of honor, not only to the present but to future generations."[9] He had no difficulty imagining the response to his exploits if he was able to discover gold. His seniors approved the plan, while emphasizing the purely military nature of the expedition.

The question of gold had become increasingly important nationally, not only because of the huge national debt left over from the Civil War—debt that was denominated in gold—but because of the depression that had hit the economy with sudden and overwhelming force. The economic catastrophe was caused in part—or at least precipitated—by the overextension of the nation's premier banker, Jay Cooke & Company, whose efforts to finance the dubiously necessary Northern Pacific Railroad involved not only major investment and commercial bank loans but also the sale of smaller-denomination bonds to Middle America—the same investors who financed much of the Civil War through bonds sold by the same Jay Cooke & Company. Cooke's collapse set off a domino effect caused by interlocking credit arrangements among the nation's banks. Some of Cooke's troubles were caused by the rise of international interest rates, for the Bank of England, the leading international lender, more than doubled its rates, meaning that banks here that borrowed from the B of E raised their interest rates even higher and squeezed out the less creditworthy as well as legitimate business that relied on credit, as most did. The former went out of business, while the latter cut back on production, laid off workers, and tried to ride out the storm. The Bank of England raised its rates in part because of the collapse of Russian and Austrian banks that had defaulted on loans from *their* investors and bank lenders. Ironically, those banks failed in part because their customers—the great estates of the nobility—defaulted on their loans. And they defaulted on their loans because cheap agricultural exports coming from the United States undermined the Russian and Austrian agribusinesses that had traditionally relied on higher prices and easy credit from their banks—banks whose credit standards were far too lax. Failure of the European agribusinesses led to the subsequent failure of the banks, which found the collateral they held—farm land—was virtually worthless. The banks could not recoup their loans, because they could not sell their collateral. And so they shut their doors.

The rise in European rates meant that domestic US banks also increased their rates, and that directly affected Cooke's cost of money and ability to raise new loans. Cooke's other problems were caused by negative publicity regarding his Northern Pacific Railroad. In the first place, some analysts began to question the essential concept of the NPRR, revisiting the initial objections that it was a line from nowhere to nowhere. In the second place, standing between the two "nowheres" were the hostile Sioux. The surveys into the Yellowstone Valley had been attacked by Sioux warriors under Sitting Bull and other hostile leaders—chiefs who wanted nothing to do with the treaty Red Cloud, Spotted Tail, and others had signed. Nor did they want anything to do with the reservation—except for some of the younger warriors who returned to the reservation in the winter to subsist on government rations. The Sioux were incensed by the railroad surveys, for they understood the dire consequences of a finished road through their hunting grounds, a road that would not only frighten away the game but, just as bad, bring hordes of white settlers into the country. Custer's report of the 1873 Yellowstone fighting certainly burnished his image as an Indian fighter, but it made investors in the NPRR nervous—they wondered how the NPRR could ever be finished and become a viable commercial proposition that was therefore able to repay its bond debt, both interest and principal. How long would the hostile Lakota stand in the way? Even if the army was eventually able to subdue the hostiles, time was money, and the NPRR bonds were under pressure. Bond holders watched their principal values erode. Investors began selling NPRR bonds—getting out while the getting was good. Jay Cooke tried to prop up the sagging bond values of the NPRR but ultimately ran out of cash and credit, and so collapsed. NPRR bonds fell to forty cents on the dollar, and thousands of investors lost millions. When Jay Cooke & Company closed its doors forever, hundreds of US banks also collapsed during the ensuing depression. Unemployment soared. Meanwhile western crops began to fail because of a devastating infestation of grasshoppers—a plague that would last four years. City laborers and farmworkers alike were out of work and in some cases destitute and starving. Nebraska farmers were especially hard hit, which added to the miseries they suffered from Sioux raids.

The Sioux were infuriated not only by the NPRR but also by the corruption and venality of the Indian agents appointed by the Indian Bureau under the Department of the Interior. Graft was widespread, and even those Sioux who wanted peace and wanted to remain on the reservations were radicalized by this infamous and widespread corruption. Much of the agency corruption was caused by politicians in Washington who benefited

indirectly by distributing lucrative agency positions to their political supporters and directly through bribes and kickbacks. These same politicians
also benefited from the construction of the transcontinental railroads and
local spurs. In some cases they received gratuities of cash; in others, stock,
but the climate of Washington was so rife with fraud and corruption that it
was regarded as business as usual and conducted without a blush of shame.
This same climate of fraud spilled over into the management of the reservation, further exasperating numbers of Sioux and sending them into the
welcoming arms of Sitting Bull, or sending them south to the settlements,
where they could exact repayment of a different kind. Even the chiefs who
wanted to maintain order among their bands could not control their young
men, not only because those young warriors were incensed over their treatment but also because the culture of the Sioux allowed and in fact encouraged the young warrior to seek acclaim through warfare. Even though they
had plenty of excuses to go on the warpath, they didn't need them; it was
in their blood. The Sioux and their allies, therefore, were not blameless
victims. Far from it. Their culture cried out for war and celebrated the successful warrior. His amour propre depended on success against enemies,
and for the Sioux almost everyone, red or white, was an enemy. The victor
would invariably mutilate his victim, leaving a dreadful and shocking
reminder to following white men that they were dealing with a different
kind of culture, one that celebrated and rewarded savagery and brutality.
Moreover, their culture was based on nomadic hunting; they claimed huge
swaths of western land even though they could only rarely visit any one
vicinity. To a white farmer or rancher this was a sinful waste of potential; the Indians did nothing with the land. They didn't believe in such
a thing. This attitude toward the land and its resources was the principal
gulf between the two cultures. To the whites the land was a resource to
be developed; to the Indians the land was a living benefactor to be venerated and left as is. Of course the Sioux were dependent on the buffalo, and
for that reason the army and government encouraged a policy that would
lead to the buffalo's virtual extinction—both by commercial hide hunting
and by settlement of the Plains. Railroads and towns would soon drive
the dwindling herds away. The loss of the buffalo was an economic and
spiritual catastrophe for the Lakota. And just as bad, the Black Hills had

always been a fallback hunting ground, when buffalo were scarce. Rich in elk, deer, and antelope, the Hills were the Lakota's "meat pack." To lose the Black Hills would redouble the economic and cultural disaster.

Frustrated with constant warfare and ineffective treaties, President Grant introduced a Peace Policy that in essence was designed to turn the nomadic warriors into stationary farmers of freehold land as well as into good Protestants, or at the very least, Catholics. Moreover, their children would be sent away to school to learn the "white man's road." This policy was well intentioned but wildly out of touch with the culture of the Sioux, and most of them resented and rejected it.

So the hostile Sioux were either recalcitrant warriors under Sitting Bull or radicalized young reservation men who detested the elements of the Peace Policy and hated the villainous agents and post traders who cheated them in every way possible. More fundamentally still, they resented being told where they could and could not go. Who were these Wasichus to restrict the movements of a people who had roamed through hundreds of western miles, following the buffalo and defeating their enemies? If they were being cheated, it was fair turnabout to subsist on the government's scanty rations in the winter and go out on the warpath in the spring when "the grasses showed their tender faces again," and their horses regained their fitness.[10]

As immigrants streamed into the country, many driven here by the depression in Europe and enticed by agents of the railroads who intended to sell them land along the various rights of way, the lack of opportunity and employment drove many of them to join the army, even though it was for most a stopgap, since army pay was low and living conditions on the frontier often wretched. Many would desert at the first opportunity; others were hardcases who suffered brutal discipline in addition to the inherent dangers of life on the frontier. Disease, discharge, and desertion combined to keep the army chronically undermanned. Moreover the Congress that was busy lining its own pockets was at the same time reducing the army's level of readiness. The cheeseparing budgets, the low level of troop allocations, the scattering of the troops initially throughout the South on Reconstruction duties and subsequently throughout the frontier meant that morale and training were constantly at low levels, and there weren't enough troops to go around when it came time to prevent the flood of miners who rushed into the Black Hills, once Custer's news had spread. What's more the army had no stomach for the job, and most senior officers were sympathetic to the argument that the nation needed the gold of the Black Hills, if it was really there. Besides, even if the gold was mere fantasy, there was no way to stop the individual entrepreneurs who believed in it. Nor did the army believe that it should try. Finally Grant agreed that the job was impossible and quietly removed the army from the Hills. A few months later Custer's disaster at the Little Bighorn shocked and then infuriated the country.

Looking back on such momentous events, such as Custer's epic defeat, it's always tempting to try to find some structure, perhaps some meaningful plot lines that allow the creation of a satisfying narrative, perhaps even something that rises to the level of tragedy. In this case, was there linkage between Custer's Black Hills Expedition and the Little Bighorn? Some, but not very much. Did Custer really "dig his grave in the Black Hills"? Not really. Certainly the Black Hills Expedition angered and radicalized portions of the reservation warriors and, almost certainly, added to the numbers of summer roamers who joined Sitting Bull in the hostile camps. But Custer's Thieves' Road was only one of many grievances the Lakota had. Custer and his men did not die because the Lakota and Cheyenne were angry at him over the Black Hills. He died because he attacked a village that was three times larger than he expected; he died because he neglected to do a thorough reconnaissance; he died because his two subordinate commanders failed him, although given the numbers engaged against the cavalry, it's doubtful that even the combined force of the Seventh Cavalry could have escaped defeat, if not annihilation. And Custer died because of overconfidence in himself and the troops, and because he accepted the army's widely understood belief that a village under surprise attack would scatter, that Indian warriors would first look to saving their families and not unite into a cohesive fighting force. Like most unexamined assumptions, military conventional wisdom was, and is, subject to unpleasant, and sometimes shocking, rebuttals.

But there was linkage between Custer's disaster and the subsequent action of Congress. Frustrated with the recalcitrance of the reservation chiefs over the sale of the Hills, Congress in August of 1876—a mere six weeks after the Seventh Cavalry's catastrophe—passed what in effect was an ultimatum: sell the Hills or starve. In other words, if the Sioux did not agree to sell, Congress, which controlled the purse strings, would not authorize further annuities and rations. In the context of the Custer catastrophe Congress's action was transparently punitive—not only an act of frustration but also one designed to retaliate against the entire Sioux tribe, even though the reservation chiefs had little if anything to do with the Little Bighorn. Faced with a Hobson's choice, the chiefs sold and thereby put a period to the story of Custer's Black Hills expedition. Though all the world knew that the chiefs who "touched the pen" did not represent the entire nation and in fact were only a small minority, Congress was satisfied, and the title to the Black Hills was transferred to the United States. So Congress declared.

Given the environment it's not hard to understand the events that flowed from Custer's discovery of gold and the Jenney expedition's subsequent verification of the Black Hills' riches. And given the various historical factors on all sides of the question, it's hard to imagine how things could have happened differently. Perhaps the story has the inevitability of a tragedy. Perhaps from the moment the gold was discovered, it was inevitable that the Black Hills as the Lakota knew them would be gone forever. On the other hand, it does not seem inevitable that the outcome had to unfold the way it did. Congress might have at least made a fairer offer to the Sioux—a higher payment or a large royalty—some covering of velvet over the iron fist. But in the context of the Custer defeat and the ongoing war against the hostile Sioux, the government was in no mood to negotiate fairly. Or to negotiate at all.

Even so, the commissioners assigned to present the government's final offer for the sale of the hills were moved by the speeches of the various chiefs they met, men who knew they had no choice but who were not going to surrender without a protest. The various chiefs came forward individually to "touch the pen" and signify agreement, but each, like some condemned prisoner, had a few words to say before signing. As one of the commissioners wrote: "The recital of the wrongs which their people had suffered at the hands of the whites, the arraignment of the government for gross acts of injustice and fraud, the description of treaties made only to be broken, the doubt and distrusts of present professions of friendship and good-will were portrayed in colors so vivid and language so terse, that admiration and surprise would have kept us silent had not shame and humiliation done so."[11] Honest men, the commissioners were unhappy and uneasy about their assignment, but they managed to accomplish it, in the end. And so the Black Hills were lost to the Lakota forever.

Were the Lakota more sinned against than sinning? From the perspective of a century and a half, the answer must be yes, although western settlers at the time would not have agreed. But in the entire saga of the Black Hills, its prelude and aftermath, none of the parties, red or white, emerges blameless. In that sense, the Hills are a metaphor for the settlement of the west. There was more than enough cruelty, violence, and guilt to go around. Looking back, Black Elk said: "I told my vision through songs. . . . I sang it four times, and the fourth time all the people began to weep together, because the Wasichus had taken the beautiful world away from us."[12] Later, when he became a Catholic missionary, he would have found another passage that also applied—Ecclesiastes 7:22: "There is not a just man upon earth that doeth good and sinneth not."

NOTES

INTRODUCTION

1. Throughout this book I will generally use the modern-day names of the states, even those that were not yet states and were organized as territories. (Current North and South Dakota were simply Dakota Territory.) This simplifies locations and avoids repetition of the awkward phrase "what would become the state of South Dakota."

2. James Calhoun, *With Custer in '74: James Calhoun's Diary of the Black Hills Expedition* (Provo, UT: Brigham Young University Press, 1979), p. 103.

3. Ibid., p. xvii.

4. Robert M. Utley, *Frontier Regulars: The United States Army and the Indian, 1866–1891* (Lincoln: University of Nebraska Press, 1984), p. 244.

5. Calhoun, *With Custer in '74*, p. 9.

6. Donald Jackson, *Custer's Gold: The United States Cavalry Expedition of 1874* (New Haven, CT: Yale University Press, 1966), p. 128.

7. Ibid., p. 10.

8. Ibid., p. 6.

9. Most likely Sherman was thinking in terms of Chief Justice John Marshall's 1831 ruling that the Indians had an "unquestioned right to the land they occupy, until that right shall be extinguished by a voluntary cession to our government." More on this later.

10. Calhoun, *With Custer in '74*, p. 90.

11. Elizabeth B. Custer, *Boots and Saddles: Or, Life in Dakota with General Custer* (New York: Harper and Brothers, 1885), p. 96.

12. Jackson, *Custer's Gold*, pp. 8, 9.

13. Calhoun, *With Custer in '74*, p. 39.

14. Francis Parkman, *The Oregon Trail / The Conspiracy of Pontiac* (Des Moines, IA: Library of America, 1991), p. 148.

15. Ibid., p. 230.

16. Jackson, *Custer's Gold*, p. 14.

17. Calhoun, *With Custer in '74*, p. 10.

18. Utley, *Frontier Regulars*, pp. 260, 261.

CHAPTER ONE: WAR, TAXES, DEBT, AND THE RESULTANT LURE OF GOLD

1. Robert D. Hormats, *The Price of Liberty: Paying for America's Wars* (New York: Henry Holt & Co., 2007).

2. Donald Jackson, *Custer's Gold: The United States Cavalry Expedition of 1874* (New Haven, CT: Yale University Press, 1966), p. 89.

3. *New York Times*, April 2, 2012.

4. James M. McPherson, *Battle Cry of Freedom: The Civil War Era* (Oxford: Oxford University Press, 1988), p. 614.

5. Hormats, *The Price of Liberty*, p. 89.

6. McPherson, *Battle Cry of Freedom*, p. 306.

7. Ibid., p. 61.

8. Hormats, *The Price of Liberty*, p. 67.

9. McPherson, *Battle Cry of Freedom*, p. 67.

10. Ibid., p. 68.

11. Ibid., p. 89.

12. Ibid., p. 69.

13. Ibid., p. 71.

14. Ibid., p. 75.

15. Ibid., p. 76.

16. Ibid.

17. Ibid., p. 78.

18. Ibid., p. 79.

19. This happened in Mexico during the American Civil War. The Juárez government suspended interest payments on loans from France, which led to the French army invading Mexico and setting up a puppet emperor, Maximilian. In peace times the United States would have invoked the Monroe Doctrine, and there would have been trouble with France. But with the Civil War raging, the US government looked the other way. This adventure was precisely the sort of thing Jeffersonians feared—the undue influence of financial interests on international politics, that is, when the French bankers howled, France sent an army to collect the loans.

20. If an investor has a bond paying 5 percent (its coupon) and wants to sell it at a time when interest rates have risen, the bond holder would find no one interested unless the bond's price is reduced so that the yield is in line with new issues of the same maturity and credit quality.

21. The Confederate thrust from Texas into New Mexico in 1862 was in part designed to move north to capture the Colorado gold fields. The Confederates were turned away at the Battle of Glorieta Pass when Colorado volunteers led by Colonel John Chivington outflanked the Rebels and destroyed their supplies. Chivington was later the leader of the despicable Sand Creek massacre of Black Kettle's Cheyenne.

22. Hormats, *The Price of Liberty*, p. 82.

23. Ibid., p. 83.

24. M. John Lubetkin, *Jay Cooke's Gamble: The Northern Pacific Railroad, the Sioux, and the Panic of 1873* (Norman: University of Oklahoma Press, 2006), p. 3.

25. Hormats, *The Price of Liberty*, p. 90.

CHAPTER TWO: GOLD IN MONTANA, DISASTER IN WYOMING

1. Robert M. Utley, *Frontier Regulars: The United States Army and the Indian, ʼ–1891* (Lincoln: University of Nebraska Press, 1984), p. 99.

2. Ibid.

3. Mark Twain, *Roughing It* (Oxford: Oxford University Press, 1996), p. 103.

4. The quote, according to most sources, is "Nothing in life is so exhilarating as to be shot at without result" from *The Malakand Field Force*, 1898.

5. To fire a Minié ball the soldier first bit off a paper cartridge filled with black powder, poured it down the barrel, and then dropped the Minié ball on top and tamped it down with a ramrod. (The Minié ball had a soft metal base that expanded on firing and engaged the grooves of the rifled barrel.) Then the soldier added a cap to the firing mechanism, pulled back the hammer, and fired. In close-quarters fighting, the time involved in this process could be lethal to the soldiers. Indian opponents were not slow to understand the time elements.

6. The Army Act of 1869 did away with regimental bands, but from then on nearly every regiment raised money to support them privately.

7. Utley, *Frontier Regulars*, p. 98.

8. Dee Brown, *The Fetterman Massacre* (Lincoln, NE: Bison Books, 1971), p. 43.

9. Utley, *Frontier Regulars*, p. 108.

10. Ibid., p. 100.

11. Historian Dee Brown writes that Fetterman and Captain Fred Brown killed each other with shots to the temple to avoid being taken alive.

12. Brown, *The Fetterman Massacre*, p. 188.

13. Ibid., p. 197.

14. Utley, *Frontier Regulars*, p. 108.

15. Ibid., p. 107.

16. Brown, *The Fetterman Massacre*, p. 106.

17. John G. Neihardt, *Black Elk Speaks: Being the Life Story of a Holy Man of the Oglala Sioux, the Premier Edition* (Albany: State University of New York Press, 2008), p. 74.

18. Brown, *The Fetterman Massacre*, p. 223.

19. Donald Jackson, *Custer's Gold: The United States Cavalry Expedition of 1874* (New Haven, CT: Yale University Press, 1966), pp. 127–36.

20. Ibid.

21. Dorothy M. Johnson, *The Bloody Bozeman: The Perilous Trail to Montana's Gold* (Missoula, MT: Mountain Press Publishing Co., 1983), p. 306.

22. Bob Drury and Tom Clavin, *The Heart of Everything That Is: The Untold Story of Red Cloud, an American Legend* (New York: Simon and Schuster, 2013), p. 359.

CHAPTER THREE: THE ADVERSARIES

1. Royal B. Hassrick, *The Sioux: Life and Customs of a Warrior Society* (Norman: University of Oklahoma Press, 1988), p. 80.

2. John G. Neihardt, *Black Elk Speaks: Being the Life Story of a Holy Man of the Oglala Sioux, the Premier Edition* (Albany: State University of New York Press, 2008), p. 27.

3. John C. Cremony, *Life among the Apaches* (San Francisco: A. Roman & Company, 1868), p. 117.

4. Dee Brown, *The Fetterman Massacre* (Lincoln, NE: Bison Books, 1971), p. 198.

5. Hassrick, *The Sioux*, p. 81.

6. Francis Parkman, *The Oregon Trail / The Conspiracy of Pontiac* (Des Moines, IA: Library of America, 1991), p. 242.

7. Hassrick, *The Sioux*, p. 161.

8. Alvin M. Josephy Jr., *The Indian Heritage of America* (Boston, MA: Houghton Mifflin, 1991), p. 116.

9. Ibid., p. 14.

10. Hassrick, *The Sioux*, p. 30.

11. Ibid.

12. Ibid., p. 194.

13. Ibid., p. 248.

14. Anyone interested in investigating the Sioux religion in greater depth should examine Royal Hassrick's excellent book *The Sioux* (see n. 1, above), from which much of this discussion has been derived.

15. Ibid., p. 73.

16. Joseph M. Marshall III, *The Lakota Way: Stories and Lessons for Living* (London: Penguin Group, 2002), p. 56.

17. Ibid., p. 42.

18. Interestingly, this method of luring ducks into gunshot range actually works. The Nova Scotia tolling dog was bred to do just that. "Tolling" means attracting through antics on the shore.

19. Hassrick, *The Sioux*, p. 78. Ethnologist George Bird Grinnell, who knew and studied the Pawnees, gives a different account of this incident in his book *Two Great Scouts* (see n. 29, below). He says that the Pawnee men were out hunting and the victims of the Sioux attack were 150 women and children.

20. Hassrick, *The Sioux*, p. 79.

21. Marshall, *The Lakota Way*, p. 194.

22. Neihardt, *Black Elk Speaks*, p. 67.

23. Hassrick, *The Sioux*, p. 14.

24. Ibid., p. 15.

25. Marshall, *The Lakota Way*, p. 70.

26. Hassrick, *The Sioux*, p. 90.

27. Neihardt, *Black Elk Speaks*, p. 70.

28. Ibid., p. 74.

29. George Bird Grinnell, *Two Great Scouts and Their Pawnee Battalion: The Experiences of Frank J. North and Luther H. North, Pioneers in the Great West, 1856–1882, and Their Defence of the Building of the Union Pacific Railroad* (Lincoln: University of Nebraska Press, 1973), p. 244.

30. Marshall, *The Lakota Way*, p. 107.

31. Hassrick, *The Sioux*, p. 108.

32. Ibid., p. 254.

33. Neihardt, *Black Elk Speaks*, p. 84.

34. Hassrick, *The Sioux*, p. 107.

35. Marshall, *The Lakota Way*, p. 44.

36. Hassrick, *The Sioux*, p. 256.

37. Neihardt, *Black Elk Speaks*, p. 155.

38. George Armstrong Custer, *Nomad*, ed. Brian W. Dippie (Austin: University of Texas Press, 1980), p. 20.

39. Robert M. Utley, *Frontier Regulars: The United States Army and the Indian, 1866–1891* (Lincoln: University of Nebraska Press, 1984), p. 22.

40. Ibid., p. 84.

41. Ibid., p. 24.

42. Robert M. Utley, *Cavalier in Buckskin: George Armstrong Custer and the Western Military Frontier* (Norman: University of Oklahoma Press, 1988), p. 44.

43. Utley, *Frontier Regulars*, p. 16.

44. James Calhoun, *With Custer in '74: James Calhoun's Diary of the Black Hills Expedition* (Provo, UT: Brigham Young University Press, 1979), p. 99.

45. Ibid., p. 97.

46. Ibid., p. 127.

47. Ibid., p. 57.

48. Elizabeth B. Custer, *Boots and Saddles: Or, Life in Dakota with General Custer* (New York: Harper and Brothers, 1885), p. 100.

49. Theodore Ewert, *Private Theodore Ewert's Diary of the Black Hills Expedition of 1874*, ed. John M. Carrol and Lawrence A. Frost (Piscataway, NJ: CRI Books, 1976), p. 25.

50. Ibid., p. 35.

51. Ambrose Bierce, *The Devil's Dictionary* (New York: Hill and Wang, 1957), p. 202.

52. Terry Mort, *The Wrath of Cochise: The Bascom Affair and the Origins of the Apache Wars* (New York: Pegasus Books, 2013), p. 214.

53. E. Custer, *Boots and Saddles*, p. 98.

54. Utley, *Frontier Regulars*, p. 47.

55. Mort, *The Wrath of Cochise*, p. 216.

56. Utley, *Frontier Regulars*, p. 49.

57. E. Custer, *Boots and Saddles*, p. 290.

58. Utley, *Frontier Regulars*, p. 48.

59. Mort, *The Wrath of Cochise*, p. 214.

60. E. Custer, *Boots and Saddles*, p. 163.

61. The most famous female captive was Cynthia Ann Parker, who married a Comanche warrior and gave birth to Quanah Parker and never wanted to return to white civilization. But Cynthia was captured when she was nine and over the years forgot most of her English and became thoroughly acculturated by the time she married. Most adult captives, however, suffered the treatment Libbie and her colleagues greatly feared.

62. Ewert, *Private Theodore Ewert's Diary*, p. 35.

CHAPTER FOUR: THE GILDED AGE

1. John M. Lubetkin, *Jay Cooke's Gamble: The Northern Pacific Railroad, the Sioux, and the Panic of 1873* (Norman: University of Oklahoma Press, 2006), p. 53.

2. Mark Twain, *The Gilded Age and Later Novels*, ed. Hamlin Lewis Hill (Des Moines, IA: Library of America, 1990), p. 144.

3. Josiah Bunting III, *Ulysses S. Grant* (Albuquerque, NM: Henry Holt & Co., 2004), p. 123.

4. Ibid., p. 90.

5. Twain, *The Gilded Age*, p. 262.

6. Ibid., p. 95.

7. Ibid., p. 135.

8. Ibid., p. 262.

9. Lubetkin, *Jay Cooke's Gamble*, p. 159.

10. Robert M. Utley, *Frontier Regulars: The United States Army and the Indian, 1866–1891* (Lincoln: University of Nebraska Press, 1984), p. 94.

11. Andrew Paul Hutton, ed., *The Custer Reader* (Lincoln: University of Nebraska Press, 1992), p. 201.

12. George Armstrong Custer, *My Life on the Plains or Personal Experiences with Indians: Custer's Memoir of His Campaigns against the Indian Tribes of the Western Plains* (Norman: University of Oklahoma Press, 1986), p. 175.

13. It's worth noting that $10,000 in 1870 was worth something like $180,000 today. It was good to be in Congress.

14. Twain's coauthor of *The Gilded Age*, Charles Dudley Warner, was responsible for the quote "Everybody talks about the weather, but nobody does anything about it." Twain used the line in a lecture and so generally gets credit for it.

15. Ambrose Bierce, *The Devil's Dictionary* (New York: Hill and Wang, 1957), p. 158.

16. Mark Twain, "Pudd'nhead Wilson's New Calendar," in *Following the Equator* (Mineola, NY: Dover Publications, 1989), chap. 8, p. 99.

17. Lubetkin, *Jay Cooke's Gamble*, p. 294.

CHAPTER FIVE: POLITICS, PHILANTHROPY, AND CORRUPTION

1. John Gregory Bourke, *On the Border with Crook: General George Crook, the American Indian Wars, and Life on the American Frontier* (Lincoln: University of Nebraska Press, 1971), p. 464.

2. Dee Brown, *The Fetterman Massacre* (Lincoln, NE: Bison Books, 1971), p. 214.

3. George Armstrong Custer, *My Life on the Plains or Personal Experiences with Indians: Custer's Memoir of His Campaigns against the Indian Tribes of the Western Plains* (Norman: University of Oklahoma Press, 1986), p. 171.

4. Ibid., p. 33.

5. The source for these examples of fraud is "The Indian Ring in Dakota Territory 1870–1890," published by the South Dakota State Historical Society, http://www.sdsh-spress.com/. Interestingly, there's a county in North Dakota named for Burleigh. Its county seat is Bismarck, not far from Fort Lincoln, and is the western terminus of the Northern Pacific Railroad.

6. Ibid.

7. Ibid.

8. Custer, *My Life on the Plains*, p. 176.

9. This decision was associated with the notorious Trail of Tears saga, because by deciding that the Cherokees were not a sovereign nation the Court was ruling that they had no standing at the Supreme Court to redress their grievances against the State of Georgia's

infamous land grabs. Marshall began his remarks by saying he sympathized with the Cherokees but could not rule on the merits of the case.

10. Royal B. Hassrick, *The Sioux: Life and Customs of a Warrior Society* (Norman: University of Oklahoma Press, 1988), p. 72.

11. Custer, *My Life on the Plains*, p. 22.

12. Ibid., p. 14.

13. Ibid., p. 19.

14. Ibid., p. 21.

15. Robert M. Utley, *Frontiersmen in Blue: The United States Army and the Indian, 1848–1865* (Lincoln: University of Nebraska Press, 1981), p. xii.

16. Ibid.

17. Ibid.

18. The fight at Beecher's Island consisted of fifty frontiersmen who were army employees and six hundred to seven hundred Cheyenne and Sioux. The fight lasted nine days and only ended when a troop of the celebrated "Buffalo Soldiers" raised the siege. The frontiersmen were commanded by Major George "Sandy" Forsyth, who would accompany Custer in the Black Hills Expedition.

19. Josiah Bunting III, *Ulysses S. Grant* (Albuquerque, NM: Henry Holt & Co., 2004).

20. Shelby Foote, *The Beleaguered City: The Vicksburg Campaign, December 1862–July 1863* (New York: Modern Library, 1995).

21. John Keegan, *War and Our World: The Reith Lectures 1998* (New York: Vintage Books, 2001), p. 27.

22. In 1873 Hare was appointed Bishop of Niobrara, a territory comprising northern Nebraska and the Dakotas. Hare arrived in Yankton at the same time as the Seventh Cavalry.

23. M. A. DeWolfe Howe, *The Life and Labors of Bishop Hare: Apostle to the Sioux* (New York: Sturgis and Walton, 1911), chap. 3.

24. Custer, *My Life on the Plains*, p. 21.

25. Howe, *The Life and Times of Bishop Hare*, chap. 3.

26. Robert M. Utley, *The Indian Frontier 1846–1890* (Albuquerque: University of New Mexico Press, 1983), p. 133.

27. Ibid.

28. Elizabeth B. Custer, *Boots and Saddles: Or, Life in Dakota with General Custer* (New York: Harper and Brothers, 1885), p. 227.

29. Robert M. Utley, *Frontier Regulars: The United States Army and the Indian, 1866–1891* (Lincoln: University of Nebraska Press, 1984), p. 91.

30. Ibid.

CHAPTER SIX: THE NORTHERN PACIFIC RAILROAD

1. Robert M. Utley, *Cavalier in Buckskin: George Armstrong Custer and the Western Military Frontier* (Norman: University of Oklahoma Press, 1988), p. 112.

2. Robert M. Utley, *The Indian Frontier1846–1890* (Albuquerque: University of New Mexico Press, 1983), p. 105.

3. The most egregious atrocities, such as the Sand Creek (1864) and Camp Grant (1871) massacres, were committed by militia or civilian mobs. And while there were women and children casualties at Washita, there were also fifty-three women and children

prisoners. There were no prisoners taken at Sand Creek. The only survivors escaped. The only prisoners taken at Camp Grant were two dozen or so Apache infants, who were then sold into slavery. The Camp Grant mob consisted of a half dozen white civilians, roughly fifty Mexicans and approximately one hundred Papago Indians.

4. B. H. Liddell-Hart, *Sherman: Soldier, Realist, American* (Boston: Da Capo, 1993), p. 429.

5. This question of terminology is reminiscent of George Orwell's comment that "thought can influence language, but language can influence thought." Indeed, it seems that language is often used as a substitute for thought. "Politics and the English Language," *Horizon* magazine, April 1946.

6. Robert M. Utley, *Frontier Regulars: The United States Army and the Indian, 1866–1891* (Lincoln: University of Nebraska Press, 1984), p. 52.

7. Bob Drury and Tom Clavin, *The Heart of Everything That Is: The Untold Story of Red Cloud, an American Legend* (New York: Simon and Schuster, 2013), p. 186.

8. Liddell-Hart, *Sherman: Soldier, Realist, American.*

9. William T. Sherman, *Memoirs of General W. T. Sherman* (Des Moines, IA: Library of America, 1990), p. 902.

10. John M. Lubetkin, *Jay Cooke's Gamble: The Northern Pacific Railroad, the Sioux, and the Panic of 1873* (Norman: University of Oklahoma Press, 2006), p. 36.

11. Ibid., pp. 58, 59.

12. Scott Reynolds Nelson, *A Nation of Deadbeats: An Uncommon History of America's Financial Disasters* (New York: Alfred A. Knopf, Inc., 2012), p. 161.

13. Lubetkin, *Jay Cooke's Gamble*, p. 68.

14. Ibid., p. 72.

15. Ibid., p. 63.

16. Ibid., p. 145.

17. Nelson, *A Nation of Deadbeats*, p. 165.

CHAPTER SEVEN: CUSTER AGONISTES

1. Robert M. Utley, *Cavalier in Buckskin: George Armstrong Custer and the Western Military Frontier* (Norman: University of Oklahoma Press, 1988), p. 36.

2. Albert Barnitz and Jennie Barnitz, *Life in Custer's Cavalry: Diaries and Letters of Albert and Jennie Barnitz, 1867–1868*, ed. Robert M. Utley (Lincoln: University of Nebraska Press, 1977), p. 52.

3. Utley, *Cavalier in Buckskin*, p. 39.

4. Josiah Bunting III, *Ulysses S. Grant* (Albuquerque, NM: Henry Holt & Co., 2004), p. 114.

5. Louise Barnett, *Touched by Fire: The Life, Death, and Mythic Afterlife of George Armstrong Custer* (New York: Henry Holt & Co., 1966), p. 211.

6. Utley, *Cavalier in Buckskin*, p. 150.

7. Elizabeth B. Custer, *Boots and Saddles: Or, Life in Dakota with General Custer* (New York: Harper and Brothers, 1885), p. 11.

8. Ibid.

9. Utley, *Cavalier in Buckskin*, p. 41.

CHAPTER EIGHT: THE YELLOWSTONE EXPEDITION

1. John M. Lubetkin, *Jay Cooke's Gamble: The Northern Pacific Railroad, the Sioux, and the Panic of 1873* (Norman: University of Oklahoma Press, 2006), p. 185.

2. Robert M. Utley, *Frontier Regulars: The United States Army and the Indian, 1866–1891* (Lincoln: University of Nebraska Press, 1984), p. 23.

3. Andrew Paul Hutton, ed., *The Custer Reader* (Lincoln: University of Nebraska Press, 1992), p. 188.

4. Elizabeth B. Custer, *Boots and Saddles: Or, Life in Dakota with General Custer* (New York: Harper and Brothers, 1885), p. 18.

5. Ibid., p. 29.

6. Hutton, *The Custer Reader*, p. 187.

7. Dee Brown, *The Fetterman Massacre* (Lincoln, NE: Bison Books, 1971), p. 63.

8. Hutton, *The Custer Reader*, p. 185.

9. Ibid., p. 190.

10. E. Custer, *Boots and Saddles*, p. 290.

11. Lubetkin, *Jay Cooke's Gamble*, p. 182.

12. Robert M. Utley, *Cavalier in Buckskin: George Armstrong Custer and the Western Military Frontier* (Norman: University of Oklahoma Press, 1988), p. 123.

13. John Keegan, *Winston Churchill: A Life* (New York: Viking Press, 2002), p. 174.

14. Custer's cordial relations with the press differed markedly from those of his commanding general, Sherman, who detested journalists for a variety of reasons, not least because one of them had described him as insane. During the Battle of Vicksburg Sherman heard that a boat carrying four Northern journalists had been sunk by Confederate artillery, to which Sherman responded, "In our affliction we must console ourselves with the pious reflection that there are more where they came from." Shelby Foote, *The Beleaguered City: The Vicksburg Campaign, December 1862–July 1863* (New York: Modern Library, 1995).

15. Lubetkin, *Jay Cooke's Gamble*, p. 160.

16. Ibid., p. 189.

17. In a very sharp pinch, cottonwood bark could serve as food for the horses. The tribesmen often had to rely on this food for their ponies during difficult winters. Even so their horses lost weight and strength, which is why the hostiles waited until the grass turned green again in the spring and their horses recovered; only then could the hostiles head out to war.

18. Lubetkin, *Jay Cooke's Gamble*, p. 188.

19. Utley, *Cavalier in Buckskin*, p. 119.

20. Lubetkin, *Jay Cooke's Gamble*, p. 186.

21. Hutton, *The Custer Reader*, p. 191.

22. Ibid., p. 188.

23. Lubetkin, *Jay Cooke's Gamble*, p. 191.

24. Utley, *Cavalier in Buckskin*, p. 200.

CHAPTER NINE: THE YELLOWSTONE BATTLES

1. Elizabeth B. Custer, *Boots and Saddles: Or, Life in Dakota with General Custer* (New York: Harper and Brothers, 1885), p. 238, George Custer's last report in afterword.

2. Robert M. Utley, *Cavalier in Buckskin: George Armstrong Custer and the Western Military Frontier* (Norman: University of Oklahoma Press, 1988), p. 119.

3. A competent combat commander, Benteen detested Custer, and his comments about Custer should always be taken with a grain of salt. Students of the Little Bighorn fight will remember Benteen as commander of one of the three battalions. He received Custer's last message and was culpably slow in responding. He was also the driving force behind the successful defense of Reno's Hill.

4. Utley, *Cavalier in Buckskin*, p. 117.

5. Andrew Paul Hutton, ed., *The Custer Reader* (Lincoln: University of Nebraska Press, 1992), p. 206.

6. Ibid., p. 207.

7. Ibid., p. 208.

8. E. Custer, *Boots and Saddles*, p. 283.

9. Hutton, *The Custer Reader*, p. 209.

10. E. Custer, *Boots and Saddles*, George Custer's last report in afterword.

11. Ibid., p. 217.

12. Andrew Paul Hutton, ed., *The Custer Reader* (Lincoln: University of Nebraska Press, 1992), p. 218, Custer's article in *Galaxy* magazine.

13. Ibid., p. 218.

14. E. Custer, *Boots and Saddles*, George Custer's last report in afterword.

15. Utley, *Cavalier in Buckskin*, p. 120.

16. E. Custer, *Boots and Saddles*, p. 283.

17. Ibid., p. 284.

18. Ibid.

19. Ibid.

20. Ibid., p. 285.

21. Ibid., p. 286.

22. Ibid., p. 289.

23. Ibid.

24. George Armstrong Custer, *My Life on the Plains or Personal Experiences with Indians: Custer's Memoir of His Campaigns against the Indian Tribes of the Western Plains* (Norman: University of Oklahoma Press, 1986), p. 171.

25. John M. Lubetkin, *Jay Cooke's Gamble: The Northern Pacific Railroad, the Sioux, and the Panic of 1873* (Norman: University of Oklahoma Press, 2006), p. 260.

26. Scott Reynolds Nelson, *A Nation of Deadbeats: An Uncommon History of America's Financial Disasters* (New York: Alfred A. Knopf, Inc., 2012), p. 166.

27. Utley, *Cavalier in Buckskin*, p. 125.

28. Norman K. Risjord, *Dakota: The Story of the Northern Plains* (Lincoln: University of Nebraska Press, 2012), p. 143.

29. Custer's rebuttal to Hazen came after the crash of '73 and the bankruptcy of the NPRR, but the bankruptcy trustees had every hope of saving the railroad and were grateful for any positive publicity from a celebrity officer like Custer. Indeed, during the Black Hills Expedition Custer was photographed sitting in front of his extensive tent marked "NPRR."

CHAPTER TEN: ANATOMY OF A CRASH

1. One of Trollope's many novels was *The Way We Live Now*. Though having the usual conventions of the Victorian novel, in point of view it resembles Twain's *The Gilded Age* in satirizing the greed and corruption operating in London and especially in "The City," which was, and is, London's equivalent of Wall Street. The novel was published in serial form before coming out in book form in 1875 and is therefore roughly contemporaneous with *The Gilded Age*. Financial shenanigans and fraud were not limited to the United States. Far from it.

2. Anthony Trollope, *The Way We Live Now*, Modern Library ed. (Random House, 1996). "Apicius" was a Roman "epicurean"—in the gustatorial, not the philosophical sense.

3. Robert M. Utley, *Cavalier in Buckskin: George Armstrong Custer and the Western Military Frontier* (Norman: University of Oklahoma Press, 1988), p. 109.

4. Ibid., pp. 153–55.

5. Charles P. Kindleberger and Robert Aliber, *Manias, Panics, and Crashes: A History of Financial Crises* (Hoboken, NJ: John Wiley & Sons, 2005), p. 163.

6. Scott Reynolds Nelson, *A Nation of Deadbeats: An Uncommon History of America's Financial Disasters* (New York: Alfred A. Knopf, Inc., 2012), p. 163.

7. Ibid., p. 162.

8. Ibid.

9. Ibid., p. 167.

10. Ibid., p. 168.

11. Kindleberger and Aliber, *Manias, Panics, and Crashes*, p. 21.

12. Nelson, *A Nation of Deadbeats*, p. 175.

13. Josiah Bunting III, *Ulysses S. Grant* (Albuquerque, NM: Henry Holt & Co., 2004), p. 140.

14. Nelson, *A Nation of Deadbeats*, p. 166.

15. Norman K. Risjord, *Dakota: The Story of the Northern Plains* (Lincoln: University of Nebraska Press, 2012), p. 133.

16. James Calhoun, *With Custer in '74: James Calhoun's Diary of the Black Hills Expedition* (Provo, UT: Brigham Young University Press, 1979), p. 116.

CHAPTER ELEVEN: BUILD-UP

1. Elizabeth B. Custer, *Boots and Saddles: Or, Life in Dakota with General Custer* (New York: Harper and Brothers, 1885), p. 189.

2. Watson Parker, *Gold in the Black Hills* (Pierre: South Dakota State Historical Society Press, 1966), p. 39.

3. Ibid.

4. E. Custer, *Boots and Saddles*, p. 168.

5. James Calhoun, *With Custer in '74: James Calhoun's Diary of the Black Hills Expedition* (Provo, UT: Brigham Young University Press, 1979), p. 91.

6. Ibid., p. 92.

7. E. Custer, *Boots and Saddles*, p. 290.

8. In the event the grazing varied from good to poor on the journey across the Plains—until they got to the Black Hills. As Calhoun wrote in his July 14 diary, twelve days into the

expedition, "If the grazing had continued of poor quality, I believe the mules would soon play out. The amount of forage issued to the public animals is very small."

9. Calhoun, *With Custer in '74*, p. 100.

10. Ibid., p. 93.

11. Donald Jackson, *Custer's Gold: The United States Cavalry Expedition of 1874* (New Haven, CT: Yale University Press, 1966), p. 23.

12. Ibid., p. xvii.

13. Ibid., p. xviii.

14. Joseph M. Marshall III, *The Lakota Way: Stories and Lessons for Living* (London: Penguin Group, 2002), p. 190.

15. Keith H. Basso, *Wisdom Sits in Places: Landscape and Language among the Western Apache* (Albuquerque: University of New Mexico Press, 1996), p. 190.

16. Ibid., p. 156.

17. Theodore Ewert, *Private Theodore Ewert's Diary of the Black Hills Expedition of 1874*, ed. John M. Carrol and Lawrence A. Frost (Piscataway, NJ: CRI Books, 1976), p. 2.

18. Shirley A. Leckie, *Elizabeth Bacon Custer and the Making of a Myth* (Norman: University of Oklahoma Press, 1993), p. 166.

19. Calhoun, *With Custer in '74*, p. 117.

20. Ibid., p. 118.

21. Ibid.

22. Ibid., p. 119.

23. Paul Horsted, Ernest Grafe, and Jon Nelson, *Crossing the Plains with Custer* (Golden Valley, CA: Golden Valley Press, 2009), p. 11.

24. Ibid., p. 14.

25. Calhoun, *With Custer in '74*, p. 104.

26. Ibid., p. 96.

27. Ewert, *Private Theodore Ewert's Diary*, p. 26.

28. Calhoun *With Custer in '74*, p. 104.

29. Donald Jackson, *Custer's Gold: The United States Cavalry Expedition of 1874* (New Haven, CT: Yale University Press, 1966), p. 19. Note that Jackson writes that there were four hundred Sioux, but army correspondence reports only one hundred.

30. Horsted, Grafe, and Nelson, *Crossing the Plains with Custer*, p. 36.

31. Calhoun, *With Custer in '74*, p. 100.

32. Ibid., p. 99.

CHAPTER TWELVE: SOLDIERS, SCOUTS, AND SCIENTISTS

1. James Calhoun, *With Custer in '74: James Calhoun's Diary of the Black Hills Expedition* (Provo, UT: Brigham Young University Press, 1979), p. 127.

2. Donald Jackson, *Custer's Gold: The United States Cavalry Expedition of 1874* (New Haven, CT: Yale University Press, 1966), pp. 22, 23.

3. Ibid.

4. A grain is the traditional unit of measurement for both powder and bullets. There are seven thousand grains in a pound.

5. It may be remembered that the previous year in the second battle of the Yel-

lowstone, Private John Tuttle, the regiment's best shot, killed three Sioux at an estimated range of six hundred yards (Custer's estimate). But Tuttle was using a Springfield rifle, not a carbine. He was killed by volley fire. Stanley's artillery ultimately scattered the massed Sioux on the opposite side of the river.

6. By comparison, the Smith & Wesson .45 "top break" design opened like a shotgun, so that all six chambers were exposed. The act of opening ejected the six empties simultaneously. That pistol could be reloaded much faster than the Colt .45. The army did buy some of these, but the Colt remained the dominant handgun.

7. Theodore Ewert, *Private Theodore Ewert's Diary of the Black Hills Expedition of 1874*, ed. John M. Carrol and Lawrence A. Frost (Piscataway, NJ: CRI Books, 1976), p. 3.

8. Jackson, *Custer's Gold*, p. 65.

9. Terry Mort, *The Wrath of Cochise: The Bascom Affair and the Origins of the Apache Wars* (New York: Pegasus Books, 2013), p. 69.

10. Robert M. Utley, *Cavalier in Buckskin: George Armstrong Custer and the Western Military Frontier* (Norman: University of Oklahoma Press, 1988), p. 17.

11. George Armstrong Custer, *My Life on the Plains or Personal Experiences with Indians: Custer's Memoir of His Campaigns against the Indian Tribes of the Western Plains* (Norman: University of Oklahoma Press, 1986), p. 383.

12. The *New York Herald Tribune* wrote this tribute to Grinnell upon his death in April 1938: "Aside from Grinnell's prophetic vision, his forthrightness, his scholarship in the field of zoology and Indian ethnography, and the drive that empowered him to carry so many causes to successful conclusion, his outstanding personal characteristic was that of never failing dignity, which was doubtless parcel of all the rest. To meet his eye, feel his iron hand-clasp, or hear his calm and thrifty words—even when he was a man in his ninth decade—was to conclude that here was the noblest Roman of all."

13. George Bird Grinnell, *Two Great Scouts and Their Pawnee Battalion: The Experiences of Frank J. North and Luther H. North, Pioneers in the Great West, 1856–1882, and Their Defence of the Building of the Union Pacific Railroad* (Lincoln: University of Nebraska Press, 1973), p. 243.

14. Jackson, *Custer's Gold*, p. 51.

15. Ibid., p. 109.

16. Paul Horsted, Ernest Grafe, and Jon Nelson, *Crossing the Plains with Custer* (Golden Valley, CA: Golden Valley Press, 2009), p. 12.

17. John G. Neihardt, *Black Elk Speaks: Being the Life Story of a Holy Man of the Oglala Sioux, the Premier Edition* (Albany: State University of New York Press, 2008), p. 83.

CHAPTER THIRTEEN: ALKALI AND COMETS, GRASS AND STARS

1. Paul Horsted, Ernest Grafe, and Jon Nelson, *Crossing the Plains with Custer* (Golden Valley, CA: Golden Valley Press, 2009), p. 13.

2. James Calhoun, *With Custer in '74: James Calhoun's Diary of the Black Hills Expedition* (Provo, UT: Brigham Young University Press, 1979), p. 21.

3. Theodore Ewert, *Private Theodore Ewert's Diary of the Black Hills Expedition of 1874*, ed. John M. Carrol and Lawrence A. Frost (Piscataway, NJ: CRI Books, 1976), p. 17.

4. The average cavalry horse's load was almost a quarter of their weight. The cavalry saddle weighed 17 pounds. Total equipment, 90 pounds, preferred weight of a trooper, 130 to 150 pounds; total weight on the horse, 220 to 255 pounds. Average weight of a cavalry horse, 1,052 pounds.

5. Calhoun, *With Custer in '74*, p. 28.

6. Harney Peak was named by the well-traveled Lt. Gouverneur K. Warren. Warren sighted the peak from a distance. The highest peak east of the Rockies, it was also the site of Black Elk's vision: "I saw that the sacred hoop of my people was one of many hoops that made one circle, wide as daylight and as starlight, and in the center grew one mighty flowering tree to shelter all the children of one mother and one father. And I saw that it was holy." John G. Neihardt, *Black Elk Speaks: Being the Life Story of a Holy Man of the Oglala Sioux, the Premier Edition* (Albany: State University of New York Press, 2008), p. 33.

7. Calhoun, *With Custer in '74*, p. 21.

8. Donald Jackson, *Custer's Gold: The United States Cavalry Expedition of 1874* (New Haven, CT: Yale University Press, 1966), p. 125.

9. Terry Mort, *The Wrath of Cochise: The Bascom Affair and the Origins of the Apache Wars* (New York: Pegasus Books, 2013), p. 86.

10. Ibid.

11. Neihardt, *Black Elk Speaks*, p. 63.

12. John S. D. Eisenhower, *So Far from God: The U.S. War With Mexico, 1846–1848* (Norman: University of Oklahoma Press, 2000), p. 369.

13. Ewert, *Private Theodore Ewert's Diary*, p. 16.

14. Ibid., p. 8.

15. Ibid., p. 25.

16. Jackson, *Custer's Gold*, p. 4.

17. Robert M. Utley, *Cavalier in Buckskin: George Armstrong Custer and the Western Military Frontier* (Norman: University of Oklahoma Press, 1988), p. 137.

18. Calhoun, *With Custer in '74*, p. 24.

19. Ibid., p. 130.

20. Horsted, Grafe, and Nelson, *Crossing the Plains with Custer*, p. 65.

21. Ibid., p. 35.

22. Ibid., p. 56.

23. Ibid., p. 70.

24. Ibid; the *Random House Dictionary of the English Language* definition of alkali is "Inorganic compound, any soluble hydroxide of the alkali metals: lithium, sodium, potassium, rubidium and cesium. . . . They react with acid to form salts, are caustic and can corrode tissues." When alkali leaches into a stream the water can become toxic, depending on the concentration. The key words in the dictionary definition are "caustic" and "corrodes tissues."

25. Horsted, Grafe, and Nelson, *Crossing the Plains with Custer*, p. 39.

26. Calhoun, *With Custer in '74*, p. 29.

27. Robert M. Utley, *Frontiersmen in Blue: The United States Army and the Indian, 1848–1865* (Lincoln: University of Nebraska Press, 1981), p. 42.

28. Calhoun, *With Custer in '74*, p. 25.

29. Ibid.

30. Ewert, *Private Theodore Ewert's Diary*, p. 35.

31. George Bird Grinnell, *Two Great Scouts and Their Pawnee Battalion: The Experiences of Frank J. North and Luther H. North, Pioneers in the Great West, 1856–1882, and Their Defence of the Building of the Union Pacific Railroad* (Lincoln: University of Nebraska Press, 1973), p. 241.

32. Ernest Hemingway, ed., 2nd ed., *Men at War: The Best War Stories of All Time* (Wings Books, 1992), introduction.

33. Ewert, *Private Theodore Ewert's Diary*, p. 20.

34. Horsted, Grafe, and Nelson, *Crossing the Plains with Custer*, p. 84.

35. Ibid., p. 122.

36. Ibid., p. 123.

37. Ibid., p. 124.

38. Ibid.

39. Ibid., p. 126.

CHAPTER FOURTEEN: IN THE MOON OF BLACK CHERRIES

1. John G. Neihardt, *Black Elk Speaks: Being the Life Story of a Holy Man of the Oglala Sioux, the Premier Edition* (Albany: State University of New York Press, 2008), p. 50.

2. James Calhoun, *With Custer in '74: James Calhoun's Diary of the Black Hills Expedition* (Provo, UT: Brigham Young University Press, 1979), p. 68.

3. Ibid.

4. According to Paul Horsted's excellent book *Crossing the Plains with Custer* (see n. 10, below), the local people still tend these graves today.

5. Calhoun, *With Custer in '74*, p. 40.

6. Ibid.

7. Ibid.

8. Ibid., p. 41.

9. Ibid., p. 52.

10. Paul Horsted, Ernest Grafe, and Jon Nelson, *Crossing the Plains with Custer* (Golden Valley, CA: Golden Valley Press, 2009).

11. Donald Jackson, *Custer's Gold: The United States Cavalry Expedition of 1874* (New Haven, CT: Yale University Press, 1966), p. 78.

12. Perhaps the most imbecilic and mendacious of these caricatures is Arthur Penn's 1970 movie, *Little Big Man*.

13. Jackson, *Custer's Gold*, p. 80.

14. Calhoun, *With Custer in '74*, p. 57.

15. Ibid., p. 60.

16. Ibid.

17. Elizabeth B. Custer, *Boots and Saddles: Or, Life in Dakota with General Custer* (New York: Harper and Brothers, 1885), p. 242.

18. Theodore Ewert, *Private Theodore Ewert's Diary of the Black Hills Expedition of 1874*, ed. John M. Carrol and Lawrence A. Frost (Piscataway, NJ: CRI Books, 1976), p. 98.

19. Calhoun, *With Custer in '74*, p. 41.

20. Ibid., p. 99.

21. Ibid., p. 68.

22. Ibid.

23. E. Custer, *Boots and Saddles*, p. 303.

24. Jackson, *Custer's Gold*, p. 89.

25. Paul Horsted, Ernest Grafe, and Jon Nelson, *Crossing the Plains with Custer* (Golden Valley, CA: Golden Valley Press, 2009), p. 159.

26. Jackson, *Custer's Gold*, p. 90.

27. Robert M. Utley, *Cavalier in Buckskin: George Armstrong Custer and the Western Military Frontier* (Norman: University of Oklahoma Press, 1988), p. 134.

28. E. Custer, *Boots and Saddles*, p. 253.

29. Jackson, *Custer's Gold*, p. 90.

30. Neihardt, *Black Elk Speaks*, p. 62.

CHAPTER FIFTEEN: HOMEWARD BOUND

1. James Calhoun, *With Custer in '74: James Calhoun's Diary of the Black Hills Expedition* (Provo, UT: Brigham Young University Press, 1979), p. 69.

2. Donald Jackson, *Custer's Gold: The United States Cavalry Expedition of 1874* (New Haven, CT: Yale University Press, 1966), p. 94.

3. George Bird Grinnell, *Two Great Scouts and Their Pawnee Battalion: The Experiences of Frank J. North and Luther H. North, Pioneers in the Great West, 1856–1882, and Their Defence of the Building of the Union Pacific Railroad* (Lincoln: University of Nebraska Press, 1973), p. 142.

4. Ibid., p. 242.

5. Paul Horsted, Ernest Grafe, and Jon Nelson, *Crossing the Plains with Custer* (Golden Valley, CA: Golden Valley Press, 2009), p. 152.

6. Calhoun, *With Custer in '74*, p. 71.

7. Ibid., p. 73.

8. Theodore Ewert, *Private Theodore Ewert's Diary of the Black Hills Expedition of 1874*, ed. John M. Carrol and Lawrence A. Frost (Piscataway, NJ: CRI Books, 1976), p. 70.

9. Ibid.

10. Calhoun, *With Custer in '74*, p. 75.

11. Ibid., p. 78.

12. Ibid., p. 79.

13. Ibid., p. 80.

14. Ibid.

15. Ibid., p. 86.

16. Horsted, Grafe, and Nelson, *Crossing the Plains with Custer*, p. 166.

17. Jackson, *Custer's Gold*, p. 100.

18. Grinnell, *Two Great Scouts and Their Pawnee Battalion*, p. 43.

19. Calhoun, *With Custer in '74*, p. 82.

20. Ibid., p. 83.

21. Jackson, *Custer's Gold*, p. 100.

22. Calhoun, *With Custer in '74*, p. 84.

23. Ibid., p. 96.

24. Ibid., p. 86.

25. Jackson, *Custer's Gold*, p. 102.

26. Ewert, *Private Theodore Ewert's Diary*, p. 82.

27. Ibid.

28. Ibid.

29. Ewert was four feet eight inches when he enlisted in the Union army at age fifteen. Perhaps he had grown some by 1874. And he eventually did marry, but not until after the Black Hills Expedition.

30. Jackson, *Custer's Gold*, p. 104.

31. Dogberry is a character in *Much Ado About Nothing*. He is a fatuous night constable, a fool given to malapropisms such as "Villain! Thou wilt be condemned to everlasting redemption for this." Modern readers might well be impressed by the *Bismarck Tribune*'s literary references.

32. Jackson, *Custer's Gold*, p. 108.

33. Watson Parker, *Gold in the Black Hills* (Pierre: South Dakota State Historical Society Press, 1966), p. 71.

34. Jackson, *Custer's Gold*, p. 110.

35. Robert M. Utley, *Cavalier in Buckskin: George Armstrong Custer and the Western Military Frontier* (Norman: University of Oklahoma Press, 1988), p. 141.

36. John Gregory Bourke, *On the Border with Crook: General George Crook, the American Indian Wars, and Life on the American Frontier* (Lincoln: University of Nebraska Press, 1971), p. 244.

CHAPTER SIXTEEN: INVASION

1. Donald Jackson, *Custer's Gold: The United States Cavalry Expedition of 1874* (New Haven, CT: Yale University Press, 1966), p. 104.

2. Ibid., p. 105.

3. Ibid.

4. John Gregory Bourke, *On the Border with Crook: General George Crook, the American Indian Wars, and Life on the American Frontier* (Lincoln: University of Nebraska Press, 1971), p. 247.

5. Watson Parker, *Gold in the Black Hills* (Pierre: South Dakota State Historical Society Press, 1966), p. 52.

6. Ibid.

7. Jackson, *Custer's Gold*, p. 106.

8. Ibid., p. 105.

9. Parker, *Gold in the Black Hills*, p. 98.

10. Ibid., p. 141.

11. Ibid., p. 53.

12. Jackson, *Custer's Gold*, p. 107.

13. Parker, *Gold in the Black Hills*, p. 111.

14. Ibid., p. 110.

15. Bourke, *On the Border with Crook*, p. 242.

16. Ibid.

17. Jackson, *Custer's Gold*.

18. Bourke, *On the Border with Crook*, p. 244.

19. Parker, *Gold in the Black Hills*, p. 128.

20. Jackson, *Custer's Gold*, p. 117.

21. John G. Neihardt, *Black Elk Speaks: Being the Life Story of a Holy Man of the Oglala Sioux, the Premier Edition* (Albany: State University of New York Press, 2008), p. 34.

22. Parker, *Gold in the Black Hills*, p. 129.

23. Jackson, *Custer's Gold*, p. 118.

24. Parker, *Gold in the Black Hills*, p. 139.

25. Neihardt, *Black Elk Speaks*, p. 15.

26. Bourke, *On the Border with Crook*, p. 245.

27. Neihardt, *Black Elk Speaks*, p. 62.

28. Parker, *Gold in the Black Hills*, p. 200.

29. Robert M. Utley, *Cavalier in Buckskin: George Armstrong Custer and the Western Military Frontier* (Norman: University of Oklahoma Press, 1988), p. 146.

30. Parker, *Gold in the Black Hills*, p. 71.

EPILOGUE

1. Robert M. Utley, *Cavalier in Buckskin: George Armstrong Custer and the Western Military Frontier* (Norman: University of Oklahoma Press, 1988), p. 146.

2. Jeffrey Ostler, *The Lakotas and the Black Hills: The Struggle for Sacred Ground* (London: Penguin Group, 2010), p. 99.

3. Ibid., p.101.

4. John G. Neihardt, *Black Elk Speaks: Being the Life Story of a Holy Man of the Oglala Sioux, the Premier Edition* (Albany: State University of New York Press, 2008), p. 188.

5. Watson Parker, *Gold in the Black Hills* (Pierre: South Dakota State Historical Society Press, 1966), p. 202.

6. Ibid., p. 107.

7. Ibid., p. 166.

8. Neihardt, *Black Elk Speaks*, p. 218.

9. Robert M. Utley, *Cavalier in Buckskin: George Armstrong Custer and the Western Military Frontier* (Norman: University of Oklahoma Press, 1988), pp. 211, 212.

10. Neihardt, *Black Elk Speaks*, p. 143.

11. Parker, *Gold in the Black Hills*, p. 139.

12. Neihardt, *Black Elk Speaks*, p. 198.

BIBLIOGRAPHY

❦

Barnett, Louise. *Touched by Fire: The Life, Death, and Mythic Afterlife of George Armstrong Custer*. New York: Henry Holt & Co., 1966.

Barnitz, Albert, and Jennie Barnitz. *Life in Custer's Cavalry: Diaries and Letters of Albert and Jennie Barnitz, 1867–1868*. Edited by Robert M. Utley. Lincoln: University of Nebraska Press, 1977.

Basso, Keith H. *Wisdom Sits in Places: Landscape and Language among the Western Apache*. Albuquerque: University of New Mexico Press, 1996.

Bourke, John Gregory. *On the Border with Crook: General George Crook, the American Indian Wars, and Life on the American Frontier*. Lincoln: University of Nebraska Press, 1971.

Brown, Dee. *The Fetterman Massacre*. Lincoln, NE: Bison Books, 1971.

Bunting, Josiah III. *Ulysses S. Grant*. Albuquerque, NM: Henry Holt & Co., 2004.

Calhoun, James. *With Custer in '74: James Calhoun's Diary of the Black Hills Expedition*. Provo, UT: Brigham Young University Press, 1979.

Cremony, John C. *Life among the Apaches*. San Francisco: A. Roman & Company, 1868.

Custer, Elizabeth B. *Boots and Saddles: Or, Life in Dakota with General Custer*. New York: Harper and Brothers, 1885.

Custer, George Armstrong. *My Life on the Plains or Personal Experiences with Indians: Custer's Memoir of His Campaigns against the Indian Tribes of the Western Plains*. Norman: University of Oklahoma Press, 1986.

———. *Nomad*. Edited by Brian W. Dippie. Austin: University of Texas Press, 1980.

Drury, Bob, and Tom Clavin. *The Heart of Everything That Is: The Untold Story of Red Cloud, an American Legend*. New York: Simon and Schuster, 2013.

Eisenhower, John S. D. *So Far from God: The U.S. War with Mexico, 1846–1848*. Norman: University of Oklahoma Press, 2000.

Ewert, Theodore. *Private Theodore Ewert's Diary of the Black Hills Expedition of 1874*. Edited by John M. Carrol and Lawrence A. Frost. Piscataway, NJ: CRI Books, 1976.

Grafe, Ernest, and Paul Horsted. *Exploring with Custer: The 1874 Black Hills Expedition*. Golden Valley, CA: Golden Valley Publishing, 2002.

Grinnell, George Bird. *By Cheyenne Campfires*. Lincoln: University of Nebraska Press, 1971.

———. *Two Great Scouts and Their Pawnee Battalion: The Experiences of Frank J. North and Luther H. North, Pioneers in the Great West, 1856–1882, and Their Defence of the Building of the Union Pacific Railroad*. Lincoln: University of Nebraska Press, 1973.

Hassrick, Royal B. *The Sioux: Life and Customs of a Warrior Society*. Norman: University of Oklahoma Press, 1988.

Hormats, Robert D. *The Price of Liberty: On the Trail of Vikings, Conquistadors, Lost Colonists, and Other Adventurers in Early America*. New York: Henry Holt & Co., 2007.

Horsted, Paul, Ernest Grafe, and Jon Nelson. *Crossing the Plains with Custer*. Golden Valley, CA: Golden Valley Press, 2009.

Howe, M. A. DeWolfe. *The Life and Labors of Bishop Hare: Apostle to the Sioux*. New York: Sturgis and Walton, 1911.

Hutton, Andrew Paul, ed. *The Custer Reader*. Lincoln: University of Nebraska Press, 1992.

Jackson, Donald. *Custer's Gold: The United States Cavalry Expedition of 1874*. New Haven, CT: Yale University Press, 1966.

Johnson, Dorothy M. *The Bloody Bozeman: The Perilous Trail to Montana's Gold*. Missoula, MT: Mountain Press Publishing Co., 1983.

Josephy, Alvin M. Jr. *The Indian Heritage of America*. Boston, MA: Houghton Mifflin, 1991.

Keegan, John. *War and Our World: The Reith Lectures 1998*. New York: Vintage Books, 2001.

———. *Winston Churchill: A Life*. New York: Viking Press, 2002.

Kindleberger, Charles P., and Robert Aliber. *Manias, Panics, and Crashes: A History of Financial Crises*. Hoboken, NJ: John Wiley & Sons, 2005.

Leckie, Shirley A. *Elizabeth Bacon Custer and the Making of a Myth*. Norman: University of Oklahoma Press, 1993.

Liddell-Hart, B. H. *Sherman: Soldier, Realist, American*. Boston, MA: Da Capo, 1993.

Lubetkin, M. John. *Jay Cooke's Gamble: The Northern Pacific Railroad, the Sioux, and the Panic of 1873*. Norman: University of Oklahoma Press, 2006.

Marshall, Joseph M. III. *The Lakota Way: Stories and Lessons for Living*. London: Penguin Group, 2002.

McPherson, James M. *Battle Cry of Freedom: The Civil War Era*. Oxford: Oxford University Press, 1988.

Mort, Terry. *The Wrath of Cochise: The Bascom Affair and the Origins of the Apache Wars*. New York: Pegasus Books, 2013.

Neihardt, John G. *Black Elk Speaks: Being the Life Story of a Holy Man of the Oglala Sioux, the Premier Edition*. Albany: State University of New York Press, 2008.

Nelson, Scott Reynolds. *A Nation of Deadbeats: An Uncommon History of America's Financial Disasters*. New York: Alfred A. Knopf, Inc., 2012.

Ostler, Jeffrey. *The Lakotas and the Black Hills: The Struggle for Sacred Ground*. London: Penguin Group, 2010.

Parker, Watson. *Gold in the Black Hills*. Pierre: South Dakota State Historical Society Press, 1966.

Parkman, Francis. *The Oregon Trail / The Conspiracy of Pontiac*. Des Moines, IA: Library of America, 1991.

Risjord, Norman K. *Dakota: The Story of the Northern Plains*. Lincoln: University of Nebraska Press, 2012.

Sherman, William T. *Memoirs of General W. T. Sherman*. Des Moines, IA: Library of America, 1990.

Twain, Mark. *The Gilded Age and Later Novels*. Edited by Hamlin Lewis Hill. Des Moines, IA: Library of America, 2002.

Utley, Robert M. *Cavalier in Buckskin: George Armstrong Custer and the Western Military Frontier*. Norman: University of Oklahoma Press, 1988.

———. *Frontier Regulars: The United States Army and the Indian, 1866–1891*. Lincoln: University of Nebraska Press, 1984.

———. *Frontiersmen in Blue: The United States Army and the Indian, 1848–1865*. Lincoln: University of Nebraska Press, 1981.

———. *The Indian Frontier 1846–1890*. Albuquerque: University of New Mexico Press, 1983.

INDEX